For Generations:
Jewish Motherhood
Edited by Mandy Ross and Ronne Randall

Published in 2005 by Five Leaves Publications,
PO Box 81, Nottingham NG5 4ER

in association with the European Jewish Publication Society,
PO Box 19948, London N3 3ZL. www.ejps.org.uk
The European Jewish Publication Society gives grants to
support the publication of books relevant to Jewish literature,
history, religion, philosophy, politics and culture.

Five Leaves gratefully acknowledges financial assistance from
Arts Council England

Design by Four Sheets Design and Print
Printed in Great Britain

ISBN: 0 907123 643

The cover illustration, Making Soup, is by Anita Klein,
whose work can be seen on www.anitaklein.com
and at The Boundary Gallery in London

For Generations:
Jewish Motherhood

For Generations:
Jewish Motherhood

*Edited by Mandy Ross
and Ronne Randall*

Five Leaves Publications
in association with European Je
Publication Society

ejps

www.fiveleaves.co.u

Contents

In the Beginning:
Pregnancy, Birth, Early Days

Family Life

The Shadow of the Shoah

Mothering Daughters, Mothering Sons

Forging New Links

Choices in Israel

Identity in the Diaspora

On Not Having Children

Foreword

Michele Hanson

A young man once travelled down from the north of England to visit his sister in London. His coach passed through Golders Green. On arrival he asked his sister "who were all those gangsters" that he'd seen there, in big hats and dark coats? "They weren't gangsters," said his sister. "They were Jews."

To the young man, the Golders Green Hassidim seemed to come from another world. A secular twenty-first-century Jew, like myself, could easily agree. The Hassidim might well seem to come from another world, four centuries away in sixteenth-century Poland. And for many of the mothers in this book, the struggle is to try, as Sally Berkovic does, to "reconcile two worlds that are intrinsically at odds with each other". In Sally's case, the two worlds are the feminist and the Orthodox. But other women in this book are grappling with different opposing strands within Judaism: traditional/modern, religious/secular, Orthodox/Progressive... the list goes on.

Some of us never make any such effort at reconciliation. The distances seem too great, the ideas so irreconcilable — so it is impressive to find so many women trying to find ways of being Jewish that bridge the contradictions within their own beliefs. Perhaps now, when the world seems more barmy and chaotic than ever, it's especially important to hang on to your culture, or the edge of what still is, or used to be, your religion — or to question and reinterpret it so that you *can* hold on to it. Otherwise, it can easily all be lost, and the world will be a drearier place.

Which is perhaps why Ronne Randall "stopped eating bacon and started lighting candles"; why Sally Berkovic feels that there are more important things to think about than "the exorbitant price of Passover marshmallows"; why modern Jewish mothers may not always want their sons circumcised, but still engage with the issue; and why Julia Bard goes to the Rabbinical Court to collect her *get* wearing jeans – but she still goes. Because, like many Jewish mothers nowadays, she is caught between the secular and the traditional. The *get* may be outrageously sexist and unfair, but without it her children would "carry the *mamzer* stigma until the end of time".

Bard is thinking of her children here, like virtually all the women in this book. Here are the sort of Jewish mothers who are light years from the archetype. They are not hysterical, overprotective, intrusive, food-and-bowel-obsessed *yachnas*. Instead they listen to, and have grown-up conversations and even philosophical discussions with, their children. They talk about the Talmud. They even learn from their children. These lucky children can get thousands of words in, and not even edgeways.

And it is important that they do, because they are dealing with the sorts of dilemmas that need to be resolved through a dialogue between equals. In that way, these mothers can help their children to find their own paths within Judaism — whether it's a new way or a new approach to the traditional ways — without breaking the "sacred chain" through which Judaism has passed from one generation to the next for countless centuries.

Of course it is not always easy to accept your child's choices, or for a feminist to explain the Torah to her daughters, or for a new mother to cope with circumcision, or to refuse it. I didn't like the idea of circumcision, but somehow I could not have refused to do it. The "somehow" was the part of me that did not want to reject my family's beliefs and culture. Luckily I didn't have to — I had a girl. But what would I have done if I'd had a boy? As mothers we don't only have our own dilemmas to deal with, but are also often stuck in the middle of warring factions: traditions that seem immutable, families who might never agree or compromise.

Or perhaps the women in this book are just choosing different paths, or different ways of dealing with trauma. After the Second World War, Kitty Hart lost her faith. "In Auschwitz where was God?" she writes. "People were praying and begging for their life, but no amount of praying would help in Auschwitz... That's where I lost my faith. If you were in the wrong place, you were dead. It had nothing to do with prayers." Yet, as she points out, some Auschwitz survivors "became very religious, because they thought God had saved them." Her experience shows that even when pushed by the same horrors to the very edge of life, people can come to markedly different conclusions. And despite her loss of faith, Kitty Hart still thinks of herself as Jewish.

There is a similarly striking discrepancy of views today in Israel, illustrated by Shirly Eran and Ayala Samuels. Samuels is a very thoughtful mother of sons, coping with the approach of army service, which she regards as inevitable. But Eran, although she too lives with the fear of terrorist attacks, does not want her children "to grow up believing that in order to live [in Israel] they must always fight the enemy."

Living in Israel may bring its own unique difficulties and challenges, as the pieces by Eran, Samuels, and the other Israeli contributors clearly show. But these women also express universal concerns about motherhood, just as every contributor to this book does, in her own way. They are concerns that will surely strike a chord not just with Jewish mothers, in all their glorious variety, but with other mothers, and other human beings. And perhaps that is what this book is all about.

Introduction

Mandy Ross and Ronne Randall

Every blade of grass has its angel that bends over it and whispers, "Grow, grow."
MIDRASH RABBA BERESHIT 10:6

Our book was conceived some time after the birth of Mandy's son, which inspired the story "Nativity". This story fertilised the idea of developing an entire book dedicated to Jewish motherhood — a book that would explore real experiences, as opposed to the familiar stereotypes (chicken soup goddess or *kvetch*-monster, take your pick). The book has since endured possibly the longest gestation period in human history, and its emergence into the world has entailed almost as many agonies, hopes, dreams and unbridled expectations as childbirth itself.

The first question everyone asks is, "But how is Jewish mothering different from other mothering?" In many ways, it isn't. But there is an idealised image that many people carry in their hearts and minds, as exemplified in a poem by Rosalind Preston:

Jewish Motherhood

What does that phrase convey?
A sense of timeless love
Continuing what has gone before
With all that will follow.

Pride and pleasure — fear and dread,
What will the future hold?
As the children's journeys begin
Creating Jewish history.

5

Home is where the heart resides
Warm and ever welcoming,
Each Shabbat a special time;
Favourite foods and shared memories.

Teaching by example
The joys of Jewish life
Passing on lessons learned
From a Jewish mother.

Then there is the well-known stereotype made famous by Philip Roth in *Portnoy's Complaint* and perpetuated in countless jokes:

Q: Why don't Jewish mothers drink?
A: Alcohol interferes with their suffering.

Q: What is the definition of a "Jewish sweater"?
A: It is a knitted garment worn by a child whose mother is cold.

MRS MOSKOWITZ (proudly): My son Louis is seeing a psychiatrist! He goes twice a week, and he pays fifty pounds an hour!
MRS WEINSTEIN: And this you're pleased about?
MRS MOSKOWITZ: Of course! Fifty pounds an hour he pays, and all he talks about is me!

We wondered whether these stereotypes had any basis in truth. Ronne, who doesn't consider herself a typical Jewish mother by any stretch of the imagination, nonetheless finds that she is compelled to make chicken soup whenever her husband or son is ill — so perhaps, like all stereotypes, this one contains a grain of truth. But only a grain.

Rather, we would say that what is specifically Jewish is the experience of mothering as part of continuous narrative. Jewish mothers — whether observant, progressive or secular — are part of a history and tradition stretching back over 3,000 years. These ancient traditions are woven into a more recent narrative of living memory, individual family and communal traditions, along with our collective memory of the

Shoah, and the birth and struggle of the state of Israel.

We are also mothering with reference to the future — maintaining or renewing tradition in whatever form, handing on our Judaism in a "sacred chain", *l'dor va'dor*, from one generation to the next.

We are each a link in that chain. Of course, we are not each solely responsible for Judaism's survival. But each of us contributes by her actions to the way and the form in which Judaism survives — and raising the next generation is a large element of that. As Ayala Samuels quotes in her piece on raising Jewish Israeli boys,

> *You are not required to complete the task, but neither are*
> *you at liberty to abstain from it.*
> RABBI TARFON, *PIRKE AVOT* (SAYINGS OF THE FATHERS), 2:21

* * *

We started by inviting contributions from relatives and friends, and from women within our own communities. Gradually we went farther afield, and we asked people to pass on our invitation to others they thought might be interested. As e-mails started to come from women whom we had not contacted directly, many from outside the UK, we knew that our net was spreading wider. Our excitement grew as we received and read Jewish mothers' stories from around the world. It was difficult for some women to write so personally, and a handful of authors chose to write under pseudonyms. Gradually our chapters emerged as we received more material, with common themes suggesting themselves.

It's impossible to imagine this task before e-mail was available. It has allowed us to create an international, virtual community of mothers who have contributed to the birth of this book.

* * *

Jews are sometimes called "the People of the Book". Our first chapter, *Sources*, gathers together material about mothers in the Book, or books — from the Bible, the Talmud, some Yiddish poetry, and from literature and film. These provide some background and context for the more personal accounts in the rest of the book. The first few articles chart the significant mothers in the Hebrew Bible — as well as bringing into the light some of the neglected women of the Bible and the Talmud. The multi-layered commentaries to the Bible, accumulated over many centuries, reflect the preoccupations of their male authors. We see how feminist writers and women's study groups are working to fill the gaps in the stories and commentaries. The Yiddish poems that follow show women poets writing about their own experience and dreams of motherhood, in contrast with the male voices of the Bible and its commentaries.

During the twentieth century, in literature and film, the stereotype of the Jewish mother changed and developed. Novels and early movies show the sentimentalised mother of the *shtetl* who sacrifices her own needs for those of her children. Through the century, the stereotype evolved into the emasculating *kvetcher* depicted by Woody Allen and Philip Roth. In Britain, the more likable character of Beattie, portrayed by Maureen Lipman in British Telecom's TV commercials, combines elements of these two with a *kvelling* warmth ("An ology? You got an ology?").

In the Beginning contains first-hand accounts of pregnancy, birth and those intense early days. Brenda Heller's startling piece tells the story of the survival *in utero* of one of her twins, all within the framework of the Days of Awe. Many women wrote about the charged ritual of circumcision, and we feel there is further scope to explore mothers' relationship with this ritual, and whether and how it differs from fathers'. The final two pieces in this chapter describe new ceremonies to welcome babies, including the *simchat bat.*

Family Life opens with Grace Paley, the celebrated New York writer, remembering another mother, not her own, leaning out of the window to call her child. This mother personifies the generation of immigrant mothers left behind and cruelly mocked by their aspirational offspring, whose ambitions they encouraged: "She was destined, with her meaty bossiness, her sighs, her suffering, to be dumped into the villain room of social meaning and psychological causation."

Also in this chapter, we see a woman combining the role of rabbi and mother, savouring the opportunities to say a hundred blessings a day as she cares for her babies, and creating new blessings to mark significant moments in her children's lives. A rabbi's wife writes about reconciling the different tugs of her work, the congregation and her own family. In "Hearts and Bowels", Michele Hanson longs sometimes "to be like an English Christian, in whose home, psychologically, there is no lavatory... But only for a little while." This chapter closes with a story by Michelene Wandor of an older woman's fantasy of becoming a mother once again.

In the Shadow of the Shoah begins with Kitty Hart's remarkable story of the mutual mothering that allowed her and her mother to survive Auschwitz together. Ruth Shire writes about her experience as a young refugee from Nazi Germany, and how later she integrated that experience into her own family life.

Most of the contributors to our chapter on gender issues, *Mothering Daughters, Mothering Sons,* are observant women. They write about women's struggle to reconcile feminism with Orthodox tradition, to create a positive Jewish environment for their own daughters, and to instil respect for women in their sons. Interestingly, in progressive Judaism, the emphasis on women's equality and the sexes' togetherness seems to have removed the pressing need for women's discussion that is so familiar in other areas of life. Mandy notes that when the (female) rabbi at her own Liberal synagogue ran a workshop on women wearing *tallit*, she realised that, apart from *Rosh Chodesh* groups, she'd scarcely been in a women-only space within Reform or Liberal Judaism. Masha Gessen, the final contributor to the chapter, writes about a medical issue that concerns all women, but perhaps Jewish mothers of daughters in particular.

Forging New Links opens with a humorous search for a man of worth — the challenge of finding Jewish father material. The chapter goes on to explore the stories of some of those creating new or unconventional links in the chain of Jewish inheritance — an adoptive mother, a lesbian mother and a mother who became Jewish before she had a child.

Our book developed within the period of the second intifada. Every Jew around the world must follow events in the Middle East with stricken attention. *Choices in Israel* contains voices from across the spectrum of Jewish Israeli life, exploring some of the unique issues facing mothers raising children in a Jewish rather than a minority culture. Rakefet Zohar, an Israeli novelist and kibbutznik, charts the changing expectations of motherhood on kibbutz, where the demands of Zionism and socialism left little room for feminism. A mother writes of her dread from the moment of her sons' birth — common to all Israeli parents? — of their reaching the age for army service. A settler describes the *yishuv* or settlement she helped to establish as her "eleventh child", while Shirly Eran, a peace campaigner, writes of sending her children to a Jewish-Arab school, and her dream, "not of co-existence, but of openness of mind, the ability to see beyond colour, garment or custom."

Shirly also writes about the celebrated status of Jewish motherhood in Israel, where the state funds generous access to fertility treatment (including for single women and lesbians), and where legislation on surrogate motherhood attempts to reconcile halachic requirements with "the cry of the infertile woman".[1] While these issues are

---

[1] *Halakha and Patriarchal Motherhood: An Anatomy of the New Israeli Surrogacy Law* by Carmel Shalev, 1998.

10

beyond the scope of this book, readers may wish to explore this fascinating area further.

Outside Israel, Jewish women living in non-Jewish cultures face very different questions of Jewish identity, and *Identity in the Diaspora* explores just a few of them. "Nativity" — the story from which this book sprang — takes a fictional (but very true-to-life) look at a woman's response to the all-pervasiveness of Christmas celebrations around her as her pregnancy progresses and her baby is born. The conflicts, both internal and external, that arise when a child makes religious choices different from your own are explored by several mothers in this section, and the possibilities of raising Jewish children without religion — but with a strong sense of Jewish identity — are explored as well. Finally, a trendy restaurant provides the setting for a short story about the relationship between a Jewish mother and a Palestinian mother in Britain during the intifada.

On Not Having Children presents the other side of the coin. What is the role in the Jewish community of women who don't have children, whether by choice or circumstance? Raising Jewish children is not the only way for women to maintain Jewish continuity; to suggest so is to limit women's involvement and participation.[2] There are many and varied ways to contribute to a vibrant Jewish communal life, and the fictional story and first-hand accounts in this chapter are evidence of women doing just that.

* * *

What shines out from the book, and what we are most proud of, is women's engagement with Judaism, whether religiously or culturally. These individual voices reveal a

[2]Inspired by Rabbi Sheila Shulman of Beit Klal Yisrael Synagogue, London.

great integrity in their questioning as well as their commitment.

We are proud, too, to have women from such different backgrounds between the covers of our book. This inclusivity brings a richness and breadth, and reveals how much we share, despite our many differences.

And now, as we prepare to send our baby out into the world, with many careful checks and last-minute reminders, we look forward to having more time once again to spend on preparing the chicken soup, and on other necessary maternal functions, which have been sadly neglected in the latter stages of editing this book.

Thanks to the very many people who helped us by offering friends and people to contact, and by discussing, suggesting ideas, reading, and checking, including Elinor Corfan, Ofra Golan, Rabbi Margaret Jacobi, Rabbi Sheila Shulman, Rehanah Sadiq, Hameeda Begum, Myra Connell and Karen Whiteside. Special thanks to Nesta Ross, Beattie Sayers and Sarah Ebner for all their help, and to Ross Bradshaw for his encouragement. Finally, thanks to our families for their patience and support throughout.

Mandy Ross, Birmingham
Ronne Randall, Radcliffe-on-Trent, Nottingham
December 2004

Dedications

To the preceding links in my chain: Rivka Peltzman and Reyzl Heller, the grandmothers I never knew, and my mother, Ceil (Tzipa) Peltzman, who helped me become the Jewish mother I am.
RR

For Joe and his cousins, and their links with the generations who came before.
MSR

Sources

Eshet Chayil:
A Woman of Worth
(Proverbs 31)

Ruth Shire

A woman of worth is hard to find, for she is more precious than rubies.
Throughout the vicissitudes of Jewish history, the Jewish mother has proved to be a role model — a woman of worth, who is found in the memories of her children, a lasting relationship of physical and spiritual nourishment.

Her husband trusts her in his heart and lacks no good thing.
She is trusted to be the linchpin of the household. Her good influence radiates out, holding together whole and fractured spokes.

All the days of her life she brings him good and not harm.
As a mother and wife, she endeavours to bring harmony, love and respect to all her activities, teaching by her example what is good and right.

Her children rise to revere her and her husband sings her praises.
As a figure of authority and wisdom, she can stress the need for tradition and discipline, and warn of the evils of the world, remembering the Shoah. She encourages her children in the pursuit of excellence.

Many women have done great things but you surpass them all.
From Biblical times onwards, we remember the self-sacrifices Jewish mothers have made for their children, regardless of the cost — though as an individual a mother remains special and unique.

Charm is a delusion and beauty fades.
The charm and beauty of a Jewish mother is her tireless dedication to the welfare of her children. Her beauty may fade, yet she remains a person of love and devotion, providing an ever-ready safety net.

The woman who reveres God is to be praised.
Her reverence for spiritual values will be absorbed by her children. Her teaching of righteousness and social justice is expressed in prayers and Jewish rituals to worship God, producing a confident Jewish identity and an understanding of a dignified difference, which leads to tolerance and not rejection of the "other".

Esteem her for the work of her hands,
Her work is creating a home, which serves as rest, refuge and source of renewal in an ever-changing world of ideas and attitudes; she remains flexible and yet firm in her values as she sees to the practical demands of the day. Charity to all around has always been a prime task of a Jewish mother, forever enlarging her spirit of generosity, and trying to kindle this flame in the next generation, as well as supporting the Jewish community.

And her own good deeds will praise her in public
Her deeds will be remembered, and her faults too, but her striving for the best possible in the human condition, helping to mend the world, is the fulfilment of her aim.

* * *

The *Eshet Chayil,* a woman of worth — a Jewish wife and mother — is traditionally praised by her husband on the eve of Shabbat. Hallelujah.

Mothers in the Hebrew Bible

Rachel Montagu

In memory of my mother and teacher,
Gwen Ellen Montagu,
26th April 1923 — 12th January 2003

The picture of motherhood in the Bible is positive. Women who are mothers are described in ways that mothers today can recognise and empathise with. Although the Bible mostly uses masculine language for God, God is several times compared to a mother. Some portrayals of women in the Bible are painful to read, for instance the chapters that the Christian Bible scholar Phyllis Tribble calls the "texts of terror", in which women are murdered or persecuted. Many women in the Bible are mysteriously nameless — Mrs Lot, Mrs Noah and Mrs Manoah to "name" just a few. But women as mothers and motherhood itself are portrayed in a way that values motherhood and reflects the ways in which we experience it today.

I have looked at the range of mothers and their mothering portrayed in the Bible. I want to describe some of the most significant individuals, and the ways in which their various stories still resound for mothers today.

Eve
The first biblical mother was brought into being soon after the creation, when Eve gave birth to Cain. She named him, saying, "I have created — *kaniti* — a man together with the Eternal" (GEN 4:1). Although readers may wonder what part, if any, Eve thought Adam had played, they can enjoy the way this verse describes a mother looking in wonder at her child, this being whose birth has changed her forever. She sees reflected in him something of God's

image, in which her child is created. Eve's name is derived from the Hebrew for life, "because she was the mother of all" (GEN 3:20). Once Adam and Eve had produced Cain, making human beings — previously God's prerogative — became part of human creativity.

The Matriarchs

The description of the matriarchs in the Bible is full of paradox. The four matriarchs — Sarah, Rebecca, Leah and Rachel — are the wives of the patriarchs, Abraham, Isaac and Jacob, the first people to enter into a covenant and an ongoing conversation with God. The words patriarch and matriarch are derived from the Latin words for father and mother. Yet Sarah, Rebecca and Rachel all have great diffi-culty in producing children — which one would think a matriarch's *raison d'être*. (In biblical stories, infertility is always assumed to be the woman's problem. However, the blessing in Deuteronomy 7:14, "There shall not be a barren man or a barren woman among you," implies that in the biblical period they, like us, knew that both sexes can be sterile.)

Leah and Rachel

The only matriarch who easily bears many sons is Leah. We are told that this is the Eternal's deliberate attempt to rectify the inherent imbalance in her marriage — Jacob loved Rachel, but he hated Leah, because he was tricked into marrying her by her father, Laban (GEN 29:18-31). Leah's choice of names for her sons shows her desperate hope that these children will win her husband's love.

Reuben means "The Eternal has seen my pain, because now my husband will love me" (GEN 29:32). Shimon means "This is because the Eternal heard that I was hated and gave me also this one" (GEN 29:33). Levi means "My man will be attached to me because I have borne him three sons" (GEN 29:34). Judah comes from the Hebrew root for thankful-ness: "This time I will praise the Eternal" (GEN 29:35). Her names for the two sons whom her handmaid Zilpah bore have simpler and less revealing explanations, perhaps because the explanations must be voiced to others, or at least to Zilpah, rather than remaining a private thought. Gad means "good luck" and Asher means "happiness", "because the young women will consider me fortunate" (GEN 30:11-13). Leah called her next son Issachar as she considered him to be a reward from God for giving her handmaid to her husband (GEN 30:18). Her sixth and last son she called Zebulun because "this time my husband will honour me because I have given him six sons" (GEN 30:20).

There is tremendous pathos in Leah's reiterated hope that this family of sons will gain her husband's love. But apart from the great expectations attached to them, the Bible tells us nothing about how Leah mothered her sons or her daughter, Dina. Similarly, although we are told about Rachel's desperate longing to bear a child, we see little of her relationship with her first son, Joseph. Rachel died giving birth to her second son, Benjamin.

Sarah and Rebecca
The Bible tells us more about the first two matriarchs' feelings and behaviour as mothers. But Sarah and Rebecca are not idealised mothers setting a perfect example that ordinary women should strive to follow. Rather they exemplify the emotional tensions and difficulties of motherhood.

The first thing we learn about Sarah is that she was barren. When at last she bore Abraham a son, she was delighted and explained Isaac's name, repeatedly using the Hebrew word *tsahak*, laugh. "God has made laughter for me; everyone who hears will laugh for me. Who would have said to Abraham, 'Sarah suckles children'? Yet I have borne him a son for his old age" (GEN 21:6-7). When I read this I smile in reflection of her joy. However, after Isaac's great weaning feast (a custom modern Jews might consider reviving), Sarah insists that Abraham banish Isaac's half-brother, Ishmael, whom she saw *mtsahek*. This means "playing" and comes from the same Hebrew root as Isaac's name. In English "playing" is positive, but some of its connotations — as in playing about or playing away — are more doubtful. Similarly, in Hebrew *tsahak* includes nuances such as murder and sexual immorality. Did Sarah see Ishmael as an immoral influence on her child? Or did she just see his similarity to Isaac and his status as the older half-brother as a threat to the unique role she wanted for her own son? Perhaps once Isaac was born, she regretted ever suggesting that Hagar bear Abraham a child. So she sent Hagar and Ishmael away, out of her sight, even though this risked both their lives. Whatever her reason, her love for and delight in her own child does not give Sarah that empathy towards other children in pain or danger that many women today say comes with becoming a mother.

The *Akedah*

The *Akedah*, the binding of Isaac, is an agonising drama played out between God, Abraham and his son. It is a lesson in the complete unacceptability of human sacrifice. The Sephardi Rosh Hashanah liturgy includes a beautiful poem on the *Akedah* by Judah Samuel Abbas. In it, Isaac says to his father that he is willing to be sacrificed but, "Oh, tell my mother that her joy has now departed, for the son she bore at ninety years of age has become a prey to the knife and the fire; where shall I seek for one to comfort her? How I grieve for my mother in her weeping and distress... When the fire shall have consumed my flesh take with you my ashes and say to Sarah, Behold this is the savour of Isaac."

Does this show that Isaac really was willing to sacrifice himself? Or has Judah Abbas caught here another possibility — that Isaac is trying to dare Abraham to obey God's word. Abraham may be able to take a knife to his son, but how could he afterwards face Sarah, the powerful wife whom God told him always to obey? Abraham seems to have taken leave of his senses as he prepares to kill Isaac. All Isaac can do is to invoke his mother's love to make

Abraham understand the outrageous, unloving inhumanity of what he is about to do.

A traditional *midrash* interpretation also emphasises Sarah's great love for Isaac. It suggests that it is Sarah who dies as a result of the *Akedah*, even though Isaac survives. The verses describing her death follow immediately after the account of the *Akedah* (although the Bible does not indicate the time frame). The *midrash* says that before Abraham and Isaac set out, Sarah realised what God had commanded. She asked Abraham to make her some signal visible from afar to show what had happened, so she would know as soon as possible whether God had relented. Abraham was too relieved and confused to remember the signal. So Sarah died of grief, believing her son was dead before Abraham completed his journey home.

Rebecca and her sons

Isaac and Rebecca's marriage started with romance and love. Rebecca was so smitten when she first saw Isaac that she fell off her camel. When they married, "Isaac loved Rebecca and was comforted after the death of his mother" (GEN 24:67). But like her mother-in-law, Sarah, Rebecca seemed to be barren. She only became pregnant once Isaac prayed for her. But speaking to God is not solely a male prerogative. When the twins started their lifetime of struggle by wrestling in her womb, Rebecca demanded an explanation from God of the extraordinary sensations she was feeling. She was given a prophecy that there were two nations within her, and that the elder child was to serve the younger (GEN 25:23). When the twins grew up they were very different. "Esau was skilled as a hunter, a man of the field, but Jacob was a man of integrity who dwelt in tents. Isaac loved Esau because he hunted the food he ate but Rebecca loved Jacob" (GEN 25:27-28).

This does not sound like a happy and united family. Preferring one child may sometimes be natural but it is not a recommended method of parenting. Why does

Rebecca love Jacob more? Savina Teubal[1] points out that Rebecca came from a matriarchal society where youngest sons inherited, and were traditionally their mother's favourite. Does that explain her preference? Or is it her pleasure in having a son who keeps her company in the tents? Or the lingering influence of the prophecy she received that the elder would serve the younger?

One of the more contentious episodes in Genesis is the appropriation of Esau's blessing as firstborn by Jacob and Rebecca (GEN 27). Traditional commentaries tend to assume that the end justifies the means and forgive them for the deception (or else blame Rebecca more than Jacob). These commentaries justify the deception because Jacob will make better use of the blessing than Esau; Esau showed that he despised his birthright when Jacob offered to buy it for a bowl of lentils. Moreover, Esau had distressed his parents when he "married out" (GEN 26:34-5) — another example of the Bible reflecting very contemporary emotions. When Esau threatened to kill Jacob as soon as their father was dead, Rebecca sent Jacob to her brother Laban, telling Isaac that her life would not be worth living if Jacob followed Esau's example and married "from the girls of the land" (GEN 27:46). To save his life, she deprived herself of the company of her beloved son.

The two mothers of Moses
Mothers saving their children's lives is a recurring theme in the Bible. At the beginning of the book of Exodus, Pharaoh decided he must take steps to control the Children of Israel, a large minority of migrant workers whom he perceived as a threat. First he decreed that the midwives should kill all baby boys at birth. The midwives refused on the pretext that the Hebrew women were too lively, and gave birth before the midwives'

[1]*Sarah the Priestess, the First Matriarch of Genesis*, by Savina Teubal (Ohio University Press, 1993)

arrival. Then Pharaoh ordered that all baby boys be thrown into the Nile. When Moses was born his mother, Yocheved, "saw how good he was". Maternal admiration for one's child is a universal phenomenon! Yocheved kept him safe. She hid him for three months, and then put him in the River Nile in a carefully waterproofed "ark".

Pharaoh's daughter saw the basket and rescued the child. Miriam, Moses' sister, was watching over the baby from nearby. She offered to find a wet-nurse, and so the child was safely returned for a while to the bosom of his family, although he was later adopted by the princess. It is often said that Moses was able to lead the Children of Israel because of the confidence he gained from his upbringing — brought up in Pharaoh's palace rather than as a slave. Yocheved's love and the princess's pity, the care of both his natural and adoptive mothers, made it possible for him to rescue the Jewish people.

Matrilineal or patrilineal Jews?

The story of Moses and Zipporah, his Midianite wife, exemplifies an important issue for Jewish identity. Today Orthodox and British Reform Jews follow the position stated in the Mishnah (around 200 CE), whereby the mother defines her child's Jewish status. This is often cited to prove Judaism's respect for the role and influence of mothers. Orthodox and British Reform Jews do not consider Jewish the child of a Jewish father and non-Jewish mother, although British Reform welcomes the conversion of such children while they are infants. Reform Jews in America and Liberal Jews in the UK accept as Jewish the child of a Jewish father who is brought up as a Jew. They partly justify this as the biblical view, as we will see.

In the Bible Jewish status is patrilineal. An example is the sons of Joseph and his Egyptian wife Osnat, Ephraim and Menasseh, who went on to head two of the twelve tribes. Even today on Shabbat we bless our sons, "May you be like Ephraim and Menasseh." Likewise, Solomon is succeeded by Rehoboam, his son by Naamah the Ammonite. Moses' sons, Gershom and Eliezer, appear in genealogies, even though their mother, Zipporah the Midianite, is not Jewish. However, Moses' sons do not succeed him as prophet and leader. Perhaps this is because the nature of a prophet's relationship with God, and his or her role communicating God's word, means that it cannot be a hereditary position — unlike the tribal privilege of priesthood. In contrast, a story of the matrilineal son of an Israelite mother and Egyptian father (LEV 24:10-12) suggests that his Jewish status was doubtful. So while the Bible gives great credit to mothers, it does not give mothers the role of transmitters of Judaism awarded by later Jewish tradition.

Deborah

What was the status of women in the Bible? Any modern discussion of Jewish women's public roles must take account of Deborah, a prototype of combining motherhood with a profession. Deborah stands out among the leaders described in the book of Judges. Unlike any male judge, she was a prophet as well as a judge. In the poem she sang about the victory over the Canaanite army, she described herself as "a mother in Israel" (JUDGES 5:7). No male prophet ever described himself as "a father in Israel". Perhaps this is the biblical equivalent of modern working mothers in public life, who find that their children and childcare arrangements are commented on more than those of their male colleagues. Or perhaps Deborah felt that, despite her status as prophet, judge and poet of the victory, to describe the essence of herself she must also mention that she was a mother. She depicts with cheerful relish the death of Sisera, the enemy general, at Jael's hands, but she also shows the pathos of war and death by describing Sisera's mother waiting and waiting at the window for her son to return. While Deborah had no qualms about the Jewish people's self-defence, still she sympathised with another mother's pain.

Hannah and Peninah

Rachel and Leah are not the only biblical example of tension between a wife blessed with children and a wife without. The book of Samuel describes Elkanah and his two wives, Peninah and Hannah, a family from Ramah who make their annual pilgrimage to Shiloh. Peninah, we learn, had children, but the Eternal "had shut up Hannah's womb". Elkanah loved Hannah, and he gave her a double portion of the pilgrimage feast. He obviously found it perfectly satisfactory to have one wife to bring up the children and another to concentrate all her devotion on him. When Peninah taunted Hannah at her barrenness, making Hannah weep, Elkanah asked her, "Am I not better to you than ten sons?" For Hannah, the cherished but childless wife, and Peninah, the mother blessed with offspring but no husbandly love, the ménage was not so ideal. Why else would Peninah have taunted Hannah, and Hannah become so distressed?

Hannah went to the shrine to pray for a child. She promised that if she were given a son, she would dedicate him to the Eternal all his life. When Eli the priest accused her of being drunk, she answered that she was "a woman distressed in spirit... and I have poured out my soul before the Eternal" (1 SAMUEL 1:15). This answer, and the way she prayed, standing with her lips moving silently, later became the model for all Jewish prayer.

Once Samuel was weaned — probably aged three or four — despite his tender years, Hannah left him at the shrine with a generous offering. She said that just as she had asked for him from God, so she was lending him back to God. Like Rebecca, Hannah is a mother who sacrifices the company of her child for the child's wellbeing. Thereafter she saw Samuel only on their annual pilgrimages, each time bringing him a little coat she had made. Samuel grew up surrounded by worship in the shrine, sleeping in the temple. This attuned him to God's presence so that he was able to hear God calling to him; later his way of being a prophet and leader inspired by God established the pattern of prophecy for succeeding generations. Eli blessed Hannah for her self-sacrificing devotion, and she had three more sons and two daughters. And eventually, Samuel returned to Ramah and settled there (1 SAMUEL 7:17), so we know that in the end he was able to rejoin his family.

Life and death

Recently there has been increasing recognition in the Jewish community of the significance of miscarriages and stillbirths. Traditionally, these deaths were not mourned with the same ritual intensity as other deaths, often failing to meet the needs of those who experience such a loss. But there is a biblical precedent for giving comfort to a mother grieving after a newborn's death. Bathsheba conceived King David's child while still married to Uriah the Hittite. The newborn child became ill, and died. In the single moment of tenderness described between them, David comforted Bathsheba for the loss of her son (2 SAMUEL 12:24).

Solomon and the two mothers

King Solomon was famous for his God-given wisdom. The Bible gives as proof of his wisdom his understanding of maternal love. Two prostitutes appeared before him (1 KINGS 3:16). They shared a house and both had recently given birth; both the babies were wanted, and the death of one of them was a tragedy for his mother. The other mother then accused her housemate of stealing her living child. This mother was more articulate, and she described how she realised that the dead child was not hers — "I continued to look at him and I understood" — describing the fascinated attention so familiar to all new mothers. As both women claimed the living child, Solomon ordered him to be cut in half with a sword so that they could share him, half each. The dead child's mother says, "Mine will not be, yours will not be, cut (him) in half." But the live baby's mother says, "Give the living child to her, but don't kill him."

26

Why did she say this? Because "her womb grew warm/ tender" (1 KINGS 3:26, author's literal translation). or, as the new Jewish Publication Society translation says, "she was overcome with compassion." *Rechem*, the Hebrew word for womb, is linked to *rachamim*, the word for mercy — how much more a positive symbolic link than the verbal connection between *hysteron*, the Greek word for womb, and hysteria. His mother's gut reaction, her visceral response, her womb-compassion, was to save him. Renouncing him was preferable to watching him be killed.

The dead child's mother is often described as "the bad mother". This seems unduly harsh. Either on the day of her child's birth, or on the third day afterwards, the day for the "baby blues", she found her son dead "because she had lain on it". The baby she wanted to see sliced in two was not hers. Wanting your housemate's child to be as dead as your own may be morally bad, but it is not bad mothering — more like acute post-natal depression combined with guilt and the shock of bereavement.

On not having children
There is no biblical precedent for the women of our generation who declare that they do not want to become mothers. There is, however, by implication, a word of comfort for women who long for children but are unable to have them. Jeremiah mentions "Rachel weeping because of her children, refusing to be comforted for her children because they are not" (JER 31:15). Does this mean children who have died, or children who have never been born? The text does not specify but continues, "Restrain your voice from sobbing and your eyes from weeping because there is a reward for that which you do." This could mean that motherhood is not the only constructive task in life from which a woman gains fulfilment.

Mothers and daughters
There are many biblical stories about mothers and their sons, but few about mothers and daughters. One of the few

27

is in the Song of Songs, where the woman in love wants to bring her beloved into her mother's house and into the room where she herself had been conceived (SONG OF SONGS 3:4). The Song of Songs, known as a poem of romantic love, also bears tribute to the love and feeling of close identity between mother and daughter.

Ruth and Naomi

The Book of Ruth explores another type of mother-daughter relationship, that between mother-in-law and daughter-in-law. Cruel jokes about mothers-in-law abound, but as exemplified by Ruth and Naomi, this can be a very beautiful relationship, a chance to make a mother-daughter connection in a new way. After Naomi and her daughters-in-law were widowed, Naomi decided to return from Moab to Bethlehem. She suggested that her daughters-in-law return to their mothers' houses to remarry. We cannot tell whether this is altruism or to avoid returning to Bethlehem accompanied by foreign women. Ruth responded with the words sometimes included in wedding services, "Where you go I will go..." expressing her devotion and commitment to Naomi.

Back in Bethlehem, Ruth went out gleaning, perhaps for subsistence, or perhaps to get herself some social life. A frequent source of tension between mother- and daughter-in-law is advice that could be more diplomatically phrased. When Ruth returned home and described Boaz's kindness, commentators note how tactfully Naomi encourages her to accompany Boaz's female workers, rather than his male harvesters.

Eventually Boaz married Ruth, redeeming her from her status as childless widow, and Ruth then bore a son. The women of Bethlehem understood that this child would be Naomi's redeemer. They blessed Naomi, saying that not only would the child provide materially for her old age but he, "the son of Ruth who is better to Naomi than seven sons", would restore her soul (RUTH 4:15). The redemption of a childless widow by a male relative is described elsewhere in the Bible as a practical solution to prevent the dead husband's name dying out and to maintain property inheritances. Here, though, it is a question of loving relationships. This child's birth is a restorative after so much bereavement, enabling Naomi to cope positively with a life without her sons and to lose some of the bitterness she felt when she first returned from Moab (RUTH 1:19-21).

Naomi put the child to her bosom and "became his *amanet* (nurse)" (RUTH 4:16). Did she actually suckle him? This verse was cited as a biblical precedent when the ethics of surrogate motherhood were first discussed. Contemporary women have breastfed grandchildren or their adopted children, but the Bible does not give any reason why Ruth should not feed her son herself. The verb *aman* means to support; perhaps the child was as much a support to Naomi's morale as she was to his physical well-being.

God as mother
God is described in the Bible by both masculine and feminine analogies; a majority of the feminine images are maternal ones. "As a mother comforts her child, so I will comfort you" (ISAIAH 66:13); "Can a woman forget the baby at her breast, show no compassion for the child of her womb? Even they may forget but I will not forget you" (ISAIAH 49:15). In the book of Job the creation of the world is compared to coming forth from the womb. These analogies show the power of maternal devotion by using it to demonstrate God's steadfast compassion and care for humanity.

Conclusion
The mothers portrayed in the Bible show many different aspects of motherhood that contemporary mothers can understand. The Bible says that mothers are to be honoured and their teachings heeded. Some biblical mothers love their children, sometimes to the point of

self-sacrifice. Women in the Bible have roles beyond motherhood, but being a mother is a significant source of fulfilment for them. Their maternal feelings are not always expressed ideally — and so we see them not as unattainably perfect mothers, but as human beings just like ourselves.

Other Mothers:
A Feminist Reading of
Biblical Stories[1]

Ayala Ronen Samuels

Jewish tradition tells us that Jews as a nation have three fathers and four mothers. The reference to the fathers is very prominent in the daily prayer. In the Amidah service, the core of the daily prayer, God is blessed for being *magen avot* — the protector of (our) fathers. Liberal versions of the Amidah have added a blessing for God as being *pokayd imahot* — the caller on (our) mothers. (The verb *pokayd* refers to God as responsible for the fertilization of the four and all mothers.) As the original blessing for the fathers mentions names — Abraham, Isaac and Jacob — so does the Liberal addition, mentioning Sarah, Rebecca, Rachel, and Leah. An almost equally famous song found in the Haggadah, the book read at the Pesach seder, asks, "Who knows four?" The correct answer is "I know four, four mothers." Thus, every child who has a Jewish education learns that "we" have four "mothers".

In fact, we have more than four foremothers. Reading the Bible, I find other women heroines to identify with, and I direct my questions about womanhood and motherhood vis-à-vis their life stories. But, as the text reflects a patriarchal society and culture, it is extremely male-

[1]This chapter is based on years of study in the Women's *Beit Midrash Nigun Shel Nashim* ("The Women's Melody") in HaMidrasha, Oranim, Israel. The fresh reading and creative midrash offered here are inspired by work done in the *Beit Midrash* over a long period of time. My deepest gratitude goes to my teachers and colleagues there, specifically to Tlalit Shavit and Rivka Lubitch for their inspiration and guidance in creative midrash-making.

centred. When women are mentioned, very little information is given about their reality and their ways of coping with it. Their point of view is in most cases neglected and forgotten. For example, Sarah is mentioned many times in Genesis. But mostly we look at Sarah from her husband's point of view. Once, we are told her reaction to what is going on: when she hears the angels promise her husband that she will give him a child, she laughs a bitter laugh of disbelief (GEN 18:12). But astoundingly, the Bible fails to tell us anything about her reaction to the horror story of the binding of her son, Isaac.[2]

What follows is a closer look at the stories of two biblical women, Bilhah the handmaid and the great mother of Shunem. Both are marginal figures in the sense that their stories serve and illustrate the stories of more important figures. The Bible offers little information regarding their life and perspective. The rabbis of the Talmudic era, too, in their careful reading of the Bible, have neglected their point of view and had no interest in them as people, as women, or as mothers.

Bilhah — the non-mother of her sons

Bilhah was the handmaid given to Rachel by her father, Laban, when she married Jacob. The Torah is very specific in saying that Laban gave *his* handmaid, Bilhah, as a handmaid to his daughter. In what ways was she *his*? Was she merely a property? The Torah leaves the question unanswered. Later, when Rachel realises she is *akara* (infertile), while her sister bears three boys to their common husband, she asks her husband to use her handmaid as a birthing instrument: "Behold my handmaid Bilhah," says Rachel to Jacob, "go into her; that she may bear upon my knees and I also may be builded up through

---

[2]The rabbis of the Talmudic era did deal with this issue in midrash, suggesting that Sarah died upon hearing the story of the binding (see *Midrash Tanhuma, VaYare* section).

her" (GEN 30:3). The plan works not once but twice. Bilhah is impregnated twice and gives birth to baby boys, Dan and Naphtali.

It is worth emphasising here the Bible's laconic reference to this most complicated, scary, and exciting process, childbearing. Was it a quick conception? How many menstrual periods did Bilhah go through until there was a definite pregnancy? Did she receive special nutrition during her pregnancy? Was her workload eased? Was it an uncomplicated pregnancy? How did delivery start? Did her waters break in public? And, finally, how on earth did she feel when her newborn was taken away from her to be named by her mistress? The Hebrew text gives only two words: *Vatahar va-teled* (She got pregnant and she gave birth). In our women's *Beit Midrash* this limited description is taken as a final proof that the text was not written by women.

Officially, the children Bilhah gave life to are Rachel's sons, though it is safe to assume that Bilhah nursed them and took care of them in their early childhood. They were two of the twelve sons of Jacob and, as such, became the fathers of two of Israel's tribes. Yet Bilhah is not considered a mother of the Israelites. She is not one of the four mythological mothers (Sarah, Rebecca, Leah and Rachel). She was perceived as a non-mother to her children. The reason for this strange, painful status is that she is not officially married to the father of her sons. But there may be something else that distinguishes her — together with Zilpah, Leah's handmaid — from the mothers: both of them were at no point *akara*, infertile. In the Bible, the state of being *akara* is not perceived as a biological or mental difficulty. Rather, it is understood and discussed as a manifestation of God's will. Therefore, when Rachel begs Jacob to give her children "or else I die", he scorns her: "Am I in God's stead, who hath withheld from thee the fruit of the womb?" (GEN 30:1-2). God does not bother to block the handmaids' wombs even temporarily, and that may account for their ordinary, rather than sanctified, status.

33

In closely examining the story of Bilhah, we can try to retell her life. Using the old method of rabbinic midrash, we can use the biblical words, few as they are, to open windows to her life and magnify her character and reality. This process is termed "creative midrash" and is based on the original Hebrew text and traditional methods of midrash.

The first midrash is concerned with the reason Laban chose Bilhah as a maid for Rachel. In Hebrew, the name Bilhah is spelled exactly like the word *balaha* (extreme fear). The two words also sound very similar.

> "His handmaid to be her handmaid" (GEN 29:24 AND 29:29)
> — Laban gave Zilpah to Leah and Bilhah to Rachel. The students in Bruria's *Beit Midrash*[3] wondered: How did Laban know that Bilhah was the right one for Rachel? They learned from her name that Bilhah understood anxieties and fears. Laban sensed that Rachel was bound to be insecure and anxious about her power and her fate. So he gave her Bilhah to help her deal with her anxieties and resolve her fears.
>
> (And why did he choose Zilpah to give to Leah? Leah's eyes were weak, so her tears were often dripping [*zolfot*]. Therefore, Laban gave her Zilpah to contain her tears and her pains.)

The midrash about the handmaids' names highlights the discussion about the life of these four women together. The men control their lives and routinely make decisions that shape their daily reality. According to the Torah text, none of the women — either wives or handmaids — was asked whether she wanted to share her life with Jacob and with his other women. They found themselves forced into each other's company and needed to struggle for control

---

[3]Bruria is the only woman mentioned in the Talmud as a scholar. My teacher, Rivka Lubitch, uses the name "Bruria's *Beit Midrash*" in her creative midrash. Of course, there was not — and could not have been — a *Beit Midrash* named after a woman scholar in pre-modern times.

(via the chance to spend a night with the man) or success (giving him sons). Discussing their relationships sheds light on the unexposed feminine point of view. This specific midrash also underscores the difficulty in living with the insecurity, the lack of control and the sadness accompanying this situation.

> There is more that we can say about the choice of Bilhah for Rachel: Rachel was a beautiful woman (GEN 29:17), and so was Bilhah, her handmaid. How do we learn that Bilhah was good-looking? From the fact that three generations of men were attracted to her:
>
> The grandfather — The expression "his handmaid" suggests that Laban was intimately involved with Bilhah before he gave her to Rachel.
>
> The father — "And he went into her." This is Jacob having intercourse with Bilhah.
>
> The son — "Reuben went and lay with Bilhah, his father's concubine" (GEN 35:22).

This midrash, presumably speaking about Bilhah's looks, brings into focus Bilhah's life in full. The Torah tells the story of Bilhah from other people's points of view. She is being given, handed over, and sexually used again and again. Her voice is never heard in the text, and we don't even know her fate. Was she alone in her old age? Did her sons love and protect her (but not from their older brother)? Where was she buried? The most creative midrash is silent on these questions. We today can merely point to the unknown and give voice to the silenced.

Why is Bilhah's story important? Why do we care enough to read it so closely and meticulously? Why imagine her feelings and add missing details? The fresh feminist reading has two aims. First, it asks questions neglected by previous, male, readers. In opening the text to female questions, interpretation and commentary, we make it more interesting and more accessible to women readers, thus adding validity to them as significant interpreters and creators of culture. Second, a midrash like this about Bilhah empowers not only her forgotten character, but also the life of women in strikingly similar situations: we want to express the insult and pain felt by all mothers who have no legal claim to their own children and struggle to survive in social systems that use them, ignore their point of view and eventually abandon them.

The Great Mother of Shunem

In the Second Book of Kings (4:8-37) we find a short and very dramatic story. It is one in a chain of tales about the prophet Elisha. Here, we are introduced to the "great woman of Shunem",[4] who recognises Elisha as a man of holiness and initiates a relationship between the two of them. From the very beginning, it is a bond of non-verbal understanding and *chesed* — grace. The woman is referred to as "great", but the Bible never explains why she merits the title. Is she physically big? Is she very wealthy? Is she known for her wisdom and courage? Moreover, she has no name, and, unusually, even though she is married, her husband's name is unknown as well. Apparently, she is not the hero of the story.

The relationship between Elisha and the "Shunammite" begins with her insightful recognition of him and is characterised by acts of grace: the Shunammite "holds" the prophet and gives him bread to eat. As he apparently passes through Shunem frequently, she extends her care for him and offers him a place to stay. It is at this point that the story becomes surprisingly detailed. The Shunammite tells her husband that she "knows" the "man of God" passes by "always". Therefore, she suggests, or rather, decides, "Let us make... a little chamber on the roof, and let us set for him a bed, and a table, and a stool, and a candlestick," to be ready for when Elisha comes to town (2 KINGS 4:10).

---

[4]Shunem is believed to be south of Mt Carmel, near Binyamina in modern Israel.

The detailed furnishing of the room is significant. On the one hand, it shows feminine, almost motherly, care: women know that a guest, specifically a regularly returning one, needs proper accommodation, and the Shunammite is a practical woman. On the other hand, the situation of a woman bringing a man into her home is loaded with erotic innuendos, even before we learn that her husband is "old" (4:14). What does the woman expect to get in return for her grace? The prophet himself wonders, and invites his hostess to his chamber to find out.

The discussion between Elisha and the Shunammite takes place in the roof chamber, as he lies on the bed and she stands in the doorway. As a barrier between their bodies and souls stands the prophet's servant, Gehazi. In the small space, Gehazi is told to ask the woman what she wants in return for her kindness. Does she need mediation with the authorities, perhaps? No, she needs nothing, she replies, as she "sits among her people", hinting, perhaps at her elevated status and independence.

Apparently the conversation is over at this point and the woman leaves. Then Gehazi contributes information he had gathered: the woman has no child, and her husband is an old man. Again Elisha asks his servant to call the woman, and she comes to his room and stands in the doorway, reluctant to come any closer. "At this season, when the time cometh round, thou shalt embrace a son," he says to her (4:16), using the same wording that Abraham's guests, the angels, used when they promised that Sarah would bear a child (GEN 18:10). The Shunammite, giving voice to years of disappointment and pain, replies: "Nay, my lord, the man of God, do not lie unto thy handmaid." [5]

[5]The Shunammite has many sisters in the Bible: Sarah (GEN 18), Rachel (GEN 30), Samson's mother (JUDGES 13) and Hannah (1 SAMUEL 1). They all became mothers (in other words, their infertility was resolved) with the will and help of God, but they all had to pay a price for this. The Shunammite's bitter answer reflects her understanding of this, as if she can hear Sarah's laughter and taste Hannah's tears right there, in the roof chamber.

The child is born on time, and several years pass in uneventful happiness. But the day comes when the child leaves his mother's protecting embrace and joins his father in the field, where he says to his father, "My head, my head," and is taken back to his mother, only to die on her knees. All this is told in the terse, dry style of the Bible, and serves as an introduction and prompt to the next encounter between the great woman of Shunem and Elisha.

The mother lays her dead child on the prophet's old bed and hurries to meet the man of God, not stopping even to explain her intentions to her husband. When they meet, Elisha tries first to distance himself from the situation by using Gehazi both to talk to the woman and later to save the child. But the Shunammite is too desperate now to settle for less than the best chance she has. She holds on to Elisha's feet, and he knows something terrible has happened. She gives him no details, merely saying, "Did I desire a son of my lord? *Did I not say: do not deceive me?*" (4:28; emphasis mine).[6] Elisha says nothing to her, but sends his servant to the boy, at which she vows: "As the lord liveth and thy soul liveth, *I will not leave thee!*" (4:30, emphasis mine).

Elisha's saving of the dead child is the focus of the biblical story, as it gives evidence of his divine powers and is a *ness galui*, an evident miracle. But we can use the detailed description to add another reading: Elisha goes to the *roof chamber* and sees the dead boy on the bed. He lies on the body, puts his *mouth* on his mouth, his *eyes* upon his eyes, his *hands* upon his hands, and he *stretches* himself upon him. He gets up, walks around and repeats the process. The boy sneezes and opens his eyes. Gehazi calls the mother and she bows down, picks up her son, and leaves. This is the (happy) end of the biblical story.

[6]See also the cry of the mother of a dying child to Elijah, and his saving of the child (1 KINGS 17:17-24).

The story of Elisha and the Shunammite has attracted curious readers before.[7] I find a beautiful description of a relationship confined by society's taboos and norms, but with no boundaries to limit the intensity and the energy in the relationship. It is a story of a man and a woman in a very basic human situation: she recognises him. She sees right through him and knows his powers. He, on the other hand, cannot see her, perhaps because he does not look. But once he learns her pain, he summons all his powers to help her. Both of them are very careful. Both have a lot to lose if the connection goes out of control and takes over their lives. Eventually, both gain enormously from the relationship. From beginning to end, there is *shechinah*, holy spirit, in the space between them. The child, alive and well, is a revelation of the deepest contact of their souls. He is the fruit of their love if the relationship was expressed through intercourse, and even if it was not. It is the woman's inner energy, in the form of acts of grace, that causes the man to see what she really lacks — a child. And he is able to give her that, after she has given up all hope. Later, when the boy dies, the mother sees it as a part of her relationship with the prophet. The detailed description of the revival is again loaded with erotic undertones and it adds another dimension to our understanding of what had happened in the roof chamber during the prophet's previous visit.

The Shunammite is a single mother in a deep sense of the word. She is married, but she alone raises the child until she thinks he is ready to meet the world — his father. The father is in the house, a part of the family, but not a "significant other" to the child. We learn that when the boy complains to him, "My head, my head," and the father, instead of trying help his son himself, instructs his

[7]See, for example, two articles in *Ha'aretz* literary magazine by Admiel Kosman (28 November 1997 and 20 May 1999), as well as the responses to the first article, by S Alony (5 May 1997) and R Alexander (26 December 1997).

servant to take the boy to his mother. Later, the father is curious enough to ask why his wife leaves in a hurry to see the prophet, but he does not ask about the sick — now dead — child. The wife's relationship with her husband is the exact opposite of the bond she has with the prophet. Similarly, the father's connection with his son is a sad mirror to that of Elisha. Neither man has a true relationship with the boy, but the prophet cares enough to give the boy life, even if only as a way of calming and satisfying his mother. The husband cannot offer her even that.

Finally, the Shunammite offers us a dramatic example of lonely, stubborn, unyielding motherhood. A very strong and proud woman, she does not admit her innermost sorrow, childlessness. Within the confines of her society she does what she sees as right. But when her child, the one she earned with grace and courage and raised with very little help from her husband, is at great risk, she breaks out of her boundaries to save him.

The story, thousands of years old, is touching in its depiction of the potential for love and grace between a man and a woman. It is also surprising to realise how it captures the essence of so many families everywhere: a remote father, engulfed in his world and his struggle to support the family, loses touch with his wife and child. The woman, alone in holding together the home and the family, creatively finds her own way to do what is right and overcomes a terrible crisis. One of the reasons I personally love the story is that it has such a happy ending, but one that leaves room for all the stories that cannot end happily, because there is no "man of God" around.

Endnote

Religion, tradition, myths and history are male-centred and ignore female perspective and interests. As a result, we do not have enough heroines to be inspired by, rebel against and model our lives upon. If modern women refuse to confine their cultural world to the past fifty years alone, they have to dig in, clean out the debris and creatively interpret what was created before the time of feminist writers.

We need to search for other mothers — "other" in more than one sense: not just figures other than the ones men have taught us to admire, but mothers whose stories must be examined from a critical and different point of view, and heroines representing other than the mainstream choices for women today. Bilhah and the great woman of Shunem offer us the opportunity to do just this — to make them our Other Mothers.

"Because She Entices
Him with Words":
Mothers in the Talmud

Rabbi Dr Margaret Jacobi

It is a truism, but still needs stating, that the Talmud[1] was
written by men, for men, about a man's world, in which
women were peripheral or incidental. This applies perhaps
even more to mothers. So the mothers in the Talmud are
mothers of sons, not daughters (though fathers and
daughters do appear). The Talmud is not a social document, but is largely legal; its stories, though frequent,
serve the purpose of reinforcing its world view.

Little is found in the Talmud about mothers, even
though it is clear that the Jewish mother is seen as essential to her son's development. Her partnership with the
father in bringing up children is recognised: "There are
three partners in the creation of a human being: God, the
father and the mother" (KIDDUSHIN 30B).

Most of what we find is in anecdotes, and there are two
key and contrasting passages which we will consider. The
first presents an idealised picture, the second a series of
more realistic ones.

Kimchit[2]
They said concerning Rabbi Ishmael the son of Kimchit:
once he was discussing matters with a certain Arab in the

---

[1]The Talmud here referred to is the Babylonian Talmud (compiled
in two parts — the older part, the Mishna, probably completed by
the year 200 CE, the second, the Gemara — a commentary —
finished around the 6th or 7th century CE) compared to the
"Jerusalem Talmud", compiled earlier in Palestine.

[2]The story of Kimchit is found in Yoma 47a. A fuller version is
found in the midrashic collection Vayikra Rabbah (20:11), with

market and some spittle fell from his mouth onto him.[3] Yeshovav his brother went (into the Temple) and served in his place, and their mother saw (her sons as) two High Priests in one day. And it is said further concerning Rabbi Ishmael the son of Kimchit that once he was discussing matters with a certain man in the market and some spittle fell from his mouth onto him. Yosef his brother went and served in his place and their mother saw (her sons as) two High Priests in one day. It is taught: Kimchit had seven sons and all of them served as High Priest. The sages said to her: "What have you done, that you should deserve this merit?" She said to them: "All my days, the beams of my house have never seen a strand of my hair." They said to her: "Many have done this, but it has not profited them."

Kimchit is seen as selfless and modest, and as a result her sons are privileged to serve as High Priest. She hides herself from the world, so that not even the beams of the house see her hair. Her reward is that her sons are in the most exposed position they can be, serving as High Priests before the whole of Israel. But the irony goes further: her sons are known as the sons of Kimchit, not of their father. He is not even named, let alone given the honour alongside Kimchit. It is unusual, though not unknown, for sons to carry their mothers' names. But when the norm is for men to be known as the sons of their fathers, and by implication, recipients of their teaching, it is significant that Kimchit's sons are known only by her name. Despite her glory being "inner",[4] clearly the influence she had on her sons became public. The reward was not only that her sons were dedicated to God, but that they were recognised as her sons, reflecting her merit — which was not so inner after all.

some slight changes, e.g. in the names of the sons. Here, too, the verse from Proverbs: "The glory of the daughter of a king is inner" is applied to Kimchit.
[3]So disqualifying him from Temple service.
[4]See footnote 3.

But there is a sting in the tale: serving as High Priest was dangerous. If the High Priest made an error in performing the Yom Kippur service, it was thought he was liable to die. This echoes another story of seven sons, like that of Kimchit, set in the time of the Second Temple. This story is found not in the Talmud but in the Apocrypha, books which were not considered suitable for inclusion in the Hebrew Bible. Here we find the story of Hannah,[5] each of whose sons undergoes a gruesome martyrdom at the hands of the Greeks. Their mother urges them not to abandon their faith, but rather to give up their lives. In both stories, a mother has the honour of giving up seven sons to God. In the case of Hannah, the sons give themselves willingly to death; in the case of Kimchit, the sons survive. But in both, the mother is idealised as selfless and the honour lies in being able to offer her sons in service to God.

Honouring one's mother

If the story of Kimchit offers an idealised picture, reality breaks through in a passage in tractate Kiddushin (30B-32A) about *kibbud av va-eym* — honouring one's father and mother. Near the beginning of the section, two commandments regarding fathers and mothers are considered: "Each person shall honour their mother and their father" (LEV 19:3) and "Honour your father and your mother" (DEUT 5:16). There is a difference in the commandments, which the Talmud picks up:

Rabbi [Judah haNasi] said: "It is revealed and known to the One who spoke, and the world came to be, that a son honours his mother more than his father, because she entices him with words; therefore the Holy One who is to be blessed placed the honour of the father before that of the mother. It is revealed and known to the One who spoke, and the world came to be, that a son reveres his

[5]II Maccabees chapter 7. She is unnamed in the Apocrypha, and her name does not appear until 1510.

father more than his mother, because he teaches him Torah; therefore the Holy One who is to be blessed put the reverence of the mother before that of the father."
(KIDDUSHIN 30B)

The distinction is made between a mother, who is loving and tender towards her sons, and a father, who is a strict teacher, inspiring fear rather than love. However, the word "entice" also has other overtones. The Hebrew root *sh-d-l* means to persuade gently, and to win over with words. But it is also used in the Talmud in relation to Potiphar's wife's attempted seduction of Joseph. Rashi, the great eleventh-century CE commentator, makes this nuance more explicit in explaining the word with the Hebrew root *f-t-h*. As an example of the latter word, he quotes Exodus 22:15, which, ironically, refers to a man seducing a woman.

There are therefore clear sexual overtones in the phrase and perhaps oedipal feelings. These are more clearly present in the story of Rav Assi and his mother, described below. It forms a contrast with Kimchit, who was so careful about keeping herself covered that not even a hair of her head was exposed. Although the distinction between mothers and fathers seems at first simply to reflect a gentler view of mothers, the words hint at a certain discomfort. It is borne out by what follows. When we come to consider exactly what it means in practice to honour one's mother, the picture of a mother is not so comfortable.

The exemplar of how to fulfil the commandment is, significantly, a non-Jew, named Dama ben Netinah. It is told of him: "He was once wearing a gold embroidered silken cloak and sitting among Roman nobles, when his mother came, tore it off from him, struck him on the head, and spat in his face, yet he did not shame her."

We do not know the cause of his mother's behaviour, nor whether Dama ben Netinah's actions had provoked her. But it is clear that forbearance is expected from the son. The anecdotes which follow, relating to both fathers

45

and mothers, make this clear. One relates to Rabbi Tarfon, one of the greatest rabbis of the second century CE:

> Rabbi Tarfon had a mother for whom, whenever she wished to mount into bed, he would bend down to let her ascend; and when she wished to descend she stepped down upon him. He went in and boasted about it in the school. They said to him: "You have not yet reached half the honour due: has she thrown a purse before you into the sea without your shaming her?"

A story in the Jerusalem Talmud[6] about Rabbi Ishmael, a contemporary of Rabbi Tarfon's, goes further:

> The mother of Rabbi Ishmael complained about her son to the rabbis. "Rebuke him for he does not do me honour." The rabbis demanded, "Is it possible that Rabbi Ishmael does not show honour to his mother? What has he done to you?" She replied, "When he goes to the House of Study, I want to wash his feet and to drink the water in which I have washed them, and he will not permit it." The rabbis said to him, "If that is her wish, honour her by allowing her to do it."

Both stories indicate that a son cannot go too far in honouring his mother. But the second story adds another dimension — a mother wishing to honour her son. Rabbi Ishmael's mother was obviously proud of him, and wished to show it by actions which seemed to Rabbi Ishmael to demean her. Yet his colleagues felt that if that was her wish, he should allow her to do so. He showed her honour by respecting her wishes, by allowing her to dote on him in an extreme way. Sometimes, it is hard for sons to accept their mothers' extravagant affection for them. But, the Talmud suggests, mothers are honoured when they are allowed to express their feelings for their sons in whatever way they wish.

[6]Kiddushin 61b.

46

Rav Assi

A story of more complicated feelings follows in the Babylonian Talmud:

> Rav Assi had an aged mother. She said to him: "I want ornaments." So he made them for her.
>
> "I want a husband."
>
> "I will look out for you."
>
> "I want a husband as handsome as you."
>
> Thereupon he left her and went to Palestine (from Babylonia).
>
> On hearing that she was following him, he went to Rabbi Yochanan and asked him: "May I leave Palestine for abroad?"
>
> "It is forbidden," he replied.
>
> "But what if it is to meet my mother?"
>
> "I do not know," said Rabbi Yochanan.
>
> Rav Assi waited a short time and went before Rabbi Yochanan again.
>
> "Assi," said Rabbi Yochanan, "you have determined to go. May the Omnipresent bring you back in peace."
>
> Then Rav Assi went before Rabbi Eleazar and said to him, "Perhaps, God forbid, he was angry?"
>
> "What, then, did he say to you?" he asked.
>
> "The Omnipresent bring you back in peace," was the answer.
>
> "Had he been angry," replied Rabbi Eleazar, "he would not have blessed you."
>
> In the meantime, Rav Assi learnt that his mother's coffin was coming. "Had I known," he exclaimed, "I would not have gone out."

Rav Assi's mother is making difficult demands on him. He tries to cope by bringing her ornaments, and by promising to find her a husband. But when she asks for a husband as handsome as he is, he can no longer cope and leaves for Palestine. Perhaps it is not just the demands that are a problem, but that there seems to be a sexual undercurrent to them, which gradually becomes more explicit: his mother's demand for a husband as handsome as her son seems to express her sexual feelings towards him.

47

But he cannot escape by going to Palestine. She follows him. On hearing this, he expresses a desire to leave Palestine. Is it to flee his mother who is pursuing him, as he sees it? Or is it rather, as he subsequently claims to Rabbi Yochanan, to meet his mother? The narrative is ambiguous, perhaps reflecting Rav Assi's feelings. He may have felt impulses in both directions, though clearly it would have been more acceptable to Rabbi Yochanan to say he wished to meet his mother — both as a reason to leave the Holy Land and as a commendable action in its own right.

But whilst he is debating with his teachers, he hears that his mother has died. His final remark is somewhat anti-climactic. It suggests that he regrets leaving the Holy Land, but gives no indication of regret at his mother's death. Perhaps he felt none, but instead felt relief that he no longer had to cope with her demands.

The narrative also hints at another theme behind Rav Assi's ambivalence, which is picked up later in the passage: the relative roles of parent and teacher. The Talmud discusses the relative importance of the two roles. Teachers are paramount in rabbinic culture. Fathers are respected in their role as teacher, and referred to as "my father my teacher". If they fail to teach, then the teacher is accorded greater respect. Mothers, since they do not (usually) learn or teach Torah, have a secondary role. Here, Rav Assi's teachers take on a parental role. He seeks advice from them and they give it. When he fears that Rabbi Yochanan is angry with him, it causes him concern. Perhaps Rav Assi feels a conflict between the demands of his mother and those of his teachers. With his mother's death, the conflict is at an end.

The picture that emerges of mothers in the Talmud is one which is increasingly part of society today: children — sons in the rabbinic world — care for their parents. Their parents' demands can be irrational and embarrassing, perhaps due to the onset of dementia. The Talmud recognises how hard it is for the children. Yet it makes no concessions. Parents deserve unlimited care despite or because of what may become of them.

The mothers of Tarfon, Ishmael and Assi are a far cry from Kimchit, the idealised, retiring, modest mother. They are the mothers we encounter as we and they grow older, albeit with exaggerated behaviour which stretches the imagination. Jewish mothers — indeed any mothers — are not always comfortable to be with. They can be most challenging when they most wish to show their love. The stereotype of the all-embracing Jewish mother is one that the Talmud seems to recognise. But the Talmud is clear: to honour them is to let them show their love. That remains a challenge for Jewish sons — and daughters — today.

Tender Voices:
Mothers in Yiddish Poetry

Translations by Sheva Zucker

Rashel Veprinski

Fun mayne shlanke glider

Fun mayne shlanke glider veynen kinder nit geboyrene,
Vos viln durkh mayn layb di vayse velt derzen
Un ufblien unter der zun
Mit kepelekh gekroyzlte,
Eygelekh breyt-farvunderte,
Shvartsinke un bloy.
Nor tif in zikh farneyn ikh yene klore shtimelekh
Mit toyznt shtimen
Fun a fiberishn drang,
Tsu blaybn eybik, eybik,
Azoy meydlesh-beygik,
Fray far shvung, kapriz, —
Un far dayne libndike hent —

To zoln mayne nekht un teg
Do vern hastiker farshvendt,
Az dortn vu ir vart, —
Ahinter vayse toyern, —
Kumen zol ikh yung tsu aykh.
Ikh vel aykh
Shtil tsuzamennemen unter mayne mame-fligl
Un af epes veynen glaykh mit aykh.

50

Rashel Veprinski

From My Slender Limbs

From my slender limbs cry children yet unborn,
Who want, through my flesh, to glimpse the white world
And blossom forth under the sun
With curly heads,
Little eyes wide with wonder,
Blue and black.
But deep within me I say no to those clear little voices
With a thousand voices
Out of a frenzied striving
To stay always, always,
So girlishly supple,
Free for the lilt, for the whimsy, —
And for your loving arms —

So let my nights and days
Here be more hastily squandered,
So that there where you wait, —
Beyond white gates, —
I may come, still young, to you.
And I will take you my children
Quietly under my mother-wings
And cry over something, together with you.

Rashel Veprinski

Ven...

Ven ikh zol kinderlekh geboyrn,
Yedn yor a kind, biz ikh vel hobn tsen —
Vi vunderlekh dos volt geven.
Ikh volt zey durkh di teg, ayngezoygn, ayngevigt,
In ovnt volt ikh laybelekh fun vol far zey geshtrikt,
Hemdelekh un vindelekh volt ikh gevashn,
Far tog, ven ale shlofn,
Volt ikh zey tsehongen af di shtrik
Un volt a vaylinke geshtanen,
Gekukt in hoykhn himl
Tsi s'vet haynt regenen,
Un s'volt mayn harts bahaltn ongekvoln
Fun dem shirkh-shorkh vos der vint makht
Ufblozndik di hemdelekh un vindelekh
Vi di fonen fun a zeglshif, —
Di fonen fun mayn zeglshif —
Vi vunderlekh dos volt geven.

Rashel Veprinski

If...

If I were to bear children,
Every year a child, until I had ten —
How wonderful it would be then.
By day I would nurse them and rock them in their cradle,
At night I would knit them undervests of wool,
And wash their little shirts and diapers,
At daybreak, when everyone was still asleep,
I would hang them out on the line
And would stand for a while,
Looking at the sky above
To see if it was going to rain today,
And secretly my heart would delight
In the rustle of the wind
Unfurling the little shirts and diapers
Like the flags on a sailboat, —
Like the flags on my sailboat —
How wonderful it would be then.

Rashel Veprinski was born in 1896 in the town of Ivankov, not far from Kiev, in Ukraine. She came to New York in 1907, and at the age of thirteen she went to work in a shop. At fifteen, she began writing poetry, and was first published in 1918 in the journal *Di naye velt (The New World)*. She wrote several books of poetry, an autobiographical novel, short stories, and articles, and was published regularly in Yiddish periodicals. From the 1920s until his death in 1953, she lived with the famous Yiddish writer Mani Leyb. She was the mother of one daughter by an earlier marriage. Rashel Veprinski died in the early 1980s. The poems are from her collection *Di Palitre (The Palette)*, published in 1964 (I L Peretz Publishing House, Tel Aviv).

Rajzel Zychlinsky

Mayn Kind Klapt

Mayn kind klapt mit farmakhte vies
In dem toyer fun der velt.
S'iz Kislev —
Di verbes tsitern in frost
Un es shmekt di tseshternte kelt.
S'klapt dos harts fun mayn kind:
Efn!

Baym rog fun gas hob ikh zikh
Mit der akhter levone getrofn.
Mit yidishe oygn kuk ikh
Der levone in ponem arayn:
— Mayn kind, dos blut in dayne odern iz zaft
Fun gloybn un payn,
Gelaytert bay di taykhn fun Bovl
Un bay di bregn fun Nil.
S'hot mayn mame in a shtetl in Poyln
Gedavnt in a shil,
Di shil iz geven fun holts
Alt zeks hundert yor
Un di beyner fun di zeydes
Hobn geloykhtn in tol.

Di shil iz farbrent,
Der tol tsetrotn.
Af opgemekhte kvorim
Hoyern nor shotns.

— Kh'shtel pamelekh di trit.
Ikh gey laykht azoy vi a shtral,
Vi a vanderer in midber,
Vos hot gefunen a kval.

continued on page 56

54

Rajzel Zychlinsky

My Child Knocks

My child knocks with closed lashes
At the gate of the world.
It's Kislev —
The willows quiver in the frost
And the starry cold is fragrant.
The heart of my child beats:
Open!

At the corner of the street
I met the eighth moon.
With Jewish eyes I look
The moon in the face:
— My child, the blood in your veins is the juice
Of belief and pain,
Purified in the rivers of Babylon
And at the shores of the Nile.
In a town in Poland my mother
Prayed in a synagogue,
The synagogue was made of wood
Six hundred years old
And the bones of my grandfathers
Shone in the valley.

The synagogue is burned,
The valley is trampled.
Over rubbed-out graves
Only shadows hover.

— Slowly I walk,
Treading lightly like a sunbeam,
Like a wanderer in the desert,
Who has found a spring.

continued on page 57

55

Rajzel Zychlinsky

Mayn kind klapt mit farmakhte vies
In dem toyer fun der velt —
Der himl iz ful nokh mit shtern un haftokhes,
Vi a mol, iber Yankevs getselt.

Rajzel Zychlinsky

My child knocks with closed lashes
At the gate of the world —
The heavens are still full of stars and promises,
Like long ago, over the tents of Jacob.

Rajzel Zychlinsky was born in Gombin, Poland, in 1910. Her first book of poems, published in 1936, included a foreword by the celebrated poet Itsik Manger, in which he hailed her work as "a new, authentic revelation of the feminine poetic countenance in Jewish Poland." She left her home in Warsaw during the Second World War with her husband and child, the latter undoubtedly the inspiration for the poem reprinted here. The family took refuge in Soviet Russia. In 1947 Zychlinsky returned to Poland, but after a year left for Paris. In 1951 she emigrated to New York. She lived there until the last few years of her life, when she moved to Berkeley, California, to join her son. She published several volumes of poetry in Yiddish; a good selection of her poems has been published in English in the book *God Hid His Face: Selected Poems of Rajzel Zychlinsky*, translated by Barnett Zumoff, Aaron Kramer, and Zychlinsky's son, Marek Kanter (Santa Rosa, California: Word & Quill Press, 1997). She died in California in 2001. The Holocaust is a major theme in Zychlinsky's work. The poem reprinted here is from *Shvaygndike Tirn (Silent Doors)*, a collection published with the help of the Yiddish PEN Club in New York in 1962.

"The Most Unforgettable Character I've Met": Literary Representations of the Jewish Mother

Nadia Valman

"The Most Unforgettable Character I've Met" is how, in the opening words of his monologue, the eponymous narrator of Philip Roth's *Portnoy's Complaint* (1967) pays tribute to his mother. Unforgettable, of course, in the sense of oppressive and inescapable. Roth's notorious literary *kvetch*, which ascribes the ills of the modern American Jewish man to the self-sacrificing, suffocating, passive-aggressive Jewish matriarch, in many ways typifies the twentieth-century literary image of the Jewish mother. And yet it wasn't always that way. Sophie Portnoy's neurotic devotion to the cause of protecting the physical health and religious purity of her beloved son has its roots in a very different image of Jewish motherhood in nineteenth-century Europe.

In his utopian novel *Altneuland* (Old-New Land), published in 1902, the Zionist ideologue Theodor Herzl imagined a future Jewish state peopled not by the hopelessly depressed, unhealthy and self-loathing Jews of nineteenth-century Europe, but vigorous, optimistic young men and women. After much discussion of the ideological, economic and cultural basis of the Jewish state, however, the novel ends, significantly, with the death of the young Zionist pioneer's Jewish mother. "She sustained us in affliction, for she was Love," he eulogises at her funeral. "In better days, she taught us humility, for she was Pain... She was an invalid. But Pain did not degrade her. It exalted her. Often she seemed to me the symbol of the Jewish people in the days of its suffering."[1] Herzl's novel not only suggests an intrinsic connection between the heroic sacrifices of the Jewish mother and the creation of a new generation full of striving nationalist idealism. He also regards the Jewish mother as the embodiment of Jewish history itself.

This idealisation of the Jewish mother goes back even further. In mid-nineteenth-century middle-class culture, the reverence of domestic femininity was at its height. Like her Christian contemporaries, the Victorian Anglo-Jewish novelist Grace Aguilar prescribed an exalted role for the Jewish woman and exhorted her female readers to take pride in the magnificent task that had been entrusted to them as mothers. In her book of female scripture biography, *The Women of Israel* (1845), aimed at the Jewish woman reader, she declared: "To the women of Israel... is entrusted the noble privilege of hastening 'the great and glorious day of the Lord,' by the instruction they bestow upon their sons, and the spiritual elevation to which they may attain in social intercourse, and yet more in domestic life."[2] In her domestic fiction aimed at the general reader, Aguilar demonstrated the role of wife and mother, who acted as moral governor to the family, monitoring the upbringing of children, encouraging them to develop virtuous habits and to resist sin, and figuring as God's proxy in the home. In her novella *The Perez Family* (1844), Aguilar repeated the same formula in her portrait of a Jewish family beset by the trials of poverty and assimilation, but ultimately saved by Rachel, its matriarch, whose

[1]Theodor Herzl, *Old-New Land (Altneuland)*, transl. Lotta Levensohn (New York: Markus Wiener Publishing/The Herzl Press, 1987 [first publ. 1902]), pp. 294-95.
[2]Grace Aguilar, *The Women of Israel or Characters and Sketches from the Holy Scriptures and Jewish History Illustrative of the Past History, Present Duties, and Future Destiny of the Hebrew Females, as based on the Word of God* (London: Groombridge, 1870; first publ. serially 1844-45), p. 579.

steadfast and simple piety in the face of suffering comes to exemplify Aguilar's idea of Jewish spirituality. The story's centrepiece, highly reminiscent of Victorian Christian fiction, is a scene in which she directs the family in their celebration of a peaceful, sober Sabbath and instructs her children in Bible-reading. "To every mother in Israel," Aguilar reminds her reader, "these powers are given."[3]

Aguilar hoped that her own powers of persuasion could contribute to improving public opinion concerning Jews in Victorian England. Certainly, by the late nineteenth century, Jewish domestic life was the one acknowledged ray of light amidst what was widely regarded as the dark and threatening problem of impoverished Jewish immigrants living in crowded conditions in the slum areas of British cities. Victorian social investigators frequently remarked on the tranquillity of the Jewish family despite such hardships. In an article published in the *Sunday Magazine* in 1892, one journalist noted that "However poor a family may be they strive to have a little feast on Friday evenings after the service in the synagogue."[4] In their survey *The Jew in London: A Study of Racial Character and Present-day Conditions* (1900), C Russell and HS Lewis commented:

> The Jew is a born critic, but he seldom finds fault with his wife, and he is, as a rule, blessed with domestic happiness. The Jewish husband spends most of his leisure at home, and, possibly owing to this fact, his wife's advice and influence count for much with him... Poverty necessarily makes home life more difficult, and the absence of privacy

[3]For more on "The Perez Family", see Michael Galchinsky, *The Origin of the Modern Jewish Woman Writer: Romance and Reform in Victorian England* (Detroit: Wayne State University Press, 1996), pp. 178-85.

[4]Mrs Brewer, "The Jewish Colony in London", *The Sunday Magazine*, XXI (1892), pp.16-23, cited in David Englander, ed., *A Documentary History of Jewish Immigrants in Britain, 1840-1920* (Leicester: Leicester University Press, 1994), p. 72.

for members of a family who have only one or two rooms of their own must often tempt them to seek distraction elsewhere. It is all the more remarkable that foreign Jews, whose houses are so often overcrowded, are able to conquer adverse influences and to set such an example of happy and contented home life.[5]

What most appealed to these Victorian observers of Jewish immigrant life was the potential for respectability indicated by the domestic culture of working-class Jews.

If, in these Victorian accounts, the happiness of the Jewish immigrant home is ascribed to the power and influence of the Jewish mother, the story begins to change in the twentieth century. Henry Roth's modernist masterpiece, *Call It Sleep* (1934) drew on Freudian theory to portray the American Jewish family as fraught by conflicts of power and desire. David Schearl, the Polish-born six-year-old at the centre of the narrative, is the object of an ongoing struggle between his violent, frustrated father and his fearful, devoted mother, whose overprotective love for her son fills the void of an unhappy marriage. David experiences his relationship with his mother as one of guilty desire, provoked alternately by her eroticism and her vulnerability. On one occasion, for example, just after one of his father's fits of rage, David's neighbour Yussie appears, demanding that David come out and play.

> He hesitated, looked up at his mother. Her breast was heaving slowly, deeply, making a slight moaning creak in her throat. Her eyes, unwinking, round and liquid, swam in the lustre of unshed tears. For a shattering instant a throng of impulses, diverse, fierce, maddening, hurtled against the very core of his being. He wanted to shrink away, to run, to hide, anywhere, under the table, in a corner, in his bedroom, to burst into tears, to scream at

---

[5]C Russell and HS Lewis, *The Jew in London: A Study of Racial Character and Present-day Conditions* (1900), pp. 186-91, cited in Englander, p. 103.

her. So many they paralysed him. He stood quivering, gaping at her, waiting for her to weep. Then suddenly he remembered! Yussie was looking at her! He would know! He would see! He mustn't![6]

It's possible to see here the roots of Philip Roth's *Portnoy's Complaint*, in which the narrator, also engaged in a generational struggle with his parents, experiences this as a desperate longing to escape the moral guilt inculcated in him by his mother.

In his monologue to his psychoanalyst, Alex Portnoy recalls the first stirrings of sexuality in his four-year-old consciousness, marvelling that his mother was "so attuned to my deepest desires!"[7] He remembers a time when

> She sits on the edge of the bed in her padded bra and her girdle, rolling on her stockings and chattering away. Who is Mommy's good little boy? Who is the best little boy a mommy ever had? Who does Mommy love more than anything in the whole wide world? I am absolutely punchy with delight, and meanwhile follow in their tight, slow, agonisingly delicious journey up her legs the transparent stockings that give her flesh a hue of stirring dimensions.[8]

Twenty-five years later, he notes, "Mommy still hitches up the stockings in front of her little boy," still humiliating her husband with her filial passion and binding her son to her with a manipulative and irresistible force.[9]

It is Sophie Portnoy's unshakeable belief in her own exemplary goodness, however, that Alex regards as the most perverse and damaging aspect of the Jewish family dynamic. She has brought him up to believe that his obedience and dutifulness are the only possible compensation for her lifetime of self-sacrifice. Roth links the prohibitions of traditional Jewish dietary laws ("The watch-its and the

[6]Henry Roth, *Call It Sleep* (London: Michael Joseph, 1934), p. 144.
[7]Philip Roth, *Portnoy's Complaint* (London: Penguin, 1969), p. 43.
[8]Ibid, p. 44.
[9]Ibid, p. 45.

be-carefuls! You mustn't do this, you can't do that"[10]) with the fearfulness engendered by centuries of persecution, and laments that

> this is my life, my only life, and I'm living it in the middle of a Jewish joke! I am the son in the Jewish joke — *only it ain't no joke!* Please, who crippled us like this? Who made us so morbid and hysterical and weak?... Doctor, what do you call this sickness I have? Is this the Jewish suffering I used to hear so much about? Is this what has come down to me from the pogroms and the persecution? From the mockery and abuse bestowed by the *goyim* over these two thousand lovely years? Oh my secrets, my shame, my palpitations, my flushes, my sweats! The way I respond to the simple vicissitudes of human life! Doctor, I can't stand any more being frightened like this over nothing! Bless me with manhood! Make me brave! Make me strong! Make me *whole*! Enough being a nice Jewish boy, publicly pleasing my parents while privately pulling my putz! Enough![11]

In Roth's novel, the inhibitions generated by anti-Semitism and Jewish law are writ large in the figure of the virtuous and forbidding Jewish mother. While Portnoy grew up hearing that his mother's fault was that she was "too good", he asserts, instead, that "to be *bad*, Mother, that is the real struggle: to be bad — and to enjoy it! That is what makes men of us boys, Mother."[12]

Although Roth's novel was regarded at the time of its publication as taboo-breaking, its gripes had become staples of American Jewish humour in the 1950s and 60s. The cultural anthropologist Riv-Ellen Prell has suggested that the stereotype of the Jewish mother emerged as a specific response to the anxieties of upward mobility, consumerism and suburbanisation in postwar American Jewish life. The Jewish mother, she observes,

[10]Ibid, p. 35.
[11]Ibid, p. 37.
[12]Ibid, p. 114.

was not the Yiddishe Mama of the Old World, to whom immigrants longingly turned with sentimental songs and harsh comparisons to American sweethearts and wives. Rather, this representation of New World prosperity was an American-born Jewish Mother who pushed, wheedled, demanded, constrained, and was insatiable in her expectations and wants. The guilt induced by the Old World was not her siren song; rather she demanded loyalty to herself and her impossible New World expectations.[13]

The "comic image of nurturance gone awry" appeared at the same time as often-expressed fears amongst American Jews that the stability of the Jewish home had been disrupted by the excess power of the Jewish woman.[14] The stereotype of the over-demanding Jewish mother perhaps even reflected disenchantment with middle-class aspirations.[15]

It's not altogether surprising, then, that a similar image is discernible in fiction by women writers as well as by men. In Lesléa Newman's novel *Good Enough to Eat* (1986), the affluent suburban Jewish mother of protagonist Liza Goldberg invariably follows a litany of local gossip on recent engagements and bar mitzvahs with a punitive question about her daughter's weight, both forming part of an oppressive heterosexual discourse of family. Liza's Yiddish-speaking grandmother, by contrast, is more often concerned with whether she is eating well and enough. The contrast between the immigrant grandmother's positive and nurturing love and the assimilated mother's effort to constrain Liza's appetite, to reshape her body towards an American ideal, maps affect onto generational change. Growing up in an era of rampant consumption wholeheartedly embraced by her mother,

[13]Riv-Ellen Prell, *Fighting to Become Americans: Jews, Gender, and the Anxieties of Assimilation* (Boston: Beacon Press, 1999), p. 143.
[14]Ibid, p. 151.
[15]Ibid, p. 176.

Liza responds by starving herself. The figure of the Jewish mother, central to the idealisation of the Jewish family in the nineteenth century, is, it seems, just as crucial in the critique of this myth for contemporary Jewish novelists. By the 1980s, moreover, women writers were voicing their own claim to the oedipal rage that had previously been the prerogative of the Jewish male.

For other women writers, however, the Jewish mother is a figure of more complex ambivalence. Vivian Gornick's memoir *Fierce Attachments* (1987) shifts between the present and the past as Gornick walks the streets of Manhattan in the company of her mother, a woman operatically devoted to the image of her own suffering. Typically, the narrator's memories are triggered by arguing. In one scene, Gornick resolutely opposes her mother's sentimental nostalgia for the life in a Jewish tenement in the Bronx that they have both left behind. When her mother laments the loosening of emotional ties between modern children and their mothers, the narrator protests that just because sons and daughters of the previous generation were more dutiful it didn't mean they had more love for their mothers. "It wasn't a better life, it was an immigrant life, a working-class life, a life from another country... Nowadays love has to be earned. Even by mothers and sons" — a comment that earns her only a withering glance of scorn.[16] At other moments, however, the author reflects that her mother's arrogant and hypercritical tone, her repeated mockery of her college-educated daughter, is her defence "when she thinks she doesn't understand something and she's scared" — a perspective on the trials of parenting across class and educational difference that clearly never occurred to Roth's Portnoy.[17]

[16]Vivian Gornick, *Fierce Attachments: A Memoir* (New York: Farrar, Straus and Giroux, 1987), pp. 44-45.
[17]Ibid, p. 73.

For Gornick, the relationship between daughter and mother is the continuous, dynamic and always fraught love affair of her life. Instead of experiencing only filial fury, she also notices their common sensibility, their similarly debilitating romanticism and melodramatic longing: "'Oh Ma!' I cry, and my frightened greedy freedom-loving life wells up in me and spills down my soft-skinned face, the one she has given me."[18] More than this, she recognises in her mother's signature gesture — "the flat edge of her hand cutting the air in that familiar motion of dismissal" (her most Jewish trait) — the expression of a moral consciousness that the author cannot but embrace with gratitude and affection: "The dismissal of others is to her the struggle to rise from the beasts, to make distinctions, to know the right and the wrong of a thing."[19] Gornick, and writers like Tillie Olsen and Grace Paley, invoke the Jewish mother as carrier not of religious values as such, but of an ethical tradition — a tradition that is manifest in the extension of their maternal role into a wider political commitment to social justice.[20]

This brief survey of literary representations has traced a shift from the idealised Jewish mother of the nineteenth century to the domestic demon of the twentieth. What makes them so interesting to consider together is the way that the figure of the mother is consistently made to stand for Jewishness itself, and all the romantic, raging or ambivalent feelings that it arouses. As Gornick writes of her relationship with her mother, "We are locked into a narrow channel of acquaintance, intense and binding."[21]

[18]Ibid, p. 48.
[19]Ibid, p. 198.
[20]On Olsen and Paley, see Janet Handler Burstein, *Writing Mothers, Writing Daughters: Tracing the Maternal in Stories by American-Jewish Women* (Urbana: University of Illinois Press, 1996).
[21]Gornick, p. 6.

Jewish Mothers
on Film

Angela English

The Jewish mother has featured as a character worthy of note from the earliest silent films right up to the present day. It is not possible to provide a definitive picture of the Jewish mother on film in this short chapter, but I hope to provide some insights into changing perceptions by exploring three films made in the USA from the 1920s to the 1980s. These three — *The Jazz Singer* (1927), *Green Fields* (a Yiddish film from the late 1930s) and *Radio Days* (Woody Allen's 1987 comedy) — all feature Jewish mothers as important characters. The creative impulses that lay behind these films were those of a variety of Jewish men. It may be interesting to speculate about their relationships with their mothers as reflected in the way these films portray Jewish mothers. As we will see, these and other films tend to idealise the role and position of mothers.

The founders of the film industry in the USA were largely immigrants or sons of immigrants who came from central and eastern Europe during the mass immigration of the late nineteenth century. Most were of Orthodox Jewish parentage and came from poverty-stricken backgrounds. Parents must have sacrificed and suffered for their children, and the Hollywood moguls were perhaps idealising the struggles of their own mothers in their films. Of the eight major film companies that came to form the Hollywood film industry in the 1920s, six were founded by Jews, few of whom continued to adhere to their Orthodox faith. Most of the movie moguls passionately wanted to assimilate and become fully fledged Americans — they wanted to live the American dream.

They had mostly anglicised their names. An example of this was the Warner Brothers, whose earlier name was "Waters", an obvious Anglicisation from another, eastern European name. Probably their parents had effected a name change. This points up the "double immigration" of the Jewish film moguls, who first came to New York from Europe and then later crossed a whole continent to go to California, where they founded Hollywood. The moguls, in shedding their Jewishness, also tended to divorce their first (Jewish) wives and marry second wives who were gentiles. As part of this move towards Americanisation, they fought shy of making films dealing with Jewish experience, and by the 1930s their films generally had jettisoned any reminder of their ethnic past. Thus *The Jazz Singer* (1927) was probably the last Hollywood film that dealt with issues around assimilation — intermarriage, generational conflict, mobility and economic achievement. While the film was groundbreaking because it was the first so-called "talkie" (though it was primarily a silent film with a small amount of spoken dialogue), it marked the end of an era in its depiction of images of Jewish life. After *The Jazz Singer,* Hollywood films from the sound era tended to ignore Jewish life.

Warner Brothers Studios, run by four brothers, Harry, Jack, Sam and Albert, made the film. Sam really believed in sound cinema and had persuaded his more sceptical brothers to invest in the production of musical short films. The studio had released synchronised sound shorts in 1926 and *The Jazz Singer* also featured songs, mostly sung by the famous Jewish entertainer Al Jolson, who plays the main role of Jakie Rabinowitz. The film also had some sequences of synchronised spoken dialogue and was the first film to do this.

The Jazz Singer is the story of Jakie Rabinowitz, a cantor's son who becomes a successful jazz singer on Broadway. His father disowns him as he seeks fame and fortune, and father and son are only reunited at the father's deathbed. Jakie takes his father's place as cantor in the synagogue for the Kol Nidre service, but there is no doubt that he will continue his Broadway career.

While Jakie's conflict is mainly with his father, his mother is a key figure in his life. She is played by the silent film actress Eugenie Besserer (who was not Jewish) and portrayed as an archetypal white-haired mother, an anxious, homely figure who is devoted to her only son but cannot defend him against his strict and rigid father. Mama is nervous of Papa, who is stern, old-fashioned and unyielding. He represents the old traditional ways. Mama has little say in important decisions. Jakie leaves home to pursue his career and perforce he leaves his mother behind.

Jakie returns home some years later as a success. It is at this point in the film that one of the main synchronised speech sequences takes place. This most important part of the film takes the form of an exchange between mother and son, and points up the key role this Jewish mother plays in her child's life. Jakie first gives his mother a necklace as a gift, and then sits at the piano to sing her one of his songs, "Blue Skies". He syncopates his singing, becoming more lively and "jazzy". "Did you like that, Mama?" he says, before launching into a long monologue detailing how he will look after her, buy her a fur coat, move her to a better home and ameliorate her harsh life. Mama listens, protesting slightly but revitalised by her son's presence. Sadly, this happy idyll ends when Papa enters and fresh conflict begins.

Mama in *The Jazz Singer* is seen primarily through her relationship with her son, which is expressed in a sentimental way. We see her slaving over a hot stove, gazing at her lost son's photograph, and weeping as she lights the candles. She gets her reward for her loyalty and acceptance of her son's new life at the end of the film. After Papa has died, we see Mama at the theatre, proudly watching Jakie (now Jack) on stage, while he sings "Mammy". For this sequence, Jolson performs in blackface, as he did throughout his career. A number of Jewish performers adopted blackface, and their reasons for doing so were culturally complex, but it may have been about identification with other oppressed groups. In blackface, performers could adopt another identity, and explore ideas and mores not necessarily their own. The song "Mammy", while talking about the Deep South ("my heartstrings are tangled round Alabammy"), is really a hymn to mother love: "Mammy, Mammy, I'd walk a million miles for one of your smiles, my Mammy." In this instance, it seems there may be common ground between the oppression of black mothers (often separated from their children under slavery) and the condition of Jewish mothers, whose self-sacrifice took a different form. In reality, the lot of Jewish mothers was hard, and Jolson's songs sentimentalise that hardship.

Jolson was hugely popular in his day, virtually a super-star. He performed other songs both in this film and in his career which praised home and mother, as in "Swanee" — "because my Mammy's waiting for me, praying for me down by the Swanee" — and "Own Back Yard" — "the bird with feathers of blue is waiting for you, back in your own back yard."

Unlike the Hollywood film industry of the 1930s, the Yiddish film companies were based in New York and catered to a small, clearly defined ethnic group. Yiddish cinema flourished for a short time in the 1930s, but was brought to an end by World War II and assimilation. The latter meant that the third generation of immigrants scarcely spoke Yiddish any more. There was a resurgence of Yiddish film in the 1980s and 1990s, but the real "golden age" was the 1930s when the large Yiddish-speaking community in New York eagerly awaited new films. A huge feature of these films was nostalgia for the "old country" and old ways, now seen through rose-coloured glasses. Between 1937 and 1939, twenty-three Yiddish films opened, some of them drawing on classics of Yiddish theatre and literature for inspiration and others arising from the *shund* plays of the late nineteenth

70

century. The latter were formula melodramas and operettas, sagas of family problems that were extremely popular with audiences, despite being highly sentimental. In these films, mothers are self-sacrificing, giving up their lives for their families — often giving up their babies or going to prison to protect the family. Titles like *My Yiddisher Mama, My Son, Her Second Mother* and *A Little Letter to Mama* point up the centrality of the self-sacrificing Jewish mother.

Edgar G Ulmer began to make Yiddish films in the late 1930s, having set up a production company in New York with two other Jewish producers expressly to make Yiddish-language movies. Ulmer was a secular Jew born in Moravia, whose career as a director in Hollywood had been cut short, and he had worked with a variety of different ethnic groups. He spoke no Yiddish, but his four Yiddish films were highly regarded.

Green Fields was released in 1937 and was adapted from Peretz Hirschbein's popular play *Grine Felder*, which had been a Yiddish classic for some years. The film stands out in contrast to many Yiddish films of the 1930s, as it is not melodramatic or stagey. It was shot largely in the open air on a farm in New Jersey with a cast of Yiddish stage actors, some of whom had appeared in silent films, but none of whom had acted in a "talkie". The film is set in the *shtetl,* a world that would have still felt familiar to the 1937 audience. A shy, unworldly yeshiva scholar travels to the country to find a new meaning to life. He meets a family of rural Jews and learns to value nature and the earth. At the end of the film he marries the daughter of the family and stays on the farm. The film celebrates *shtetl* culture and is both moving and charming.

Anna Appel, a veteran of the Yiddish theatre, plays Rochel, the mother of the family. Rochel is a traditional wife and mother. She wears a headscarf, defers to her husband and is shown cooking the Sabbath meal. She is nonetheless a lively character with a robust sense of

71

humour. Rochel is concerned throughout the film that her only daughter Tsineh is too "wild", as she runs about the farm bareheaded and without shoes. In several moving scenes between mother and daughter, Rochel ultimately gives her blessing to Tsineh. Rochel allows Tsineh to choose her own husband, even though her own experience is of an arranged marriage. She urges Tsineh to be pious and obedient, to dress modestly and to wear shoes — this will show that Tsineh is ready for marriage and, ultimately, motherhood. Tsineh is later seen suitably attired and serves the Sabbath meal to the men. However, Tsineh has earlier in the film asserted her right to literacy (she learns to write her name), while her mother cannot read or write. It is understood that she will eventually be a less traditional wife and mother than Rochel. Rochel is ultimately a positive character; a very loving mother who wants the best for her daughter and in the end enables her to make choices. However, she still fits within the "self-sacrificing" image of the Jewish mother, living for and through her children.

Woody Allen's *Radio Days* was made in 1987. Much has been written about Allen's work, though perhaps not much about his portrayal of the Jewish mother, who appears in various guises in his work. *Radio Days* shows some of the conflicts and contradictions that run throughout his films in his explorations of class, gender and ethnicity. The film is a tribute to a childhood (partly Allen's own) and shows a Jewish family in the 1940s and how radio affects their lives, hopes and dreams. The film is nostalgic and affectionate, and its portrayal of Jewishness is far more direct than in any of Allen's earlier films.

The young protagonist of the film, Joe, lives with his mother, father and extended family in Rockaway, New York, a dilapidated neighbourhood. The family has little money. Joe's mother, Tess (played by Jewish actress Julie Kavner, now best known as the voice of Marge in *The Simpsons*), is first seen in dressing gown and curlers in her rundown kitchen, washing dishes and listening to the radio. Tess is seldom shown outside the home — she is clearly a housewife and mother, does all the chores and has a life bound by her husband and family. While this doubtless reflects the time frame in which the film is set, her single sister, Bea, has a freer and more interesting life. While Tess has aspirations for Joe, her only child, she is not self-sacrificing. She derives pleasure from her family life, enjoys her fantasies of glamour gleaned from the radio and bickers warmly with her husband. Like Rochel in *Green Fields*, she encourages her son to look forward to a different future, with greater financial and educational opportunity.

It is perhaps worth mentioning here Allen's contribution to the film *New York Stories* (1989), in which three well-known directors, all involved with New York, each contributed a short film about some aspect of the city. Allen's contribution, *Oedipus Wrecks,* comically features the portrayal of a monstrous, interfering, possessive Jewish mother. Her son Sheldon (played by Allen himself) is plagued by her until one day she disappears, courtesy of a magician's trick. She is then manifest as a huge, cloud-like apparition in the skies above Manhattan, *kvetching* for all to hear about her son's life and his failings. This short film is hugely amusing, but its portrayal of Jewish motherhood is negative and extreme.

The films I have examined cannot provide a definitive view of the Jewish mother on film. The tendency to portray Jewish mothers in a sentimentalised or melodramatic way does seem to run through these films and others. The possessive, demanding and difficult Jewish mother seems a familiar, almost stock character, often tipping over into parody. And yet, in these three films, the mother is absolutely central, pivotal, to the main character's life and development — in *The Jazz Singer,* Jakie returns home to visit his beloved mother and is able to heal family rifts; in *Green Fields* Rochel, despite her own misgivings, encourages her daughter to take greater freedoms; and in *Radio Days,* Tess is the centre of a warm and enduring extended family. These Jewish mothers transcend stereotyping.

Further reading
When Joseph Met Molly: a reader on Yiddish film, edited by Sylvia Paskin (Nottingham: Five Leaves, 1999)
The Bridge of Light, J Hoberman (New York: Schocken, 1991)

Glimpses: Hagar-Hajar and Mary, Mothers in Islam and Christianity

Mandy Ross

During the period I have been editing this book, I have had the opportunity to explore some of the stories of Islam and Christianity, the other Abrahamic faiths. Many are stories which were familiar to me, but unread. I have talked about them with Muslim and Christian neighbours and friends, and I find they are starting to feel like stories from cousins' families (which, in a way, they are): familiar stories, familiar characters, but with an unexpected slant or detail or change of emphasis in the telling, which startles and intrigues me.

My antennae were tuned to motherhood, the theme of this book. Here are two glimpses — elemental moments for mothers Sarah, Hagar and Mary.

The first glimpse is the familiar story in Genesis of the jealous Sarah expelling Hagar and her child, after the birth of her own son, Isaac. Sarah said,

> "Get rid of that slave woman and her son, for that slave woman's son will never share in the inheritance with my son Isaac." The matter distressed Abraham greatly because it concerned his son. But God said to him, "Do not be so distressed about the boy and your maidservant. Listen to whatever Sarah tells you, because it is through Isaac that your offspring will be reckoned. I will make the son of the maidservant into a nation also, because he is your offspring." (GEN 21:10-13)

Abraham left Hagar and her son Ishmael in the desert of Beersheva. He gave her some food, and a goat's skin of water. When the water ran out, Hagar feared her son Ishmael would die of thirst.

> She went off and sat nearby, about a bow-shot away, for
> she thought, "I cannot watch the boy die." And as she sat
> there nearby, she began to sob... The angel of God called
> to Hagar... Then God opened her eyes and she saw a well
> of water. (GEN 21:16-19)

In the course of researching and writing a series of children's books on holy places, I read the Islamic retelling of
this story. The Qur'an alludes to this story, with the prophet
Ibrahim's supplication to Allah for his wife Hajar and his
son Isma'il (QUR'AN 14:37). The story is told in full in the
Hadith, traditional tellings which are often used as commentary to the verses of the Qur'an. In this version, Ibrahim left
Hajar and Isma'il at Mecca, later to become the centre of the
Islamic world, rather than at Beersheva as in Genesis.

In the Islamic story, Isma'il was young enough still to be
breastfeeding (which is not specified in Genesis). Hajar
drank from the waterskin to increase her milk for her
baby. When the water ran out, "she tucked up her robe
and ran in the valley like a person in distress and trouble."
She ran seven times between the two hills of the desert
there, looking for people who might help her. But she saw
no one. Then suddenly she heard a voice. "And behold! She
saw an angel at the place of Zamzam, digging the earth
with his heel (or his wing), till water flowed from that
place." Hajar drank from the stream, and her milk
increased.

Details differ between the biblical and Islamic accounts,
but it is recognisably the same, poignant story. But I was
fascinated to discover the prominence of Hajar's story in
Islam. Her ordeal forms a major part of the Hajj, the
annual pilgrimage to Mecca. Going on Hajj is one of the
five pillars of Islam. It is a central obligation which every
Muslim aspires to fulfil in his or her lifetime. Every year
on Hajj, more than two million Muslims, male and female,
personally re-enact Hajar's panicky running seven times
between the two desert hills. They share her relief as they
drink water from the Well of Zamzam, the angel's water
source.

76

The Bible shows without ambiguity that it is Sarah who expels Hagar. Interestingly, the Islamic sources do not seem to ascribe the blame so directly to Sarah. Another commentary opens like this:

> When Ibrahim had differences with his wife (because of her jealousy of Hajar, Isma'il's mother), he took Isma'il and his mother and went away. (SAHIH AL-BUKHARI 4.584)

Hajar asks Ibrahim whether he is acting alone, or whether Allah has directed him. He answers that it is Allah's will. Hajar accepts then that her fate is in Allah's hands, answering, "I am satisfied to be with Allah."

It is striking how the rivalry between the two mothers, Sarah and Hagar — from whose sons sprang the two nations of Judaism and Islam — is mirrored in present-day conflict.

Further rivalry may be apparent in the Islamic telling of Ibrahim's sacrifice, where it is Isma'il, rather than Isha'q (Isaac), who is to be sacrificed. Some sources challenge this interpretation, but it is nevertheless widely accepted among Muslims as the true version.

* * *

The second glimpse is Mary at the crucifixion of Jesus, her son. This story is told and retold in the four Gospels of the New Testament. Like many Jews, I have always resisted reading this story. But I was confronted by it when I went to listen to a friend performing in Haydn's *Seven Last Words of Christ*.

From the cross, Jesus sees his mother, Mary, standing beside his beloved disciple, John.

> When Jesus saw his mother there, and the disciple whom he loved standing near by, he said to his mother, "Dear woman, here is your son," and to John, "Here is your mother." From that time on, this disciple took her into his home. (JOHN 19:26-27)

An only son, Jesus thinks of his mother at the moment of his own violent death. He commends her to his friend. In place of the mother-son relationship which is about to be lost, Jesus gives each to the other: *here is your son... here is your mother*. I found this a shockingly disturbing moment. Part of the shock is to discover just how moving this Christian story is. Even admitting this feels like breaking a taboo within Judaism.

* * *

These two glimpses show mothers and their sons *in extremis*. They show sacred texts exploring and responding to the strongest emotions — jealousy, fear, love, loss, human need. Isn't that the job of religion, of religions, to respond to human need? If only we could concentrate on what we have in common, rather than what divides us...

Hinei ma tov uma na'im
Shevet achim gam yachad.

"How good it is, and how pleasant, when brothers and sisters live together in unity!"

Cousins too.

In the Beginning:
Pregnancy,
Birth, Early Days

A Mother and Daughter Together in Childbed[1]

Glückel of Hameln

Immediately on our arrival in Hamburg, I became with child, and my mother along with me. In good time the Lord graciously delivered me of a young daughter. I was still a mere girl, and unused as I was to bearing children, it naturally went hard with me; yet I rejoiced mightily that the Most High had bestowed on me a healthy, lovely baby.

My good mother had reckoned out her time for the same day. However, she had great joy in my being brought to bed first, so she could help me a little, young girl that I was. Eight days later my mother likewise brought forth a young daughter in childbirth. So there was neither envy or reproach between us, and we lay next to each other in the same room. But, Lord, we had no peace, for the people that came running in to see the marvel, a mother and daughter together in childbed.

[1]*The Life of Glückel of Hameln, 1646-1724, Written by Herself*, trans. and ed. Beth-Zion Abrahams (London: Horovitz Publishing, 1962; New York: Thomas Yoseloff, 1963)

Prayer to Be Said When She Nurses for the First Time[1]

Dr Giuseppe Coen

May it be Your will, Lord my God and God of my forebears, that you provide nourishment for Your humble creation, this tiny child, plenty of milk, as much as he needs. Give me the disposition and inclination to find the time to nurse him patiently until he is satisfied. Cause me to sleep lightly so that the moment he cries I will hear and respond. Spare me the horror of accidentally smothering my child while I sleep. God forbid. May the words of my mouth and the meditations of my heart be acceptable to You, my Rock and my Redeemer.

[1]From *Out of the Depths I Call to You: A Book of Prayers for the Married Jewish Woman*, edited and translated by Rabbi Nina Beth Cardin (Jason Aronson, 1995), from an Italian collection of eighteenth-century prayers for married women written by Dr Giuseppe Coen and presented to his bride as a wedding gift.

Jewish Mother's Day

Brenda Heller

My most poignant memory is Rosh Hashanah, 1987. After several years of trying to become a mum, many courses of fertility drugs, hi-tech AIH and two failed IVF attempts, I had finally succeeded in getting pregnant without medical aid. I was finally to become a Jewish mum — or was I?

In September, at three months, I started to bleed. The first time, I sought advice at Accident and Emergency. At the second bout, I was told by the call-out GP, "You shouldn't expect to carry a child at your age (forty-one to be precise). When the pains come, dial 999." The pains didn't come. All bleeding ceased for a while. But soon I found myself bleeding heavily again.

I went to *shul* that fateful Rosh Hashanah. On returning from *shul*, I was still losing blood, and eventually passed a solid mass resembling raw liver. A different emergency doctor was called and this time I was rushed to hospital.

I can't describe the utter devastation at going through so much to get pregnant, only to have a miscarriage. The casualty doctor was kind. She tried to reassure me. "Let's see what the scan reveals before we give up hope altogether."

What is the superstition surrounding those days between Rosh Hashanah and Yom Kippur? Praying that one is inscribed into the Book of Life? Our unborn daughter certainly was. Her unidentical twin was not so lucky.

Ten days later, on Yom Kippur, my husband and I went to *shul* to thank that unknown being for sparing the life of one of our twins.

I won't say the rest of my pregnancy went without a hitch. Is there any such a thing as a normal Jewish pregnancy? A bit of anaemia, a bit of blood sugar and a senior registrar called Miriam — she wasn't Jewish, but she might have been, the way she clucked and fussed over my pregnancy.

Because I was termed a "geriatric prima gravida" and also because my daughter was "small for gestation", the medics decided to induce our daughter at term. She was born on the third day of Pesach — my forty-second birthday. She was named after a paternal aunt, her first name an archaic Hebrew word meaning delight, her second name after both grandmothers and a maternal great-grandmother. I may be biased, but I think she's a very special kind of daughter.

"Your Children Will Be Jewish"

Beatrice Sayers

On a mild evening at the end of the first week of January, in a first-floor delivery room at London's University College Hospital, the tiny body I had felt wriggling and hiccupping inside me for so many months was pushed down through my pelvis and into the hands of a hospital doctor.

My waters had broken three days previously but I had not gone into labour. I'd tried to induce myself with all the usual means, but nothing worked. Eventually, I decided to sit in the empty nursery, with its empty cot and hand-me-down clothes all waiting to be filled, and focus on my body and the two hearts beating inside it.

Then the contractions began. All night I paced the house with them, excited at what nature was doing to me. I willed them to continue. Just twenty hours later I became a mother.

For me, the pain of labour was insignificant. I had read about it in textbooks and that made it bearable. What I was not prepared for was the struggle between my own background and my partner's, which was unexpectedly pushed out into the open during the months before my baby emerged.

I grew up in Finchley, north London. My being Jewish was, I felt, one of the principal facts about me. My parents belonged to a Reform synagogue, and my mother lit the candles every Friday night. At Passover, we went to my aunt and uncle's for a big family seder. But I didn't go to Hebrew lessons. They were one of the many things my parents disagreed about. When I mumbled my way through the *Shema* at the end of our school's Jewish Assembly, pretending I knew the words, everyone else seemed to know every syllable.

My mother and father had been married in an Orthodox synagogue, but were not observant. She wanted us to learn Hebrew, but he shunned any connection with a *shul*. I saw my father as part of the British establishment, and my mother as venerating the religious establishment. There were things I liked and disliked about both these positions, but instead of sorting out how I felt, I sensed only conflict, and grew up with an unresolved tension about my Jewish identity.

A third of the pupils at my secondary school were Jewish. I felt a strong affinity with them, and a sense that we were part of a wider family. But I also felt an outsider among them, because I did not know enough about Judaism, and didn't have a sense of how being Jewish affected my life and the direction it would take. "Your children will be Jewish," my mother told her two daughters. But that had little meaning for me, because I myself knew little of what it meant to be Jewish. My mother didn't tell us about our future partners or husbands, and years later the question of my child's Jewish identity would come to shape my experience of motherhood.

As a teenager, many of my friends were Jewish. But in many ways I felt more comfortable with non-Jews, as their families had fewer expectations of me; I was ashamed at my ignorance of Hebrew.

When I began to have boyfriends, I would have been nervous dating a Jew. It was hard enough anyway for me to form relationships; with a Jew there would be the extra burden of unfulfilled expectations, I thought, and an inability to cope with my family background. At sixteen, I developed anorexia nervosa, partly as a reaction to an unstable home environment and partly through an inability to see what my role in life could be.

It was not until I reached my late twenties and early thirties that, slowly and nervously, I explored how I felt about being Jewish. By this time I had been living with my boyfriend for several years; his parents were Catholics, from Ireland. My boyfriend had little interest in his nominal faith and, I later realised, was attracted to me partly because I seemed exotic, like a Jewish girlfriend he'd had before me. Our different backgrounds never seemed to be a problem for us.

The experience of organising our wedding — ten years after we met — reaffirmed my own growing sense of Jewishness. I did not want to be married by a state registrar, but it seemed our only real choice. To compensate, we filled the ceremony with Jewish ritual and spirit: my great-uncle recited the Seven Blessings, my new husband stamped on a glass, and a klezmer group played.

On the weekend after our return from honeymoon, I surprised myself by seeking out the local Liberal synagogue and attending Shabbat morning services. A few months later, I began to go to Hebrew lessons there; my husband joined me and we studied together.

It was about this time that I realised I wanted a child. I was thirty-four. My husband still wanted to put off having children but eventually agreed that now was as good a time as any. I couldn't help thinking that if we'd both been Jewish it would have been natural for us to think about a family earlier in our relationship.

Before I became pregnant, he and I had discussed how we would bring up a child: what it would be like to grow up in London (he had grown up in a village by the sea in north Devon) and what the local schools were like. But most of all, we talked about religion.

Having been taken to Catholic mass every Sunday as a child, my husband was wary of "indoctrination" and felt that a person should discover religion for himself or herself. But I knew that without a Jewish upbringing — at least experiencing or taking part in, as I had, prayer and celebration in the home, and festivals in the synagogue — a child was unlikely to feel much of what it is like to be Jewish.

Almost for the first time, I was exploring properly the fact that I had a non-Jew as a partner. The new person we created would be a mingling of genes, ideas and traditions

87

from two different people. It was not easy to work out an identity for the family we wanted to create. Eventually we agreed on some basics. We would give our child a Jewish education, teaching him or her about beliefs and ceremonies, because all children would learn about Christianity anyway. If we had a girl, we would hold a blessing for her in synagogue. And if we had a boy?

Circumcision was an issue we had enjoyed debating occasionally almost even since we first met. We had a video documentary where Jewish ritual circumcision was discussed by experts, and we used to rehearse the arguments with friends. But when the time for rehearsals was over, we still felt ill-equipped to work out between us what we wanted.

I fell pregnant without our having reached a decision. I still do not know what we would have done if our child had been male. Perhaps I would have backed off from the idea. Many fathers feel that they would like their sons to look like them, and I could see that a *bris* would be difficult for my husband to accept. But perhaps he would have dropped his instinctive dislike. In Julia Neuberger's book *On Being Jewish* she acknowledges the strength of feeling that not having a boy circumcised is tantamount to saying he is not Jewish (a situation she calls "ludicrous"). I too had strong feelings. Perhaps, as Rabbi Neuberger suggests, we would have had the surgery without the ceremony. Or, as a Liberal rabbi had suggested to me, the ceremony without the surgery. For Progressive Jews, the biblical story of Abraham's covenant with God did not need to be interpreted literally.

That year, the year I began thinking seriously about a child, was also the first time I held a seder at home. I felt increasingly that I was part of a tradition of Jewish women bearing Jewish children; and Jewish women organise a family seder. Our guests were a family friend, Jack, and his wife. Jack had come to Britain from Berlin in 1939 on the kindertransport. His father had died at Auschwitz and a Nazi killing squad had shot his sister. As we ate our

88

boiled eggs in salt water, we discussed the symbolism: the eggs, representing life, reminded us of our freedom. Jack added that we should also bear in mind those across Europe whose lives had been snatched away.

During the week of Pesach I conceived. A couple of months later, on an ultrasound screen, I saw the flicker of a heartbeat in my womb.

The following months of hormones and heaviness created heightened emotions, among them the sense that motherhood would bring me freedom from my own childhood. But it would also create displacement, because my child would have parents very different from my own, and his or her religious identity would be more ambiguous. I had the overwhelming feeling that I needed to hold on very firmly to my Judaism.

Our baby would be my parents' first grandchild; for my husband's it would be their eleventh. It soon emerged that both sets of grandparents — to my surprise and horror — thought it better to have male offspring. My mother-in-law, reacting to the news of my pregnancy, threw her arms around me and said, "Congratulations, I hope it's a boy." Her other son was the father only of girls, and I embodied their remaining hope of continuing the male line. I was furious to be viewed this way. In my state of mental vulnerability, I even started to see the world only through the eyes of others: it seemed that women who did not produce boys were reproductive failures.

Neither my husband nor I had a preference when it came to our baby's sex. But at my twenty-week scan we could not resist taking up the opportunity to be told. It showed that I was carrying a girl.

It was difficult to accept that our baby's sex would disappoint others. We had wanted a pregnancy of unconfined happiness, not of family pressures. Also, we had not yet found a girl's name we both liked. My husband focused on the search, and browsed the *Oxford Dictionary of First Names*.

Four months into my pregnancy, his father was diagnosed with cancer, and my husband took on a caring role towards his parents. His father died when I was seven months pregnant. My husband was caught between two overwhelming life events: he needed to grieve, but he was also supposed to be happy, because he was about to become a father. Meanwhile, I felt confused and abandoned: during my pregnancy he seemed to be moving closer to his family of origin, not closer to me, and closer to his Catholic roots, not closer to his new semi-Jewish family.

I went into labour with a partner not at all ready to greet a new life, and did what so many mothers before me have done: I turned to my inner resources to cope. Though married to my baby's father, I felt absolutely like a single mother.

Of course, I fell head over heels in love with our beautiful, perfect, baby girl. Motherhood was a bigger joy than I could ever have imagined. It was also more demanding, mentally and physically, than I had been warned. But nothing, not even the emotional upheavals of my pregnancy, could take anything away from the miracle of holding in my hands the new life that had come out of me.

When our daughter was nine months old, we organised the blessing we had decided to hold. We gave her a name my husband had found in his book, and which we had both fallen for immediately: Freyde (Yiddish for joy). It is also her Hebrew name. A rabbi conducted the blessing on Simchat Torah, the most joyous day in the Jewish calendar; and a Catholic priest gave a short reading as part of the ceremony.

I've found adjusting to motherhood challenging. As Freyde's only Jewish parent, and now as a single parent, I've had to think and negotiate extra hard: not just for myself, but for the maternal tradition I felt so much a part of when I conceived. My daughter has both her parents' surnames, with my anglicised Lithuanian patronymic as the last name. As well as being an expression of my feminism, for me this is a way of preserving her Jewish identity. Perhaps I've finally found out the meaning behind my mother's telling me that my children would be Jewish.

Akedah

Ronne Randall

I have known for months that this would happen — ever since that day back in September, when the very solemn young doctor in the antenatal unit gave us the results of the amniocentesis. Norm and I, he intoned, were expecting "a male child".

"You mean a boy," Norm said.

"Yes," the doctor agreed, never even cracking a smile.

So, along with choosing a name, we had started thinking way back then about finding a *mohel*, a ritual circumciser. Neither of us was a native of Nottingham-shire, where we now lived. Norm had grown up in north London, and I in New York. And though we belonged to a synagogue here, we hardly ever went. But we now had to make enquiries, for our "male child" would have a *bris*. That we knew.

Or at least *I* knew it. Norm said he wouldn't mind if our son wasn't circumcised. He was ambivalent about the whole idea of circumcision — notwithstanding his own *bris*, some thirty-six years earlier.

"You men and your penises!" was my reaction. As far as I was concerned, it was not up for debate. Our son would be initiated into our religious community, our tribe, in the same way all of our male relatives for countless genera-tions had been — with *brit milah*, the covenant of circumcision. He would be ushered in with blessings and prayers, with wine, and with the ritual removal of his fore-skin in the presence of our friends and family.

I was forty years old. I had spent my twenties and the early part of my thirties in two intense, emotionally draining long-term relationships, both with non-Jewish men. After the second one ended, I wanted time on my own, to find out who I was outside of a relationship — a sort of very delayed identity crisis.

Part of what I found out was that I no longer wanted to ignore my Jewishness, which I had neglected for so much of my life. I didn't have a religious experience — it was merely a recognition that I was indeed Jewish, that I had a rich and valuable birthright, and that it meant a lot to me. I wanted to bring my Judaism out of the shadows and into the foreground of my life.

I stopped eating bacon. I enrolled in a Yiddish class at the Workmen's Circle. I started lighting Shabbat candles. Every now and then, I found myself in a *shul*, even when it wasn't Yom Kippur. I wanted to connect with my heritage — especially with my grandparents and the other relatives I had never known, because they had died in gas chambers in Poland years before I was born.

I wanted a Jewish partner. And I wanted to have Jewish children, to carry on the line.

At some point, this last desire — strong and deep though it was — began seeming futile. As the years pushed me inexorably toward my forties and a suitable Jewish partner did not present himself, I decided it wasn't going to happen. And after a while, that started to be OK. I concentrated on my friends, my cats, and my work, which I loved and found richly rewarding — I was editor-in-chief at a large children's publishing house.

I still felt I had something to offer a child, so I got in touch with an organisation called "Jewish Big Sisters", which matches troubled Jewish girls with older mentors. If I couldn't be a mother, perhaps I could make a difference in a Jewish child's life.

But before I'd even sent off the application, a mutual friend introduced me to Norm. It felt right from the first moment. Because we were separated by our careers and a 3,000-mile ocean — he was British, and in the RAF — our courtship was highly compressed. Not so much a whirlwind as a full-scale tornado. Less than a week after we first met face-to-face (we'd been writing to one another for a few months), Norm asked me to move to England to be with him. I agreed to visit — and when I did, we decided to get married.

I had found my *bashert*. And, if we were lucky, we might have children — the Jewish children I longed for. We never talked specifically about having children — we both knew we wanted them.

I went back to New York and packed up my life. I left my job, my rent-controlled Greenwich Village apartment, my cats, my friends and family — and moved to a small semi-detached house on a half-built estate in a tiny town ten miles from Nottingham. A few months later, Norm and I were married in the north London *shul* where he had become a bar mitzvah; thirteen months after our wedding I gave birth to our son.

It felt as if many miracles had happened in a very short space of time — and the little red-haired, red-faced, very loud and demanding bundle Norm and I had produced together was the greatest one of all. My Jewish child. He looked like my father — and maybe like those lost grandparents and aunts and uncles and cousins, too.

Now, on this frosty February morning, eight days after his birth, I am still reeling from it all. Still recovering from the caesarean section I've had, still learning to cope with cracked, bleeding nipples, lack of sleep, unpredictable hormones, and turbulent emotions I've never before experienced.

Our beautiful little boy and I are still in the hospital — and this morning, so are a lot of other people who have come to join us. My elderly parents, frail but *kvelling* — my father's face is almost trembling with happiness and pride — and my brother and sister-in-law have flown in from New Jersey to be here. My Peruvian cousin Esther and her husband are here from London, along with Norm's mother and his uncle Joel. There are some people we know from *shul*, too, and the rabbi. And there is an ancient, bearded *mohel* from Birmingham — wrapped in his *tallis*, he looks like a biblical patriarch.

I am pleased. It is how it should be. They are all here to welcome my son into our midst with joy and ceremony. Our boy will be given a name and have his foreskin taken, and he will take his place in the line that stretches back for untold generations, on Norm's side and mine. The baby's name will be Daniel Simon in English, but in Hebrew he will be Shalom Daniel — Shalom for Norm's father, who died nine years earlier, and who would have rejoiced more than anyone at this event.

I hand my treasure, my precious baby, to his father, who takes him into a glass-walled room with the men while I go outside to watch with the women. Standing beside my mother, I see my brother, the designated *sandek*, or godfather, sit down and place the baby on his lap.

The baby begins to cry. My breasts begin to throb. Seeing my baby, my small, vulnerable baby, amidst all those men, I suddenly think of the story of the *Akedah*, the binding of Isaac: Isaac, whose mother also had him after she'd given up hope of having a child; Isaac, whose father was put to the most severe test by God. It feels as if that terrifying scene of sacrifice is being re-enacted right here, in a Nottingham hospital maternity ward. I hold on to my mother's arm for support.

I hear the drone of prayers, and suddenly the *mohel*'s *tallis* is over his head, and I see the glint of a steel blade. The patriarch is going towards my baby with a knife!

"No!" I sob, lurching towards them.

My mother holds me back.

"Don't be silly!" she chides, laughing. "Look at all those men in there! They all survived!"

They did indeed. And so did my son. For it is all over now, there are shouts of *Mazel tov!* Wine is being drunk, and people are hugging me. But all I want is my wailing baby. I want to hold him and comfort him and feed him — and apologise to him for the pain he's had to go through.

The *mohel* tells me about dressing the wound, and gives me a yellow herbal powder to help it heal. Norm is herding the friends and relatives together to take them back to our house and celebrate with sandwiches and cake and whisky. I nurse my baby — my Shalom Daniel — who is now content and no longer crying, and will him to be strong for the future.

Afterword

It is eighteen years later, and my "little" boy is five inches taller than I am now (and an inch taller than his dad), and every day he looks more like his other grandfather, the Shalom after whom he was named.

We never had any other children — my body wouldn't co-operate. Like the matriarch Sarah, I was to be the mother of only one son. Eventually Norm and I came to feel that perhaps this, like our relationship, was *bashert*, too. We have never stopped feeling blessed to have Daniel.

Maybe because he's been an only child, often in the company of adults, he has always seemed older and wiser than his years. He talked at eight months, and was reading before he started school — and he has continued to do both almost incessantly throughout his life. He has been passionate about many things — Celtic folklore and music, the Notts County Football Club, fencing, hip-hop. At one time he was passionate about being Jewish. Now he is passionate about being a revolutionary socialist. He's an atheist, and religion no longer has any place in his life. Norm and I understand and respect his views. We are proud of his political passion and commitment.

I asked Daniel the other day to read this piece — it is, after all, about him, and I wouldn't consider submitting it for publication without his approval. He said it was fine. "How do you feel about it?" I asked. "About being circumcised?"

He thought about it and shrugged. "It's never bothered me as a person," he said, "but I'm not particularly fond of it as a concept. I don't believe in tribalism or religious rituals any more." He paused. "But that doesn't mean I'm not Jewish. I may have rejected religion, but I'll always identify as a Jew culturally."

If he had a son, he said, he wouldn't have him circumcised — "But I would raise him to know about his Jewish heritage. Jewish culture is part of me. I hope it will be part of my children, too."

So, Norm and I have raised a potential Jewish father. What more could a Jewish mother (and father) ask?

Letter to My Son

Sara Goodman

Dear J,

You are peaceful this afternoon, sleeping in your carrycot in the window as I write to you across the years, to when you're old enough to understand. I want to tell you the reasons why you're not circumcised, why we chose not to have a *brit milah* for you.

We thought and discussed and agonised over the question through the months when I was pregnant with you, and then when you were born.

I wanted you to have the *brit* to assert your Jewishness and so that you could feel that you could take your place more easily in the Jewish community without questions or doubts from other people (or from me, or from you) — even though we know that you are Jewish by Jewish law because *I'm* Jewish. I wanted to be able to give you your Jewish heritage clear and unclouded, unassailed by doubts of my own. But I wasn't keen on the prospect of bloodletting — and only for boys — as a welcome into the Jewish community.

Your father, though, not being Jewish, was very unhappy at the thought of your body being altered, and causing you pain, for a custom that he questions — especially since I'm not the most observant or believing Jew. I was clear that the reason for the *brit* is not rational, medical or possibly even (for me) religious — rather, a very deep-seated, emotionally charged, communal requirement. So that was to be set against your father's wishes.

The *mohel* who was to perform the *brit* required both parents' consent. Eventually, T did give his consent. He said he didn't want to block the *brit* if it was going to cause me unhappiness over years and years, which was what I was afraid of. But he didn't want to be present at it, and was clearly really horrified and distressed at the thought of it.

And then, because he had acknowledged the importance of the issue to me, I found that I could start to consider the possibility of *not* going ahead. That was when I spoke to lots of relatives, rabbis and Jewish friends, to explore the consequences for me, and more importantly for you, of not having your *brit*.

I think it was the most difficult decision I've ever had to make. In the end, I felt that ethically it was wrong to have you circumcised without your consent and against your father's wishes, especially when I questioned the need and purpose of the *brit* myself to some extent. This didn't feel like a positive action within Judaism for you, me or T. Also, I started to think that the *brit* is intended as a ritual initiated by the father to foster male bonding with his son — but in our situation it would have had the opposite effect. T was worried that it would make him feel more distant from you.

We started to explore alternative ways of welcoming you as a human being, as a Jewish child, and as a child of mixed parentage — just as we might have, had you been a girl. I questioned the connection between circumcision and covenanting you to God (not sure how I could do this on your behalf anyway). And I thought about ways of helping you to belong, now as a child and later, if you choose, to the Jewish community and culture that I belong to, and which I cherish and love, and also chafe against, while remaining in many ways out in the secular world.

So now we're planning a ceremony for you in our *shul*, and a party afterwards to welcome you. It feels much better to be planning this with your father's blessing, secular but unironic, than to shed your blood without it.

On the day your *brit* would have taken place, T and I took you for your first walk in the woods. The light and air were green and fresh and leafy, and you were wide-eyed at it all, till you fell asleep in our arms, even as we handed you over stiles and gates, having forgotten to bring the sling to carry you.

J, I hope when you are older, you will understand and appreciate the reasons for our decision, even if you may have some regrets about it. You may or may not choose to be circumcised later.

Either way, I hope that your Jewishness will bring you joy and questions and richness and warmth, as it has me. Through the years, I hope we can explore and discover and celebrate your Jewishness, and *also* your mixed heritage, and your father's questioning, ethical secularism. I hope we can contribute to a Judaism which embraces complexity and differences, and which can grow and change while still maintaining the precious traditions that our ancestors, yours and mine, have observed through the centuries.

We'll light Shabbat candles tonight. You are a beautiful baby. I love you with all my heart.

Ritual, Identity and *Tikkun Olam*: The Blessings of a Mother to Her Son

Karen Worth

Being a Jew is a significant part of forming and describing who I am. So when the most important event in my life took place, the arrival of my son, Solomon, I wanted to ensure that his life would be honoured within that tradition.

The traditions of celebrating important life events (as well as yearly events) through ritual, shared with family and friends, is an important part of being Jewish to me. Yet while the existing traditions are important, I also wanted to make them relevant and specific to my life and its context. Having been raised within Liberal Judaism, I am used to adapting and developing customs and liturgy.

I wanted both the welcoming and naming ceremonies for Solomon to provide him with a solid foundation of his heritage from which he could develop his own Jewish identity. I did not want my son to be circumcised (but I won't go into the reasons for this here, as that constitutes another article). Yet I wanted him to have a very Jewish celebration, to involve family and friends and to impart to my son some of the key things I value about being Jewish. In addition to the strong tradition of critical thinking, the Jewish spirit of *tikkun olam* (repairing the world) and social justice are significant guiding factors in how I live my life. I have been involved for years in peace activities and feminist and left-wing movements. These are some of the values I want to pass to my son.

Solomon's early life was celebrated with two events. The first was at home when he was three weeks old. We wrote and collated the ceremony ourselves and our rabbi conducted it. The second was a more conventional baby naming and welcoming at synagogue, which included blessings that we wrote for him. These three writings are included here and are our attempt to provide our son with a strong foundation from which he can develop his Jewish identity.

The first piece is my welcome to Solomon. The second piece is my partner's welcome and commitment to supporting him as a Jew. My partner is not Jewish. However, she has recognised the importance of my Jewish identity to me and wants Solomon to have the same opportunity to embrace this heritage. These first two pieces were used in the home ceremony. The third piece, used in the synagogue ceremony, conveys our blessings to him and is a statement of what we hope for him, as well as a statement for us to live by in relation to him.

Karen's Welcome to Solomon
(for home celebration)

Although my understanding and concept of God is somewhat vague and confused, when I look at you, gorgeous Solomon, I truly see the Divine presence and for the first time, I understand the phrase "made in the image of God".

You are perfect.
You really are a miracle.
You are a precious gift, to me, to all your family, to your community and indeed to the world.
Thank you for coming to be with us, and for making our worlds so much bigger for having you with us.
You are perfect, and because I really believe that, I just couldn't agree to having you circumcised.
You need no adjustments or interventions to complete your perfection.
(This may be a decision which one day you will be cross with me about. Well, I guess that it will be one of many,

and I'm prepared to take that risk, to save you unnecessary pain. I hope you'll understand my motivation.)

You are fully a Jew.
May you grow and expand your horizons through learning about your culture and heritage.
May you learn how to live a righteous and significant life.
I offer you (as I have had), the great tradition of Liberal Judaism to learn from and follow, to use what makes sense to you, and to continue to adapt and develop it.
I look forward to being with you on this exciting journey.

Baruch Haba Shlomo — Welcome Solomon, Man of Peace.
Welcome to this world.
Welcome to this Jewish community,
Welcome to this home and to this family.

Wendy's Welcome to Solomon
(for home celebration)

When I think of myself as one of your parents and, in particular, my role as a non-Jew supporting your Jewish identity, several things come to my mind. The best way I can describe them is figuratively, in relation to my position to you.

I think of myself standing behind you, helping to create a Jewish home with Karen for you to grow up in and begin your own journey as a Jew.

I think of myself standing along one side of you, learning with you about the religion, the traditions, the history and culture of your people.

I think of myself standing along the other side of you, working and fighting for the liberation of all people in the spirit of *tikkun olam*: the value of your people, of repairing the world and freeing the world from oppression.

103

And finally I think of myself standing in front of you, if ever the forces of oppression and anti-semitism in particular should point in your direction.

Solomon, as a non-Jew, my welcome to you as part of the Jewish community is fourfold: to work with Karen to build a Jewish home, to learn with you, to fight for freedom with you, and to do everything I can to stand up for you and safeguard you.

Blessings for Solomon
(for synagogue baby blessing service)

Solomon...
May we keep for you a good Jewish home:
a place which will act as a rock and a firm foundation,
a place where you will always know love and respect,
a place where there will be someone with the wisdom to know when to be quiet and listen to you,
and a place where there will always be someone to catch you if you should fall.

May you be blessed with the richness of a strong and proud Jewish heritage and be nourished in the Jewish community.

May also you have the room and opportunity to think and learn in your own way as you develop into your own unique self, with your own mind and spirit.

May you take the Jewish teaching of *tikkun olam* for yourself and be blessed with the courage and wisdom to stand by what you believe, to be respectful and welcoming of all others and work in your own way towards the repair of the world.

May there always be people who will stand firm for you against any mistreatment and oppression that comes your way.

May the world be a place where you can live your biggest dreams, where peace will come in your lifetime for the people of Israel, Palestine and all their neighbours, and all the people of the world.

May you be blessed with a strong body and good health, and may you live a long life.

And also may you play, have fun and have many good friends and family to enjoy and celebrate life with.

Amen.

Becoming Jessica's Mother

Sarah Ebner

I'm a Jewish mother. But what does that make me? Proud, nonchalant, or a living, breathing stereotype?

To be honest, I'm a newcomer to this whole Jewish mother business. It's been going on for centuries; I only joined the club three years ago. But because I have a bright, gorgeous bundle of dark-haired, blue-eyed energy who is, by the way, Jewish, I've apparently turned into a cliché.

I've never been too keen on stereotypes. Many of them have a kernel of truth, but are so distorted they take on a life of their own. How did the Jewish mother become both a martyr to her children and an aggressive nag? It's a caricature which, broken down, doesn't really make sense. Yet perhaps there is something to it. Aren't all the Jewish mothers you know the hub of the household, the ones who organise and arrange, the ones who are most hands-on with the kids? Maybe that's your experience of motherhood in general, but when you're Jewish, there seems to be more to it. There are more festivals, more arranging (Friday night meals, Pesach spring cleaning), more events centred around, yes, food.

Food, as everyone knows, is a major part of Judaism, whether you're mother, father or child. From latkes to chicken soup, it's not just what you put in your mouth, but a cultural necessity. However, as if becoming a Jewish wife wasn't stressful enough, food also changes when you become a Jewish mother. Every lovingly prepared morsel takes on a greater significance as you attempt to feed the next generation. I make food for my daughter, and it is excruciating. I hope she has no idea how horrendous it is watching her reject a mouthful, and I similarly pray she

Family Life

Other Mothers

Grace Paley

The mother is at the open window. She calls the child home. She's a fat lady. She leans forward, supporting herself on her elbows. Her breasts are shoved up under her chin. Her arms are broad and heavy.

I am not the child. She isn't my mother. Still, in my head, where remembering is organised for significance (not usefulness), she leans far out. She looks up and down the block. The technical name of this first seeing is "imprint." It often results in lifelong love. I play in the street, she stands in the window. I wanted her to call me home to the dark mysterious apartment behind her back, where the father was already eating and the others sat at the kitchen table and waited for the child.

She was destined, with her meaty bossiness, her sighs, her suffering, to be dumped into the villain room of social meaning and psychological causation. When this happened to her, she had just touched the first rung of the great American immigrant ladder. Her husband was ahead of her, her intentional bulk kept him from slipping. Their children were a couple of rungs above them. She believed she would follow them all up into the English language, education, and respect.

Unfortunately, science and literature had turned against her. What use was my accumulating affection when the brains of the opposition included her son the doctor and her son the novelist? Because of them, she never even had a chance at the crown of apple pie awarded her American-born sisters and accepted by them when they agreed to give up their powerful pioneer dispositions.

What is wrong with the world? the growing person might have asked. The year was 1932 or perhaps 1942.

Despite the world-wide fame of those years, the chief investigator into human pain is looking into his own book of awful prognoses. He looks up. Your mother, probably, he says.

As for me, I was not paying attention. I missed the mocking campaign.

The mother sits on a box, an orange crate. She talks to her friend, who also sits on an orange crate. They are wearing housedresses, flowered prints, large, roomy, unbelted, sleeveless. Each woman has a sweater on her lap, for coolness could arrive on an after-supper breeze and remain on the street for the summer night.

The first mother says, Ellie, after thirty you notice it? the years fly fast.

Oh, it's true, says the second mother.

I am so shocked by this sentence that I fall back against the tenement, breathing hard. I think, Oh! Years! The next sentence I remember is said about twenty minutes later.

Ellie, I'll tell you something, if you don't want to have so many children, don't sleep in a nightgown, sleep in pyjamas, you're better off.

Sometimes even that doesn't help, says the second mother.

This is certainly an important sentence, I know. It is serious, but they laugh.

Summer night in the East Bronx. The men are inside playing pinochle. The men are sleeping, are talking shop. They have gone to see if Trotsky is still sitting on a bench in Crotona Park. The street is full of mothers who have run out of the stuffy house to look for air, and they are talking about my life.

At three o'clock in the autumn afternoon, the American-born mother opens the door. She says there is no subject that cannot be discussed with her because she was born in this up-to-date place, the USA. We have just learned

114

several words we believe are the true adult names of the hidden parts of our bodies, the parts that are unnameable. (Like God's name, says a brother just home from Hebrew school. He is smacked.) The American-born mother says those are the worst words of all, never to use them or think of them, but to always feel free to talk to her about anything else.

The Russian-born mother has said on several occasions that there are no such words in Russian.

At 3.45 the Polish-born mother stands at the kitchen table, cutting fine noodles out of dough. Her face is as white as milk, her skin is so fine you would think a Polish count had married an English schoolmistress to make a lady-in-waiting for Guinevere. You would think that later in life, of course.

One day an aunt tells us the facts, which are as unspeakable as the names of the body's least uncovered places. The grandfather of the Polish mother was a fair-haired hooligan. He waited for Easter. Through raging sexual acts on the body of a girl, his grief at the death of God might be modulated — transformed into joy at His Resurrection.

When you're home alone, lock the door double, said the milky Polish mother, the granddaughter of the fair hooligan.

On Saturday morning, at home, all the aunt-mothers are arguing politics. One is a Zionist, one is a Communist, one is a Democrat. They are very intelligent and listen to lectures at Cooper Union every week. One is a charter member of the ILGWU. She said she would leave me her red sash. She forgot, however. My friend and I listen, but decide to go to the movies. The sight of us at the door diverts their argument. Are you going out? Did you go to the bathroom first? they cry. We mean, did you go for *everything*? My friend and I say yes, but quietly. The married aunt with one child says, The truth, be truthful. Did you go? Another aunt enters the room. She has been talking to my own mother, the woman in whose belly I gathered flesh and force and became me. She says, There's real trouble in the world, leave the children alone. She has just come to the United States and has not yet been driven mad by all the requirements for total health and absolute sanitation.

That night, my grandmother tells a story. She speaks the common language of grandmothers — that is, not a word of English. She says, He came to me from the north. I said to him, No, I want to be a teacher. He said, Of course, you should. I said, What about children? He said, No, not necessarily children. Not so many, no more than two. Why should there be? I liked him. I said, All right.

There were six. My grandmother said, You understand this story. It means, make something of yourself.

That's right, says an aunt, the one who was mocked for not having married, whose beauty, as far as the family was concerned, was useless, because no husband ever used it.

And another thing, she said, I just reminded myself to tell you. Darling, she said, I know you want to go to the May Day parade with your friends, but you know what? Don't carry the flag. I want you to go. I didn't say you don't go. But don't carry the flag. The one who carries the flag is sometimes killed. The police go crazy when they see that flag.

I *had* dreamed of going forth with a flag — the American flag on July 4, the red flag of the workers on May Day. How did the aunt know this? Because I know you inside out, she said, since you were born. Aren't you *my* child, too?

The sister-mother is the one who is always encouraging. You can do this, you can get an A, you can dance, you can eat squash without vomiting, you can write a poem. But a couple of years later, when love and sex struck up their lively friendship, the sister was on the worried mother's side, which was the sad side, because that mother would soon be dying.

One evening I hear the people in the dining room say that the mother is going to die. I remain in the coat closet,

116

listening. She is not going to die soon, I learn. But it will happen. One of the men at the table says that I must be told. I must not be spoiled. Others disagree. They say I have to go to school and do my homework. I have to play. Besides, it will be several years.

I am not told. Thereafter I devote myself to not having received that knowledge. I see that my mother gazes sadly at me, not reproachfully, but with an anxious look, as I wander among the other mothers, leaning on their knees, writing letters, making long phone calls. She doesn't agree with their politics, what will become of mine? Together with the aunts and grandmother she worked to make my father strong enough and educated enough so he could finally earn enough to take care of us all. She was successful. Despite this labour, time has passed. Her life is a known closed form. I understand this. Does she? This is the last secret of all. Then for several years, we are afraid of each other. I fear her death. She is afraid for my life.

Of which fifty years have passed, much to my surprise. Using up the days and nights in a lively manner, I have come to the present, daughter of mothers and mother to a couple of grown-up people. They have left home. What have I forgotten to tell? I have told them to be kind. Why? Because my mother was. I have told them when they drop a nickel (or even a shirt) to leave it for the gleaners. It says so in the Bible and I like the idea. Have I told them to always fight for mass transportation and not depend on the auto? Well, they know that. Like any decent kids of Socialist extraction, they can spot the oppressor smiling among the oppressed. Take joy in the struggle against that person, that class, that fact. It's very good for the circulation; I'm sure I said that. Be brave, be truthful, but do they know friendship first, competition second, as the Chinese say? I did say, Better have a trade, you must know something to be sure of when times are hard, you don't know what the

117

Depression was like, you've had it easy. I've told them everything that was said *to* me or *near* me. As for the rest, there is ordinary place and terrible time — aunts, grandparents, neighbours, all my pals from the job, the playground and the PTA. It is on the occasion of their one hundred thousandth bi-centennial that I have recalled all those other mothers and their histories.

1975

How to Be a
Jewish Parent

Rabbi Marcia Plumb

What makes a Jewish parent? My husband and I feed our children chicken soup, and kosher food. We remind them not to waste food, and our mantra in the house is "family is more important than anyone else." So do I qualify as a Jewish mother, or simply a value-laden parent?

I'm not sure if food, guilt and family values are limited to Jewish mothers, but what is quintessentially Jewish is my desire to mark the passing of time, and significant moments, with a blessing or ceremony. Judaism instructs us to appreciate every action and thought. It appears that every act is to be imbued with holiness and gratitude to God. We say a blessing before and after we eat, when we first open our eyes in the morning, when we get up and get dressed, and even when we go to the toilet. There is a blessing for seeing an old friend we haven't seen in a while, meeting someone of great knowledge and someone who is "unusual in appearance". As someone who believes in retail therapy, I love the blessing that we are supposed to say whenever we get something new. According to Jewish law, we are meant to say a hundred blessings every day. Some may see this as a burden, but I find that saying these blessings reminds me to be grateful for what I have and experience in my life, and to appreciate the wonder and difficulties within creation and God's creatures.

It is not surprising then, that when I found out I was pregnant, I immediately looked for something Jewish to say. I was surprised to find nothing. There is the catch-all blessing for when something new happens (called the *Shehechianu* — it thanks God for sustaining us and bringing us to this season), but I wanted something special

119

for the gift of new life. I looked deeper and found no traditional prayers. In fact, there are no special blessings for any aspect of pregnancy or childbirth. There are the traditional *brit milah* rites for boys, and recently written naming ceremonies for girls, but nothing for the nine months and the immediate moment of childbirth.

I decided to write some of my own. Some Jews believe that the right to create new prayers stopped a thousand years ago. I however believe that every Jew has the ability and obligation to add to Judaism, in every generation. Prayers for childbirth were necessary, so off I went to create my own.

I created a fifth-month ritual in which my good friends, male and female, blessed my baby, and offered hopes for the changes that would soon take place in our family. I invited my friends to speak about how they managed major changes in their lives. We created a necklace of beautiful beads that I took with me into labour. Throughout the long twenty-three hour labour, I kept the necklace, and their prayers, near me.

When our daughter was finally born, my husband and I said blessings as he cut the cord. We wanted to wish our daughter health and strength as she would now breathe and develop on her own. We acknowledged that this was the beginning of her independence from me in particular. I told my daughter how much having her in my womb had meant to me, and how it had healed me of some of the emotional wounds within me (and healed me of my migraines as well!). I mourned the separation that would now exist between us. My husband welcomed her into our world and family. We said, "Blessed are you, *Shechinah*, who will now give this precious child her own independent life. May you, our child, be strong, brave and joyful as you begin to lead your own life."

Whenever I changed my daughter's nappy, I would say the prayer that is said when we go to the toilet. It is a prayer that thanks God for giving us "openings that open and closings that close." In other words, it thanks God for giving us veins that allow blood to flow, and tubes, including the intestine, and holes, including the anus for example, for the substances that we need to enter our bodies, and the dangerous waste products to exit. The prayer says that if the "openings" could not open, or the "closings" could not close, we would not be healthy, nor "be able to stand before You in thanks."

Saying this prayer helped me ignore the smelly nature of changing nappies (especially explosive ones!), and appreciate them instead. I was grateful for the opportunity to offer thanks for the health of my children several times a day.

There have been many other prayers and celebratory moments for our children. Another one was the prayer I said for my son on the last day of breastfeeding, when he was eighteen months old.

My prayer for Micah as he stops breastfeeding:

May he always choose food that keeps him healthy and strong. May he continue to choose what gives him nurturing and fills his needs. May he always seek out what is right for him and what he is ready for, whether he knows it or not.

Asher et yatzar et ha isha vo nekavim nekavim,
Brucha At Shechinah
Blessed are you, *Shechinah*, who creates milk ducts that flow and nipples to suck and breasts that provide what is needed. Bless you, *Shechinah,* for giving me and my body the ability to feed my children, give them what they need to enable them to be strong and healthy. Thank you for giving me the strength and mental health to let them go when the time is right, or even before it is right. May I always be strong and healthy enough in mind and body to give them what they need.

Finally, I'd like to share with you the prayer that I created when we cut my son's hair for the first time. I once heard of the three cuttings that a Jewish mother (or father) finds most poignant — cutting the umbilical cord, the *brit milah*, and the first haircut. Cutting their hair for the first time, for me, felt as though my children were moving from babyhood to childhood. Also, after that first haircut, they looked slightly different from how they did before the cut. I was proud of them, and wanted to mark the significance of their movement from one stage of development to another. This prayer focuses on the cutting of his fringe, which had grown so far that it covered his eyes.

A prayer for Micah's vision

May you see your path ahead clearly. May nothing block your way. If your visions for yourself become cloudy, may you have the inner strength to trust yourself and God. May you know that the *Shechinah* is always with you on your journey through life. May the angels that surround you always guide you — Michael on your right giving you strength and courage, Gabriel on your left giving you comfort and sustenance, Raphael bringing you healing from behind and Uriel lighting your way ahead. And may you always know that wherever you are, home is there with you, for home exists within you. We will always love and treasure you.

We pray with our children often, and they come to services with us on Shabbat and festivals, as often as their attention span and levels of tiredness will allow. When they do attend, one of my daughter's favourite moments and mine is when she stands with me, wraps herself in my *tallis* and plays with the fringes. I find this very powerful, as the predominant image of nostalgia for many Jewish children, particularly boys, is that of being in synagogue and playing with the *tallis* of their father or grandfather. Many boys in particular remember wearing the *tallis* for the first time on their bar mitzvah, a ritual in which many girls were denied participation. My hope is that my daughter will find the *tallis* so familiar and laden with love that she will wear it easily in the future and that it will be a source of comfort rather than the discomfort that many women feel today when they are invited to don one.

When I first began studying for the rabbinate, there were very few women rabbis, and I had met only two or three. One of the most powerful images that I retain from my early years as a student training to become a rabbi was when I saw, for the first time, a pregnant rabbi on the bimah (pulpit). Her stomach was very large, and she was standing on the bimah holding a Torah scroll. To me, it felt as if I was seeing Creation, as if I had been at the Garden of Eden itself. The pregnant woman rabbi was carrying human life and spiritual life at the same time. She was holding future life within her body, and the spiritual foundation of our people in her hands. At that moment, I felt my first sense of the power of being a woman rabbi. Women rabbis represent life, creation, and hope. Whether women rabbis have children or not, the potential of Woman to create and nourish life is linked to the potential that rabbis (and particularly women rabbis) have to create deeply intimate and nurturing relationships with people.

Letter to My Children

Isobel Braidman

October 2003

Dear Avi, Yossi and Raffi

I have been asked to write an article on Jewish mother-hood. The invitation came some time ago and I thought that I had everything neatly organised in my mind; some witty comments about typical Jewish mothers, how clever I had been in juggling career, home, supporting Dad in his rabbinical activities, all at a time, over twenty years ago, when the notion of working mothers was far less well accepted than it is now. Two serious medical episodes during the last year, both totally unexpected, have, as you all know, meant that I can no longer look at these things in the same way. All the more so because we are at that time of the Jewish year, the time of assessment and appraisal, when our conduct is examined and our deeds weighed and measured.

As a child, my father told me that Rosh Hashanah is when the Almighty writes our names in the Book of Life, which is left open. On Yom Kippur the Book is sealed, but on Shemini Atzeret, the Eighth Day of Solemn Assembly, the Almighty opens it again, just to have one final check, a proof-read, to make sure that there are no errors. It is an over-simplified metaphor for evaluation of one's life and the confrontation of mortality, which is the signature of this last festive month, part of which we have been able to share together. Yet the words still echo with me... "What is our life? What is our justice? What is our success? What is our endurance? What is our power?...." We ask these things on Rosh Hashanah and the Day of Atonement, with special significance. I ask them in the certain knowledge that I need not have been inscribed in the Book of Life last time and may not be this time. So I weigh my deeds and question the significance of my activities.

I regard my life as a triangle, although not necessarily one with equal sides. There is my partnership with your father, my career as a scientist and teacher, and my role as parent to you. My relationship with your father is too wonderful to describe. It transcends the ordinary and the irritating and enables me to be everything else that I am. The fact that he is a rabbi is immaterial to my relationship with him; I would love him the same had he been a dustman. My scientific and teaching activities allow me to do the things which I enjoy, namely research, the leap into the unknown, which has always excited me, and teaching, which enables me to help form the next generation of clinicians and research scientists. Then there is my role as parent.

I know now that of all the things I have done, giving birth to you, helping to nurture you, being mother and parent to you, are the most important. You will notice that the role of rebbetzin does not feature, and you have always been aware that I have been somewhat atypical. The demands on my time have required me to prioritise activities; congregations and congregants come and go, as do jobs, but family is permanent. So enabling us to celebrate Shabbatot and *chagim* together, finding and giving space for you to express your Judaism in your own individual ways, has been first and foremost. This is not to say that being part of a rabbinical household has not had its advantages; it has enabled me to celebrate my Judaism in song, and given me insights into our rich traditions, some of which, I hope, I have passed on to you.

Having a career, however, had an additional advantage for me, in that it provided me with an intense focus of interest and activity. Had I not had this, then I fear that I would have cramped you in the traditional manner of Jewish mothers. "What is the difference between a

125

rottweiler and a Jewish mother?" the joke goes. "A rottweiler eventually lets go." And, "How many Jewish mothers does it take to change a light bulb?" Answer: "None, you go out and enjoy yourself, dear, and I'll just sit here in the dark." Of course, I (and therefore by implication, you) are the product of generations of such mothers. The worn depression in the wooden handle of the ancient *hackmeisser* (chopping knife) brought by my grandparents from the *heim* attests to the generations of my foremothers who chopped liver for Shabbat and prepared gefilte fish for festivals. These Jewish mother jokes, however, could be made just as easily about Italian mothers, or Punjabi mothers, or Irish mothers, all of whom have their distinctive foods, and are central to the lives of their families. So what is so significant about my activities as a Jewish mother?

The only answer I can give you is that they are conducted in the framework of Jewish time: our weeks of Shabbatot, our months of festivals, our year. To keep my triangular life, part of which is in a totally different time frame, from collapsing, has necessitated strict organisation on our part, often not far short of the logistical requirements of a military campaign. Commercial transactions are avoided on Shabbat, so shopping must be planned accordingly, as with preparation of meals, likewise many other domestic arrangements. I would like to say that this has always run smoothly, but you know that our habit of "continental" evening mealtimes provides evidence to the contrary. In terms of our relationship with you, the complexities of bringing up a family in the late twentieth century, and against a background of frantic activity, has meant that the nurturing "mother" role had to be provided by whichever of us (Dad or I) was available at the time. While you were growing up, mothering was the result of partnership between your father and me.

An essential rule of our family life was, and still is, that our family celebration of Shabbat and the *chagim* are regarded as more important than anything else, even congregational activities. The festive meal is of course essential to this, so, regardless of all other activities, the family is together for erev Shabbat dinner and the Shabbat meal. Of course, now that you are away from home, the presence of the complete family around the table is a luxury and an event, the memory of which your father and I both savour long after you have gone. The scene is set with festive food, which occupies much time, both in the planning and preparation, but which seems to disappear with an astonishing rapidity. The mood is of discussion, questions (never restricted just to Pesach) and fun, interspersed with surreal, almost Pythonesque humour. It is that wonderful combination of our family, united in celebration of our ancient festivals, but, at the same time, each one of us expressing his or her unique way of being Jewish.

On hearing that we would not be attending a particular synagogue *simcha* on a Shabbat, as we would not be able to be there together as a family, one rather disgruntled Council member remarked that we were mistaken in our priorities: our children would develop other interests and would soon no longer wish to celebrate Shabbat with us. He was right about one thing; you have left home and are going your separate ways. Unlike the Jewish "super rottweiler" of a mother, I am having to let go. He was mistaken, though, about the ultimate goal. You have to find your own path and we have to let you go, not to keep returning to our way, but so that you can provide the warmth, love and space for your own children, through which you will celebrate Shabbat and *chagim* in your own unique fashion, so that you can have the pleasure of your festive mealtimes with your children, as we have had with you. If I have achieved anything in my life, it is to enable you to do that.

Hearts and Bowels

Michele Hanson

Sometimes I pretend I am not a Jewish mother, especially when writing my *Guardian* newspaper column about my English family. If I own up to being a Jewish mother, people will nail me to the stereotype. "Ah! That's why she screams and shouts," they will say. "That's why she's crippled by anxiety, hysterical, intrusive and obsessed with food, crap and clean bottoms."

My mother is all these things. So are millions of other non-Jewish mothers, but I have tried very hard to avoid most of them, vaguely because I don't want to fuel the dreaded stereotype, but mainly because it isn't pleasant for a daughter if your mother keeps stuffing you with food or asking for a daily report on bowel movements and personal hygiene. But I can't beat the anxiety. It is overwhelming and everlasting and I'm not sure whether it's Jewish. I suspect it might be.

On the other hand, there are positives about being a Jewish mother — see how I am obsessed with the label — the larder is always full, the hospitality is fabulous, the food high standard, we rarely eat pre-cooked or packaged drek, we are not dull and repressed and my mother makes fabulous gefilte fish. I have never, ever tasted better. I have learned how to do it. This is one of the few traditions I have maintained. Otherwise, I do nothing Jewish. I never say prayers, I don't believe in God, I am not a Zionist, I have renounced my right of return, I have little to do with the Jewish community, except to take my mother to *shul* on Yom Kippur. I am not married, my daughter's father is not Jewish.

So do I care if my daughter is considered Jewish or not? Oddly enough, I do. Once, when she was about four and skipping along in the park holding my hand, she suddenly said, in a very cross voice, "I don't want to be Jewish." What a dreadful disappointment. A total rejection of her background, grandparents, great-grandparents, culture and me. But luckily it didn't last. Now she seems quite happy to be Jewish. She writes about Jewish experiences, she wants to visit Germany, she wants to see Auschwitz. God knows why. Will I go with her? she wants to know. There's no one else she really feels she wants to go with. So I say yes. I am curious about this ghastly place. I'm surprised that my daughter is so interested in the Jews and their past, when I have hardly banged on about it.

For some years we shared our house with a friend of mine and her two young sons. My daughter wrote of my friend and me that we were an English atheist and a Jewish atheist. I read in a newspaper that Judaism is a religion not a culture, but I back my daughter on this one. I feel Jewish although I do hardly anything about it. I felt it before the baby was born. What if I had had a boy? Would I have had him circumcised, although I hardly do anything Jewish? Yes I would, and it would have been difficult. I had my baby in the West London Hospital, where a Doctor Jolly was in charge. He insisted on breast-feeding and no circumcision. To have it done I would have somehow had to sneak my baby down to the ward on the floor below where a less bossy doctor allowed you to do what you wanted. And if I hadn't had my baby circumcised, then what would my mother have done? She'd have gone mad. She would never have been able to hold this baby, never mind look at it or put its nappy on or bath it, so disgusted would she have been by its condition. And I felt enough of what she felt to want the same. So I would have had it done definitely. Despite a friend who swore that he would never speak to me again if I mutilated my child.

But luckily I never had to make that decision. I had a girl. Marvellous. Marvellous that I had a baby at all, because I was desperate to have one and my mother was even more desperate that I should do so, because she absolutely could not bear that I should be childless and she should never be a grandmother. Every other grandchild that appeared caused her pain, because it wasn't hers. The pressure on me to have a baby was immense. So what a relief at last, at thirty-six, to have a baby.

But is that necessarily Jewish? Perhaps the longing to be a grandmother is, but the wanting to be a mother is fairly general. Fortunately my mother's desperate longing to be a grandmother worked in my favour. She had given up on almost every condition. Even whether the father was Jewish, even whether he was my husband, until she had only two criteria left. "I don't care who he is," said she, "as long as he's white and kind." Who knows, in time she may not even have cared what colour he was, but when the longed-for grandchild arrived she didn't care who the father was, or where he was, because this baby was the most perfect baby on earth — better than all others in the ward, better than all her friends' grandchildren. And I have to agree. She was, on this occasion, absolutely right.

In some other areas, she was wrong. I have tried to avoid these mistakes, or at least reduce them. No screaming (unavoidable at times), no hysteria, no poking into personal affairs, no in-depth questioning about bodily functions, no expressions of disgust about bodies and sex, no barging into personal space. I feel, although I know officially that this is not so, that these problems areas are Jewish. When I wrote my newspaper column about my difficulties in coping with a teenage daughter — my hysteria, anxiety, over-indulgence, over-protectiveness — no one assumed that we were Jewish, so I assume that these are not exclusively Jewish traits.

My mother was nervous of my revealing that we were Jewish for different reasons. She is still frightened that if the world were to know, we would get a brick through our window. Having fled Russia at the turn of the century and been involved in the battle of Cable Street, she has reason to be frightened. But my daughter and I do not. Living here in north London I don't feel that we need protecting from that sort of lunatic. There are all sorts of other lunatics that I am frightened of: psychopaths, rapists, drug dealers. Of all the girls in the world, I feel that they may easily home in on my daughter. So I now sympathise more with my mother's panic and anxiety. She lives here, always panicking in the background, so I have my own terror and hers to deal with. If I am frightened of maniacs, then she is more frightened, but now I know why. This is the one thing that no one warns you about when you become a mother — that you will be worried for the rest of your life, Jewish or not.

Notice I haven't mentioned my father, who was very amusing but more often withdrawn and a terrific sulker. My mother was a screamer. I thought them entirely normal, until I read *Portnoy's Complaint*. Portnoy's mother was rather similar to mine, lurking outside the lavatory, worried to death about what's going on in there, and it is this awful physicality that I think of as Jewish mothering: food, bowels, lavatories. Probably that is specific to my mother, not to Jewish mothers in general, and I have caught it, despite my constant efforts not to behave like that. Here I am, even writing about it. Sometimes I long to be like an English Christian, in whose home, psychologically, there is no lavatory. I long to be that sort of mother. But only for a little while.

The Need to Nurture

Lucy Abrahams

All over Stanmore
Jewish not-quite grandmothers
Accessorize with babies
In a spate of summertime baby borrowing.

Clarins self-tanned skin
Cuddles up to soft pink bundles in bonnets.
Sophisticated perfume
Mixed with Huggies wipes
Colours the air feminine pretty.

These north-west London ladies
Sail around in their Mercedes.
Cappuccinos and car seats,
Weekend-treat flowers and feeding bottles,
Extra nappies and glossy magazines.

Little grabby fists reach for diamonds —
Expensive taste.
Equally content are the cooers
And cooed at.
No need for the zoo,
Happy sitting on laps.

The Mother

A short story by
Michelene Wandor

I got the idea after I went to the bar mitzvah of my friend's
grandson. She's younger than me, but she had her son
when she was sixteen. Had to leave school. You did then.
Well, you probably do now. Anyway.

Her Joseph was being bar mitzvahed. "Her" Joseph.
Like he was her son. Like he belonged to her. Anyway, I
didn't bother to try to understand. I could see how she was
proud of her Simon, her son, the professor of English, just
like I am proud of Ruthie, my daughter, the estate agent
(where she gets her ruthless streak from, I'll never know).

Anyway, so I go to Joseph's bar mitzvah, and we sit in
the Reform *shul*, together with the men. It never feels
quite right, but we do. I should explain. My parents were
religious and brought me up Jewish, but I never took
much notice. Apart from a wedding and now and again a
funeral, I don't go to *shul*.

So the service is a bit in English and a bit in Hebrew,
and even though I don't believe a word of it, I can follow
the Hebrew, because I learned Hebrew when I was little,
and I feel quite at home with its rhythms, and there's even
a lady rabbi who does some of the stuff, though her voice
isn't really up to it, she doesn't resonate like the big guy
does, and when he throws his *tallit* over his shoulder, it's
like Moses clambering down the mountain holding the
tablets all over again.

While I'm a bit bored with all the Shabbas stuff, I look
at the cupboard, or wardrobe or whatever you call it where
the Torah is — the scroll they carry round. They leave the
big gilt silver things in there, and carry round a much
smaller wood and red velvet one. So over this cupboard —

133

I suppose where the altar would be if it was a church — there are the beginnings of the Ten Commandments in Hebrew, and while I'm bored, I check them in my *siddur*, and yes, these are the various thou shalts and shalt nots, but in Hebrew, of course. It doesn't matter what you do in English. It's only the Hebrew that really matters, I suppose, even in a Reform *shul*.

Then it's Joseph's turn: a sweet round face, large eyes, light brown curly hair, his white *kupple* on his head, his voice light and confident and soaring as he sings all the prayers in his mini-cantor's voice, leading the congregation. It sounds lovely to me, but, to be honest, I begin to get more bored, and, to keep myself interested, I start wondering how I would feel if this was Ruthie's little boy. Ruthie is a good career woman, make no mistake. She has a job and a flat and a boyfriend, and, in summer, a suntan. They don't want children, she tells me. This is the legacy of feminism, she tells me, that they are absolutely happy as they are, and they don't need children. So you can see, when I start imagining how I would feel, it's more like how I might feel if, if, if. Not that it bothers me. It's her life. I don't need to babysit or change nappies again.

Joseph finishes, and the lady rabbi gives him a hug and starts talking to us in English about Joseph and his family. I wonder what it would be like to have a little boy, to peel filthy football kit off the floor and throw it into the washing machine, to buy birthday presents for a boy, what it's like when their voices break. I don't really get to the end of my wondering before the service is over, and we all go out into the hall next door, where there is sweet Israeli wine and orange juice and a wonderful spread of salads and cold chicken. By this time I'm hungry so I forget about all the wondering.

The following Saturday I go shopping as usual. This is as close as I get to going to *shul*. That's just a joke. So there's a new mall that's just opened near us, next to Junction 3 on the motorway. It's amazing. It's like fairyland. It's like an enchanted castle, with glass and steel, stone fingers in concrete curling round towers, which look like a cross between a Kent oasthouse (I saw one once on a postcard) and Rapunzel's castle, where she stood at the top and the prince stood on the ground and called to her to let down her hair. Ruthie always liked that story.

You drive into the car park, and then you walk along an avenue with trees, and just before you go through the huge, high glass doors, there is a children's playground, slides and swings and sandpits, and a pond with goldfish and railings round it. It's just like fairyland, even though you can see McDonalds and Garfunkels through the glass. The food may be fast, but when you get inside, nothing feels fast.

Inside, it's calm. Nobody is rushing. Even with the high ceiling, a vault, I suppose it is, like they have in churches, even with the wide, paved roads or walkways or whatever you call them, even with all the people and fountains and feet on the stone, it feels calm and peaceful. You could forget you were there to buy things. There is a big map by the entrance, but I'm no good at maps, so I don't bother to look at it. I just start walking.

At the junction of the roads or walkways, there are mini-roundabouts, each with a little garden in the middle, and semicircular benches for people to sit down on. The whole place feels like a big family outing; old people, middle-aged people, young people, children, toddlers, babies and shirty teenagers. Boy, was Ruthie a shirty teenager. She taught me that word. Shirty. Opinions, arguments.

So I'm looking for Marks and Spencer, and I'm looking up at the ceiling, or the vault or whatever it is, and I'm so busy doing this, that I don't look where I am going, and I bump into a little pram, and that makes me look where I am.

"I'm sorry," I say to the mother who is pushing the pram, a little blue pram, a buggy I think they call it now.

"That's all right," she says. "He'll sleep through anything."

So I go and have a look. There he is, lying there asleep,

135

with a little blue and purple blanket over him.

"How old is he?" I ask. Just like that. I'm not one for talking to strangers, by the way.

"Oh," she says, "he's eleven months."

"He's lovely," I say. He just looks like a baby, but somehow he looks lovely.

She smiles, and then she walks one way and I walk another.

A bit further on, I sit down and have a cup of coffee in a sort of modern Viennese café, and they're playing *The Blue Danube* waltz, which reminds me of my mother, because she used to sing that to Ruthie when she was trying to get her to go to sleep. *Da da da dee dum, dee dum, dee dum.* It always worked, though sometimes it took a lot of *dee dums*. I wonder whether that mother with the buggy sings to her baby, whether he's got a granny. Granny. I can't imagine being called Granny. The only thing I can imagine being called by a little baby is Mummy. That feels right.

I finish my coffee and decide to start my shopping. Marks and Spencer.

I'm looking round again, but this time also looking where I'm going, and then there, at one of the junctions, is the mother again, sitting on one of the benches, and breast-feeding the baby. He's got dark hair, streaked over his head, with little curls round his ears. She is stroking the top of his head. I remember Ruthie, tiny, warm, her legs bending right up over her body, sucking, holding my finger.

I smile as I go past. I go into Marks and Spencer, I walk around, looking at the new skirts and blouses, pushing them along the rail, I wander through the food floor, the chicken tikka trays, the cellophane bags of apples, the tubs of raspberry yoghurt dessert. I can't remember what I came in to buy, so I go back out.

Next door is a baby clothes shop, and there she is again. She's pushing the buggy through the doors. She smiles at me, and I follow her in. She stops by the high chairs. She

136

notices me and smiles.

"Is he asleep again?" I ask.

"Oh, yes," she says. "Look at this. You can use it as a high chair, and then you can undo the chair, and turn it into a table and a chair, for later. That's really good."

"Is he walking?" I ask. I'm asking a lot of questions. She doesn't seem to mind.

"Not yet. He stands up and takes a few steps, holding on."

"What's his name?"

"It's Joe," she says. "I might buy this."

"Shall I keep an eye on him while you pay?" I ask.

"Would you mind?"

"Of course not."

"Thanks. I won't be long. He won't wake up."

It's like we've always known each other. She's quite happy leaving him with me. She walks across to the counter, and starts talking to an assistant who goes off through a door at the back.

The handle of the buggy feels really comfortable. I push it a little way, and it glides really easily. I remember pushing Ruthie, when we went out shopping, in a much heavier push-chair. I push the buggy round the stands displaying baby pyjamas, little dresses, soft blue and yellow shoes. The mother turns round and waves at me. I wave back, and she turns away to wait for the assistant.

Then, before I even know it, I am outside, wheeling and fast along the smooth stone. This buggy is so smooth. Joe has a little smile on his face, his long dark eyelashes resting on his cheeks, his hands curled near his head, on either side of his face.

People smile at me as I walk along, a granny pushing her grandson. I begin to plan his room. I'll move everything out of the box room, and I'll buy one of those cots where you can take the sides down and turn it into a bed when the child gets older. I can buy him a high chair like the one his mother is buying. She's young. She can have more babies. I may never have a grandchild. I'm not sure

137

where I am now. All the roads here look the same. I should try and find the map that shows where the car park is.

I'll have to buy nappies, and bottles and milk. I remember when Ruthie learned to hold her own bottle. I remember the day she first walked without holding on. I remember the first time she called me Mummy. My own, private name, the only name I can imagine a baby calling me. The right name for a baby to call me. Mummy.

I walk along, looking at Joe, somehow managing not to bump into anyone. Joe wriggles a bit and lets out a little cry. Then he opens his eyes, blinks, sees me, and smiles. I smile back and make a little "hello" noise. I push the buggy again, and he likes the movement. He sucks his two middle fingers on his right hand, looking round, his legs kicking a little under the blanket.

"Sorry I was so long." It's her voice. "My card took ages to go through."

Joe is making happy squeaky sounds.

"Hello, darling," she says. "Was he all right?"

"Good as gold," I say. "We went for a little walk. Didn't we, Joe?" I must have walked round in a big circle, without even realising it. "Did you get the chair?"

"Yes," she says. "They're going to deliver it."

"That's good," I say. Joe has kicked his blanket off. I cover him up. "Joe's a lovely name for a little boy. It could be a name for a little girl, couldn't it? If you have a little girl next, you could call her Jo as well. Joe and Jo."

She laughs. "Yes. I could. Thanks for keeping an eye on him."

I let go of the buggy handles, and she takes over. "The handle feels all warm," she says. "Bye-bye now." And she walks away, turning round once to wave.

I wonder if she's Jewish. Not that it matters. If she's Jewish, Joe will probably learn Hebrew and have a bar mitzvah. I'd like to have held him, just for a minute. If she's Jewish, and he learns Hebrew, and if I see her again, maybe another Saturday, when I'm going shopping, then maybe she'll invite me to the bar mitzvah, and maybe I'll go to *shul* again. Babies are warm when you hold them. She didn't look Jewish.

Out in the fresh air there's a bit of a breeze. I get into the car and start the engine. I can go to Marks and Spencer's another time.

The Shadow
of the Shoah

.

Mother and Daughter in Auschwitz

An Interview with Kitty Hart

I was a child when war broke out. All the young people fled east, but we stayed in Lublin for a while. My mother was able to sneak out of the ghetto to give English lessons to a Catholic priest. This saved us from starvation. But it was predominantly the children who kept families going. Men could not venture outside or leave the ghetto. By the time I was thirteen or fourteen, I was looking after the family, getting food on the Aryan side of the city. I could have escaped into the forest with the partisans, but I felt that I couldn't leave my parents, who had become reliant on me for survival.

Prior to Auschwitz, we had false Aryan papers. My mother was given a different name on her papers. She was supposed to be my aunt, not my mother. We had to be very careful not to be too close, because it may have raised suspicions. However, eventually we were denounced, thrown into solitary confinement and interrogated separately by the Gestapo. Unfortunately my mother was tricked, and she confessed. Then the Gestapo came for me and called out my real name. They told me they knew she was my mother, but I think it was inevitable that they were going to find out. From then on we were together in prison until in April 1943, when we were sent to Auschwitz.

In Auschwitz we were immediately separated. I knew my mother wouldn't survive working outdoors even for just a couple of days. She was one of the oldest women in the camp. She only managed to get into the camp because we came directly from prison. So I knew that somehow I had to find her work indoors.

Fortunately I found a woman from my hometown, who had a privileged position. She became very protective, because it was very dangerous for an older woman such as my mother. She got her to work in the hospital compound, and that is where she remained the whole of the time in Auschwitz. I knew that she would be much safer there.

For a long time, I had no contact with my mother. She didn't know that I was alive, until one day I appeared. Very occasionally I managed to smuggle something in, and perhaps even hide there. But for her, the hospital was a more secure place, because she didn't have to stand the twice-daily roll call. When people died, sometimes they had their bread ration, and soup that she was able to use. It was a help in the battle against starvation. So it was a godsend that she was there, and sometimes I could go and hide in her hut.

I realised I had to stay alive because of my mother, at all costs, and she knew she had to stay alive because of me. You simply had to have someone to help you live. It was impossible to survive on your own.

I got typhus. Fortunately I was taken to the infectious block where my mother was working. That was when she saved me. During selections, my mother hid me under a straw mattress with a dead person on top of me, and that saved my life on several occasions. She also saved me by bringing me drinks. There were no medications, but at least she could bring me water and bread. After I recovered, I also worked in the hospital compound for some time, and it was possible to stay in contact with my mother.

Eventually I managed to join the "Canada Kommando". Here conditions were better, though we had no contact at all with the main camp. We were isolated in the area of the crematoria. Our job there was to sort clothes taken from all the people killed in the gas chambers. Occasionally we could persuade the kapos to let us take some old clothes into the main camp. The kapo knew I had my mother there, and I begged many times to be allowed into the main camp. I smuggled in many things that I knew they needed, clothing, towels, once even a tin of meat. Smuggling anything at all was strictly forbidden. It was punishable by death. But I had to take the chance, as it made an enormous difference to my mother. She could trade these things for other things she needed, including shoes, which were vital. I tried to keep her going. By this time her health had deteriorated and she was close to starvation.

One day my mother got typhus — this was inevitable as she worked in the infectious diseases hut. By smuggling various much-needed items into the hospital, I managed to get someone to look after her. At that time I saved her life. I managed to keep contact and I knew she had recovered.

In 1944, evacuations began from the camp. There were rumours that they were going to bomb the whole area. My mother was desperate to get us back together. I managed to smuggle her some jewellery. It was a very dangerous thing to do, but I knew she would be able to use it.

Because prisoners were not allowed to approach a commandant directly, my mother had to go via a privileged prisoner. For days she waited. Then one day, she stepped out with a privileged prisoner from behind a hut, and she said in perfect German, "Prisoner number 39933 begs to speak to the Camp Kommandant." He stopped, startled. I think he was impressed that a woman of her age had survived so long.

She asked, "Would it be possible for my daughter to come with me on the transport?"

My mother used the jewellery to buy us places on a list of a hundred girls being evacuated to work in a factory. Some time later, at roll call, my number was called, 39934, and I was transferred back to the main camp with my mother. Otherwise she would have gone on transfer alone.

My mother wouldn't have survived the next six months without me. The work was not arduous, but there was a strenuous walk to and from the factory. Food was very scarce, sometimes non-existent. At one point, I had the chance to escape. But I could not do it. I could not leave my mother. Others escaped, but I knew she was not able to run, and she couldn't have survived without me.

By the time we were on the Death March, in February 1945, my mother was very weak. I had to carry her with my friends much of the time. I could not allow her to lag behind, as all who did so were shot. Later we were thrown into open coal trucks and we travelled 1000 miles in eight days without food or water. We were to work in an underground ammunition plant. After more evacuations, as the Allies approached, we were put in a sealed train and left to die of suffocation. My mother was already unconscious from lack of air, but I managed to enlarge a gap in the floor, and I grabbed my mother and put her nose down by the gap to breathe.

Liberation by the Americans came on 14 April, 1945. On that day, my mother spoke to American reporters, giving the first reports on Auschwitz to the world. Very little was known before that time. For eighteen months we both worked as interpreters for the American and British military authorities and later also for Quaker Relief Teams. We came to England, in September 1946, and my mother lived with me until her death in 1974.

My mother wasn't in very good health, but she had incredible inner strength. She lost her son and her husband, but she never had a breakdown or complained. If she had any emotional problems, you would never have known it.

There was a very close bond between my elder son and my mother, because I was working and she had to bring him up. When my second son was born, I was around more, but she looked after both of them much of the time.

While my children were growing up, we always talked about what happened and what we did. We didn't discuss any of the horrible things, just the things that they could understand. We didn't talk to them directly, but within the conversation at mealtimes, with the five of us around the table, things came up about food. If the kids didn't eat,

146

we'd say, "You should have been around during the war, you'd soon eat everything." We would usually talk about food in the camps but also about general conditions and the struggle for survival. We would try and explain how vital it was for both of us to have looked after each other.

After the war I found it very difficult to attend services at synagogue. It all seemed a pretence — women dressed in their best clothes and bejewelled, some reading but many chatting. It seemed a show. It meant nothing to me and I could not tune into the prayers. I felt it was artificial and often walked out in tears.

In Auschwitz where was God? People were praying and begging for their life, but no amount of praying would help in Auschwitz. That's where I lost my faith. I couldn't just pick it up after the war. A lot of people felt like I did. On the other hand some became very religious, because they thought God had saved them. But I saw too many people die. I saw that I saved myself by my wits. If you were in the wrong place, you were dead. It had nothing to do with prayers. Therefore although I belong to the synagogue, I do not like or ever listen to sermons.

I believe in Judaism and would never contemplate changing my faith, but I have never kept a kosher home. My sons were both brought up in the Jewish faith, attending cheder and becoming bar mitzvah.

My younger son married a Jewish woman who is more religious than I am. He has mostly Jewish friends. To me it wasn't an issue when my older son married a non-Jewish woman. The issue was whether this was the right person for him. His second wife is a true-blooded German. Her parents also were refugees. She is an exceptionally nice person. I can't understand parents who cut off the children because they didn't marry into the faith. I don't play that kind of game. My grandsons have all had bar mitzvahs.

My mother and I had a very close bond over the years, but not like mother and daughter. It was much more like a friendship, more equal — because of the experiences we have gone through. It wasn't like a mother protecting me all the time, it was a two-way relationship, much more open. She lived till she was eighty-four. She lived a good life. She didn't have to work, and she had the family around her, lots of friends. She went on holidays, she didn't have any worries.

I think her teaching has been in my cooking. I have her cook book, which I use all the time. She was strong emotionally, and she helped people in the camp, not with medicine, but by talking to people. I try to think about the way she thought, and ask myself what she would have done. That has been guiding me all my life. That's her legacy.

Interviewed by Mandy Ross, 2003

Modern Jewish Motherhood — a Task and a Blessing

Ruth Shire

My experience of Jewish motherhood is twofold. There is the task of universal motherhood: caring for and nourishing your children physically and emotionally. Jewish motherhood adds other dimensions to this many-splendoured state — belonging, behaving and believing. The way of Jewish life demands certain disciplines of observances and remembrances in the cycle of a lifetime. The vicissitudes of Jewish experience throughout our long history have created a rich heritage of many laws and customs, which guide the individual in the path of righteousness. Over the centuries there have been many changes in the way we interpret the commandments — are they directly given by God or divinely inspired? As a Progressive Jew, I believe the commandments are divinely inspired and therefore can be seen from different viewpoints according to their time.

It is very problematic to get the balance right, in cooperation with your husband, to be an example to your children and provide the right education for the next generation. The Jewish way of life can be a blessing or a curse. The century of the Shoah, especially, has added the greatest tragedy to our generation and the generation to come. The imperative duty of telling the story and causing a burden to our children must be acknowledged as a serious task, which will live with us and with them forever.

I am a refugee from Nazi oppression, and have experienced the loss of home and education. I was torn from a settled, normal childhood at the age of sixteen. However, I was fortunate to be given hospitality by a fine, humane

149

Christian family who not only took me in, but provided visas and subsequent financial care for my parents in England. However, the family life of former carefree days was finished forever. My father was interned on the Isle of Man for many months. I had to live with my mother in very constrained circumstances, and to my eternal shame, I found it very hard to become a support and a substitute "parent" to her. It was an excellent lesson to learn not to lean too much on my own children later on, but to give them space in order to develop their own individual personalities.

Finally my father returned from his internment. It had been very traumatic for both him and my mother, yet more bearable than the last few years of their German experience, which included two months' incarceration in a concentration camp for my father. Though it was wartime, life took on a more normal hue again, and I was able to train as a nurse. In my new surroundings I found that several of my colleagues were from similar backgrounds and we formed a support group and called it "family", sharing triumphs and disasters. What a great lesson for future motherhood and family life.

When the time came for marriage I had to wait many frustrating years for a family. Therefore my two sons and one daughter became even more precious and valued. My husband and I tried to give them quality time and be there for them whenever necessary, a safety net in all circumstances. Our home life was carried out in an observant Progressive way and seemed to run without too many objections. It was accepted as natural to go regularly to synagogue services from an early age, observe the festivals and belong to the Jewish youth group. They did have non-Jewish friends from school, who visited and vice versa, and on birthdays they all came together. Interestingly enough, none of them ever had a serious relationship with a non-Jewish girl or boy.

My respect and understanding for other religions originated from my time as a refugee in a large Christian household, whose members treated me with a dignified difference. This tolerance became a guideline for my family. I am a grandmother now, and hope that the second generation will learn this tolerance too. Education and the Jewish community have been an important feature of life for my husband and me. Our work in the community has given us great satisfaction and gave our children an awareness of their task. Tradition becomes an inspiration when done with flexibility — though beware, lest it becomes chains, and leads to suffocation.

My most memorable moment as a Jewish mother came when I was invited for tea for the first time to my eldest son's home — just married, he just twenty-two and she twenty, and I felt a deep thankfulness and pride of being alive to see this day. My husband and I are now the Patriarch and Matriarch of the family and when we sit around one of my children's seder table we can truly say *dayenu*. Jewish motherhood has proved a blessing.

Mothering Daughters, Mothering Sons

On Skirts and Daughters

Elana Maryles Sztokman

I remember well the time I decided to stop wearing trousers in favour of skirts. At the age of nineteen, I was becoming more "religious" following my yeshiva education, and I packed up my slacks and put on those hard, straight denim skirts that were popular in my Brooklyn day school. But it wasn't long before I opted for the long, flowing, floral and paisley one-size-fits-all down to the ankle types, otherwise knows as "floor sweepers". In those skirts, I was comfortable. I could sit cross-legged on the floor, I could feel my body move in the fabric, and I was less cloistered. In a certain sense, it was more "beautiful" to me, maybe even more feminine.

It wasn't until years later, when I was a young married woman and changed my appearance again by taking off my beret and pulling on my jeans, that it occurred to me that those shapeless skirts that my Dad used to disparage as "unflattering" were actually a form of rebellion. I was making an unconscious statement. Wearing those skirts was my way of saying that how I feel is more important than how I look, that I had had enough of the tight, moulded and squeezed sensations that came with the classic Orthodox girls' uniform of the straight skirt. How odd to think that in the world of modern Orthodox Judaism, a young woman can rebel by becoming more religious.

The oppression of women via the clothing they are expected to wear is an ancient story. Although we have come a long way from corsets and bustles, and the acceptance of women's trousers in the workplace seems to indicate a growing respect for women as professional equals, still, societal expectations of women continue to be reflected in styles of dress. An ultra-Orthodox colleague of mine ironically echoed feminist sentiment when he described the way in which he feels that mini-mini-skirts, cropped tops, and sheer, tight dresses turn women into sex objects. A religious hairdresser neighbour recalled her own transition from being secular to religious as one in which she was searching for a world in which women were viewed as more than their external appearance. Hmmm, I thought, as she finished doing my colour. Would my grey hair perhaps encourage people to appreciate my mind? And moreover, must I forgo all beauty products in order to consider myself truly a feminist? Something tells me that we are beyond that — or maybe not. Maybe we were never really there.

The issue is complicated. For observant Jews, the answers are so often provided before we have finished asking the question. Jewish law tells women to cover themselves up for the purposes of sexual propriety. *Shok isha erva, kol isha erva*, says the *Shulchan Aruch*, a central authority on Jewish law — "A woman's thighs are forbidden, a woman's voice is forbidden." As predictable as these ancient assertions are, so too are their modern-day aggadic interpretations — from the apologists who try to convince us that women are actually on a "higher" (read "different") level, to the fundamentalists who chide us that this is God's will and that feminism is not a Jewish value. On the other side of the fence, post-modernists tell us that everything is subjective, that all Jewish law is context-dependent and socially constructed anyway. It's a classic example of women's subjugation — these laws succeed in turning us into silent and invisible beings for the sake of community and familial wellness. Women subject to men's gaze, woman as the object of man's desire.

Meanwhile, we women with physiques and psyches, body issues, food issues, voice issues and control issues, spend our money on therapy and yoga, diets and wardrobes, in a feeble attempt to help us sort out the pieces of the puzzle. Caught between our respect for tradition and our respect for ourselves, between adherence to codes and adherence to our own inner voices, we are returned to the ongoing tension between autonomy and submission, in search once again for our own reflections and practice of what it means to be a Jewish woman.

I see young girls in the park across the street from my house, the oldest one under the age of ten, wearing a wool tartan dress with long sleeves, thick tights and shoes, looking after two younger siblings. She's growing up too fast, I think to myself. Already she's a little mummy, already she's covering her body — and she hasn't even hit puberty yet. She won't be climbing trees, riding a bike or jumping hurdles anytime soon. Already she is taught that her body is about how others see her rather than how she feels. In summer she'll be hot from the sleeves and in winter she'll be cold from the tights. And when she wants to hide her body, when she feels flawed and imperfect, she has many tools at her disposal for covering up and hiding the perceived blemishes.

I'm grateful that my eight-year-old daughter, Avigayil, is permitted to wear trousers this year in her religious school. So far, she is empowered in terms of her own appearance, freely choosing clothes that are comfortable, warm, and physically enabling — and that look nice to her when she looks in the mirror. She seems comfortable with her body in that healthy, youthful way. But of course, the skirt rule begins next year in our school. And I worry about that. I've started to speak informally to other parents and to the principal about extending permission for trousers at least until the age of eleven or even twelve (though in reality I would prefer to do away with the rule altogether — but first things first). Why are we telling them so young that their bodies are sexual objects, that they should be paying so much attention to the way men see them? So far, I haven't met with much support for these thoughts. After all, I've been told, there are so many more important, more pressing issues on the agenda. Is this where we should be focusing our energies when we have to deal with more important questions like the curriculum, bus schedules, and homework?

Maybe it's the influence of Mary Pipher's *Reviving Ophelia* (New York: Ballantine Books, 1994) that stays with me, the notion that these early years are crucial for girls' sense of self-worth, that in a few short years they'll experience the infamous "drop" — the drop in self-esteem and self-image that puts them at high risk of eating disorders, depression, drug and alcohol exposure, and conflicts about their sexuality, among other things. The religious community is no longer able to maintain the delusion that it is somehow immune to these ills. Anorexia alone is so widespread among religious adolescent girls that all pretence of sweeping it under the carpet is gone. And maybe the growing numbers of abused women in the Orthodox community will ultimately propel us to re-examine the messages that we send our young women about self within relationships. Maybe.

Consciousness. I would like to see the Orthodox community become more attentive to girls' emotional experience. What are the girls feeling? How do they experience their own bodies? How does the girl in the park see herself? I want to be able to have the conversation about the impact of dress codes on girls within the religious educational system. So far, I haven't found too many partners for the conversation. But I'm still looking.

My three-year-old daughter, Yonina, is going through the famous "dress stage". I understand from other parents that all girls go through it. My mother reports that when I was in kindergarten, I had one dress only that I insisted on wearing every day. Thank God Yonina has two or three — that helps with the laundry. And not any dress will do, only the ones that flow high when she spins around fast, like a pinafore. Despite an early effort to gently persuade her of the merits of trousers in the rainy, snowy winter, I swiftly abandoned my cause. Like any good struggling parent, I addressed the conflict between my own vision and my child's desires by casting aside my own needs and going with hers, all the way. Now I help her find matching tights and headbands. Every morning in preschool, she runs to her friend Ruthie, and they compare dresses, colours, shoes, hair, and twirling around. It's their own sweet ritual. And despite myself, it always makes me smile. For some reason that feminist researchers may never come to understand, this stage is important in girl-hood. Besides, so far, she hasn't let the dress stop her from riding her tricycle, going down the slide, rolling on the floor, or jumping from the third stair. And I guess that's what counts.

Our messages are complicated. The laws of modesty make a point in that they encourage a form of self-respect. But they can also be inhibiting, objectifying, and oppressive. Sure, secular society often shows women as sex objects. But in the religious world, women often aren't seen at all. And so I remain torn between my desire to be seen and my desire not to be seen too much, between wanting my daughters to use their legs and not wanting them to be seen only for their legs. Finding the balance between my sometimes conflicting values is my challenge as an educator, a mother, and essentially as a grown-up girl.

Between My Daughter's World and Mine

Elana Maryles Sztokman

I collect Jewish children's literature — not just because I'm a mother of little Jewish people but also because I'm fascinated with gender in books. I tend to pick up those books that have distinct gender messages. Like the children's prayer books that show only pictures of boys. Or the stories with animal characters who are all referred to as "he". Or the ones where the mummies are shown cooking and the fathers are depicted doing everything else. What can I say? I'm a glutton for punishment. I know I'm torturing myself by accumulating that which I don't like, but perhaps it's the belief that a woman should know her enemy.

Once I found this particular book that looked different, almost promising — it's a popular Israeli cartoon series around the weekly Torah portions. I thought, the idea that Torah can be taught through lengthy cartoon strips should be a modern enough educational idea that perhaps it will also reflect some gender awareness. But alas, there was only one female character in the whole book, a tiny-waisted Disney-like damsel in distress who merited half a page including all of one dialogue bubble. After I put the book down, my oldest daughter, Avigayil, who is now ten, grabbed it and started reading it. She didn't put it down for a week. When I said to her, "Did you notice how few women and girls there are in that book?" she gave me one of those "come on, Mum" looks, and then said, "You're doing it again, that whole woman thing." Well, that put me in my place. Tempting as it is for me to force my entire ideology on her, she made it clear that she's just not interested. In fact, my zealotry threatened to induce more

160

rebellion than sympathy. So, this beautiful young creature shared with me her invaluable wisdom, and as a result she reads what she wants to read, I make few if any comments, and she decides when she's ready to talk. Although it feels as though I am leaving my feminism aside, perhaps this is an essential part of feminism — letting young women figure it out for themselves, navigate their own way.

It's taking me a while to appreciate the depth of what Avigayil is teaching me. The fact is, her reality is very different from mine. I hadn't realised to what extent this is so until one Friday night when we were walking together to a women's *tefilla*, or prayer service. Just out of curiosity, I said to her, "Tell me, what do you like better, the women's *tefilla* or the mixed group?" She responded with an explanation that I didn't understand until she repeated it for the third time. She basically said, "I like the mixed group better because the women's group is unfair — it's not nice to leave the men out." I was astounded to learn that in her life, ritual exclusion is something *men* experience by women and not the other way around. Her world is different indeed.

I can't explain to her what I have felt for so much of my life. I can't adequately describe my predominantly Barbie-doll synagogue experience growing up, where every Shabbat we would don the fancy clothes, high heels and lipstick and sit chatting behind a partition watching men have all the fun. My father is a *ba'al koreh* and *ba'al tefilla*, which means that my sisters and I would often come to hear him lead the services and read from the Torah. It took me many years of adulthood to understand why I didn't like going to *shul*, but now that I've read from the Torah many times I can say with certainty that the young teenage girl behind the partition was just dying to *leyn* like her father, just once. But back then, I didn't own the language to express my own sense of disempowerment.

But I'm not sure if all this is even important for Avigayil to know. After all, how could I possibly explain it to her, when she has watched me prepare for my Torah reading many times, she has stood with me at the bimah as I lead *Pesukei Dezimra*, she has accompanied me in chanting the blessings for being called up to the Torah — and she herself has not only wrapped the Torah and opened the Ark, but she has also led the end of the service. What would have seemed like a bizarre fantasy to me growing up has become a reality of our lives. Is it possible Avigayil will never know that Jewish women have been oppressed? Will she be able to appreciate that in so many places today they still are?

I grapple with this issue as I restrain myself. She has unknowingly witnessed scenes from my own transformation, before and after. When she was six, before I had ever read from the Torah, she had a school assignment to "describe what you see in *shul*." I started to say, well, you see a piece of lace on a wooden frame and some straw hats bobbing up and down in gossiping agreement. But I stopped myself and said, "Go and ask *Abba*." That was perhaps a cop-out. Or maybe it was an early understanding that my own issues are not necessarily hers, and that I need to think twice about how I impose my own ambivalence on her.

I don't seem to have the same grapplings with my eight-year old son, Effie. The way I see it, if we get our primary gender-identity associations from the same-sex parent, Effie will be just fine. The masculinity he receives from my husband, Jacob, is the notion that men can and should do everything — work, kids, lunches, laundry, dishes, hair, all of it. He knows that to be a man means to be nurturing and what my kids call "smoochy". Most mornings we hear, "Who is taking us to school today?" and in the evening the question that goes around is "Who's making dinner?" Jacob does not carry around the same quagmire of issues that I do, so I believe that neither will Effie. He's lucky that way. But for my daughters, I have a problem, especially with Avigayil. As my first girl, she is where I am navigating new terrain, experimenting as it were. The plight of the oldest daughter!

My tension over how much of this quagmire of mine to impose on her came up again recently as I was leaving the house to teach my class on Gender and Judaism. Avigayil often asks to come with me to work. Part of me would love to have her there, to participate in the processing that goes on with my students. Still, I am reluctant, though I can't articulate why. The other night she asked me what I was going to teach.

"Time-bound commandments, *mitzvoth ase she'-hazeman graman*," I said.

"What is that?" she said.

"Did you ever notice that there are some commandments that men do and women don't?" I explained.

"Like what?"

"Like tefillin, say."

"Oh, yeah. Why is that?"

I tried to explain how a time-bound commandment is traditionally explained around women's caretaking, knowing full well that in class later we would undo that reasoning and see that it has more to do with keeping women out of the public sphere than anything else. Nevertheless, I kept my answer as concise as possible.

"That doesn't sound so fair," she said to me. I explained that today not all women accept it any more.

"Oh, I like that," she smiled, and we left it at that. I didn't say anything else. This is her space, this is her processing, and even though I wanted to cheer and say, "You go, girl!" I restrained myself. Instead, I just gave her a hug and a kiss and said I had to go but that we would talk more about this another time and she could ask *Abba* more while I was out. And then I promised that I would take her with me to class one day.

I'm so torn between wanting to nudge her in this direction and wanting to help her find her own path. But the bottom line is, more than anything, I want to be with her in her own process. I've been searching for a way to hear her thoughts and give her space to explore worlds with me, without imposing my own issues on her. One way in which we have been doing this over the past year is by learning together, or perhaps more accurately, reading together. The text we choose to read during our *chevruta*, or "partner reading", is the Bible. We do a chapter or two each sitting, whenever we are both free and in the mood. We're about halfway through Exodus at the moment, reading about the spectacular moments when the Jews became a nation. We've seen Miriam's quick-thinking initiative, and Moses' wife circumcising their sons. We have also read about Rachel and Leah's competition over motherhood and Abraham's cruelty towards Sarah in asking her to be his "sister" instead of his wife.

There have been many times when I could have transmitted to her my own interpretations at length, and admittedly I sometimes talk more than I know I should. It's just not the place for that. Our *chevruta* is the time for her to find her own ideas. And hard as it is sometimes for me to give up that central role of teacher and the one who's "been there", or to insist on the superiority of my own thinking, when I hear her insightful words, I am left in awe by the amount I have to learn from my ten-year-old daughter. In the end, our *chevruta* time is mostly about talking together. I ask her questions, she asks me questions, and on those rare occasions when she really wants to know what I think, I tell her. But I try to remember to wait for her to ask. Usually she asks and answers her own. When she comes up with an idea that I would have myself, I gloat internally. But when she comes up with one that's different, well, that's when I'm really proud and inspired. I worked hard for my own empowerment, and although I have mostly resolved my own issues by finding comfortable places where I can be an active and full participant in Jewish life, nevertheless, I continue to struggle. But maybe for her, the journey won't be as hard.

Over the recent Shavuot holiday, we read the book of Ruth. We talked for a while about the inspiring way in which Ruth decided to leave her own history behind and cling to Naomi. We talked about the power of a loving

164

gesture, and about how Ruth chose to convert to Judaism simply because of her relationship with Naomi. Avigayil offered me words that I will treasure forever: "It's like you and me," she said. I hope so. In the end, love transcends ideology, and perhaps everything else. And maybe this is the greatest message my daughter has taught me.

And I'm so grateful for Ruth. So there is a great book about women for us after all.

Frum and Feminist:
One Mother's Dilemma

Sally Berkovic

Elisheva, my seven-year-old daughter, recently celebrated her *Chagigat Chumash* — a festive occasion at her Orthodox school where all the children in her year are formally presented with their own Bible. Interspersed with songs and dances, the children's performance was structured around a story involving the passing down of the Bible, the Torah, from one generation to the next. By way of explanation, there was a little booklet for parents in which the message was crystal clear. "Moshe received the Torah at Mt Sinai and handed it over to Joshua, and Joshua gave it the Elders, and the Elders gave it to the Prophets and the Prophets gave it to the Men of the Great Assembly. Since then, the Torah has been passed from father to son until the Redemption will come."

And the mothers? I thought to myself. And the daughters? Where do they figure in this history lesson? Where are the women in this history of Revelation? Where are the female role models for my daughter to aspire to? As an observant (I prefer this description to Orthodox) mother, how do I begin to construct an alternative reality for my daughters that stays within the realm of halachah, yet seeks to integrate the benefits of modernity? As a mother deeply connected to Jewish ritual, law and lore, how do I maintain a balance between the demands of that tradition, and the knowledge that certain traditions have the potential to alienate my daughters from their own heritage?

Elisheva's non-encounter with the Torah of her matriarchs demonstrates the power of language at such a young age. As she learns that the Torah does not belong to her, my job is made even harder as I struggle to engage my three daughters, aged eight, seven and five, in a Judaism that speaks to them as young girls who will soon emerge into womanhood. I've got a couple of tricks up my sleeve. As we walk to *shul* together on Saturday mornings, we have our "Jewish woman of the week" story. Of course, they are familiar with the biblical heroines Sarah, Rebecca, Rachel and Leah, but we've also discovered many others, including Elisheva (Aaron's wife), the scholar Bruria, the daughters of Zelophehad who argued with Moses to claim their due inheritance, the diarist Glückel of Hameln, and Yael (they particularly enjoy the gory detail that she stuck a nail through Sisera's head).

Another trick is to make sure that as every festival approaches, we spend some time discovering and re-imagining the role of women as they are relevant to the holiday. Obvious examples are Shavuot, which has canonised the story of Ruth's conversion to Judaism and her relationship with her mother-in-law, Naomi; and Purim, which celebrates the heroic role of Queen Esther (and let's not forget the subversive Vashti). But the role models are usually not so obvious, and the question remains: how does an observant mother engage her daughters in the full gamut of Jewish experience, when the lives, deeds and aspirations of Jewish women have been ignored or trivialised?

Recently, I put myself to the test. Passover was looming, and as I stood in the playground listening to the other mothers discuss cleaning the cupboards (or rather organising for the cupboards to be cleaned by someone else) and the exorbitant price of Passover marshmallows, I wondered, "Is this all there is?" On the one hand, these memories of hanging around the kitchen while my mother vigorously cleaned in the run-up to Pesach are an important part of my personal history. However, as a mother myself, I am painfully aware that my own mother knew very little about why she was doing all this cleaning — it was, "Well, just something we do." That sort of answer is no longer good

167

enough for me, and certainly not good enough for my daughters. Women (and I would suggest it's not just in the religious community) have become spectators in the Passover experience — their role in the preparation is limited to mainly menial tasks that will enable their fathers, husbands and sons to participate in the symbolic liberation from Egypt. Ironically, in an era when so many of the wealthier religious people go to kosher hotels for Passover, not even these kitchen management skills are passed on from mother to daughter.

We had been invited to a seder where we were all asked to contribute some thoughts about the text. Determined to find a "woman's story" to share at the seder, I looked at the four sons: the wise, the wicked, the simple and the one who does not know how to ask. True, the Hagaddah uses the term *banim*, which could also be translated as the gender-free "children". However, artistic interpretations and rabbinic commentaries over the centuries have always depicted these four children as four "sons". But I wondered aloud: what if they were four daughters? Would the questions be any different, and would the answers we give be any different?

To avoid any claim of originality, this idea has been around for at least twenty years since non-Orthodox American Jewish women's groups started producing feminist haggadot and creating "women's seders" to celebrate the role of women in the Passover story. The struggle I face in bringing up my daughters is to respond to these issues within an Orthodox framework,[1] where social conventions, particularly in England, are often used to justify halachic stringency. Some tell me that my attempt to fuse the old and the new is fundamentally flawed and that I am trying to reconcile two worlds that are intrinsically at odds with each other. At some level, that is true.

[1]For an exploration of these issues in an Orthodox framework, visit www.jofa.org, the website of the Jewish Orthodox Feminist Alliance, which was established in the mid-1990s.

But I feel that if I don't grapple with the issues, if I don't listen to what my heart is telling my head, I risk alienating my own daughters from their rich, complex and meaningful heritage.

So, what would these four daughters ask?

The wise daughter asks, "Why didn't the Torah count women among the '600,000 men on foot, aside from children', who came out of Egypt?"[2]

"But Mum," says Avigayil, my oldest, "the women have to count. What about the women who saved Moses? Without them, there would be no story."

Even she understands that without a memory of the experience, Jewish women cannot write their history. And so our obligation as mothers is to recount the women, to make the picture complete. The seder is a perfect opportunity to tell the story of Yocheved, the mother of Moses, who defiantly hid her child under threatening circumstances. And to remember Miriam, who watched over her brother, Moses, while he was hidden, and made sure that his own mother was hired to be his wet nurse while he was brought up in the palace. And to express our gratitude for the actions of Bitya, the daughter of Pharaoh, who found Moses floating in the Nile and adopted him.

The wicked daughter asks, "Why do you treat the men as kings on seder night? Why are you happy with the status quo?"

"Yeah, Mum," says Elisheva, my middle daughter. "Didn't you always tell us that there are women who have

---

[2]Two recent books have gathered a lot of ideas about women's relationship to Passover, and it was reading these books that formed the basis of my contribution to the seder, and by extension, the idea of this essay. *The Women's Seder Sourcebook: Rituals & Readings for Use at the Passover Seder* and *The Women's Passover Companion: Women's Reflections of the Festival of Freedom*, both edited by Rabbi Sharon Cohen Anisfeld, Tara Mohr and Catherine Spector (Jewish Lights Publishing, 2003).

challenged God to make things better for women?" In a religious community, it is too easy to dismiss the wicked daughter as someone who flouts authority and is not willing to toe the line. But I have been trying to teach my daughters that challenging the rules demonstrates that you care enough to want to do something. We can talk about changes, initiated by women, that have rocked the Orthodox establishment over the last twenty years. These include Orthodox women studying Talmud, developing alternative rituals for bat mitzvah, women's prayer groups where women are reading from the Sefer Torah. Some have dismissed these women as "wicked". But I would embrace these women as passionate advocates who care enough about tradition and halachah to ensure that women are not excluded unnecessarily.

The simple daughter asks, "Why are we talking about women's stuff?"

These daughters don't even understand that there is a story to tell about women. These are the daughters who have accepted the male definition of the Jewish experience and do not yet appreciate how the prayers, hopes and aspirations of Jewish women have been overlooked in this process.

Finally, the daughter who does not know how to ask represents those daughters who have been silenced throughout history. We have a responsibility to help this daughter to acquire the tools to question our traditions. The question-and-answer format of the seder ritual demonstrates an active, living Judaism that ideally engages all its participants. However, if we do not teach the daughter who does not know how to ask, we will lose her questions, and we will lose her.

These four daughters, like their brothers, are archetypal characters. They remind parents of their responsibility to enable each child to ask questions, and receive answers, in a style that suits his or her abilities and temperament. So I must ask: does this also mean that we have to be asking our girls different sorts of questions, and that as mothers, we have to be providing different sorts of answers for them? I'm not sure.

There are other festivals where it's possible to augment the male parameters of the celebration with women. For example, at Sukkot, there is a tradition that the *Ushpizin* visit us in our sukkah every night of the festival. This kabbalistic idea suggests that when we sit in a sukkah, God's presence is spread over it and that Abraham, Isaac, Jacob, Joseph, Moses, Aaron and King David accompany God. In recent years, families have started symbolically to invite women into their sukkah. The seven prophetesses — Sarah, Miriam, Deborah, Hannah, Avigail, Huldah and Esther — are an obvious choice to complement the seven male guests. Initiating such developments celebrates the lives of Jewish women, and reminds our daughters that women played an integral role in the history of Jewish religious life and literature. I think that Orthodox mothers have to work harder at making their daughters value the role of women, because these mothers are also products of a community that has not acknowledged women's experiences and has silenced their voices in the religious domain.

Of course, it can't only be Jewish mothers who have a responsibility to broaden their daughters' opportunities. Jewish fathers, brothers, grandfathers, rabbis, educators and youth leaders are all part of a system that has assigned a place and purpose to Jewish women. So I went to talk to the male teacher in charge of Jewish studies at my daughters' school about my concern that the language in the *Chagigat Chumash* alienated young girls. He listened sympathetically, nodded in agreement and scribbled a few notes down on a yellow Post-it note. It's a slow process, but I have to hope that these challenges to people in authority, forcing them to rethink their assumptions, will have a long-term impact.

My youngest daughter, Yonina, will have her *Chagigat Chumash* next year. I'll be waiting to see if the message on the yellow Post-it note makes its way into the script.

Being the Mother of Boys: Grievances from the Women's Section

Shana Mauer

On a warm Shabbat morning not long ago, I sat in synagogue, lost in thought, listening to the muffled voice of the *gabbay* over the *mehitzah* as he called out names for the next aliyah to the Torah. My husband and I and our three sons have been attending this synagogue for nearly a year. It is a popular, mainstream synagogue. It is a place without the slightest hint of progressive attitudes or egalitarian sympathies. The prayers are conventional. The melodies are traditional. The women's section is a slightly elevated room adjacent to the main sanctuary separated from the men by a half wall and semi-transparent white curtain. It is, in fact, a virtual model of Israel's centrist Orthodox synagogues. But, for me, sitting in my chair facing towards the men, whose chairs were directed, as is proper, towards Jerusalem, I felt as though I was in an odd chamber — a cross between a cage and theatre box seat — privy to a lacklustre dress rehearsal where the actors are brazenly indifferent to the audience.

Until recently, we had been part of another congregation, a Carlebach *minyan* that had taken decisive steps to make services an inclusive experience for the entire family. The *mehitzah* had been moved to create an even division between the men and women, with both sections facing out towards a view of Jerusalem. Both the bimah and the *aron kodesh* had been relocated next to the *mehitzah*, as close to the women's section as possible. New policies had also been implemented. One was to draw the *mehitzah* partially during the rabbi's speech, allowing the rabbi to address the whole congregation. The other was to

172

bring the Sefer Torah to the women's section following the reading of the weekly portion, allowing the women directly to pay their respects to the Scriptures.

Our main motivation for joining this synagogue had been, in short, me. I had practically ceased synagogue attendance altogether, barring a few sporadic appearances for bar mitzvahs and the High Holidays. After each spiritual venture, I would find myself angry and even more reluctant to return, distraught over the role of women in Jewish prayer and the appendage of the main sanctuary that qualified as a women's section. My husband and I, who live in a religious community in Israel, where all the local synagogues are strictly Orthodox, recognised that tackling the problem of women in traditional prayer was beyond our means. But we hoped we might find a synagogue with a more appealing women's section.

I was especially eager to find a synagogue where I could spend my Shabbat morning without feeling demeaned or discounted. As the mother of three boys, one of them already ten years old, I dreaded the prospect of listening to my sons chant their bar mitzvah Torah portions while consumed with mixed feelings of unbridled pride and festering resentment. I imagined my husband and sons in the thick of the intricate synagogue proceedings, while I sat alone on the other side of the *mehitzah*, demurely peeking through the partition, eager to catch a glimpse of my beaming bar mitzvah boy like some ultra-modest eighteenth-century matriarch. Thus, we joined the Carlebach *minyan*. Even though we lived closer to several other synagogues, it seemed to be the community where I would be most content: a *minyan* with sensitivity to the issues that elsewhere seriously hampered my ability to engage in communal prayer.

Through the baking sun of summer and torrential winter downpours, my husband trudged to the Carlebach *minyan* with my sons in tow. Often, I would stay at home. Sometimes, my youngest son was not up to the journey. Occasionally, I remained at home to prepare the table and meal for our lunch guests. And it was not uncommon for me just to opt for a quiet morning in my pyjamas, preferring a bit of solitude to Shabbat services at a synagogue that I considered passable, but still far from ideal.

After many months of this Shabbat routine, it became clear that it had been a mistake to centre our synagogue life around my concerns because, ultimately, Orthodox prayer is not about women. Services only begin when ten men assemble. The men are the presidents and *gabbays*. They serve as *shaliach tzibbor* and *ba'al koreh*. Men make the announcements, and men, who are the intended recipients, listen to them. The little boys lead the concluding *Shir HaKavod, Anim Zmirot*. Women and girls are there to attend, not participate — a fact that, as hard as I try, I cannot overlook, even when concessions are made to compensate partially for such entrenched disparity.

My husband was content with the Carlebach *minyan*, but not always eager to walk there in inclement weather. My children likewise disliked the long walk and complained that the small congregation included few of their playmates. In addition, the services were long, and we returned from synagogue when most of our friends and neighbours were already enjoying their midday repast. Like most Carlebach *minyanim*, the congregation was somewhat bohemian, eclectic and fluid, while our family was, in comparison, staid, conservative and in need of a more conventional synagogue arrangement. And though I found the *minyan*'s services more palatable than the Shabbat proceedings at other nearby synagogues, it was clear that my concerns had to be secondary, especially since my husband and sons were the main attendants. They were far more likely than me to have a bonding, long-lasting relationship with communal prayer.

Since I do not have any daughters whose relationship to prayer requires cultivation, I willingly agreed to switch synagogues. In truth, I did not feel as though the decision marked my capitulation. The whole structure of Orthodox prayer has always been an enormous compromise for me, and there is no particular synagogue to blame. I have never found comfort or solace sitting passively behind any *mehitzah*. And, as fate has not cast me in the mould of maternal role model, I have used my dissatisfaction as an excuse to retreat from synagogue life, feeling somewhat vindicated because I do not have the direct responsibility of helping a daughter connect to Jewish prayer.

So now we have joined a large, upright and proper synagogue. It is the kind of place where the men enjoy a procession of handshaking after receiving an aliyah to the Torah, and the women wear matching shoes and hats. Several of my children's classmates are there each week and my son will take his turn amongst his peers when he eventually celebrates his bar mitzvah there in the not-so-far-off future.

Surprisingly, I come to synagogue from time to time. I enjoy the opportunity to see my friends and have resigned myself to the dismal women's section. It may be true that on one Shabbat a friend had to point out that it was, in fact, my son singing *Anim Zmirot* at the end of services, since I could not hear or recognise his voice from my seat on the women's side. But my experience over the past two years has only reaffirmed what I initially knew instinctively when I embraced an Orthodox life: synagogues are the domain of men. No one ever speaks of the *ezrat gvarim* — men's section. It would be comical. The women's section is analogous to the sidelines, or the stands. Every arena might have them, but they are always, without exception, secondary to centre court.

While reflecting on my family's spiritual vagrancy, switching from one synagogue to another to try to help me find a house of worship where I might feel at peace, I am obliged to admit that, if I did not have sons, I would have been far less concerned about finding a place that provided my children with a broad comfort zone. Because my sons will have very public bar mitzvahs, I felt it was critical that we plant some roots in a synagogue that gives them a sense of belonging; a *shul* where they will feel the pomp and gravity of performing their first major rite of passage amidst their community. Typical bat mitzvah celebrations in our circles consist of a Shabbat kiddush for the congregation and an evening party for the family's friends and relatives. But, even when a local bat mitzvah involves a women's *tefilla* or Torah reading, it is not closely linked to the synagogue. For boys, the synagogue is like a club where they will all undergo their formal initiation. I wanted my children to feel that our club is a natural and obvious choice for them, not a forced or inappropriate one.

Certainly, growing up in Vancouver, Canada, where my family attended a large Conservative synagogue, I felt a comforting sense of entitlement that allowed me to perceive every aspect of Judaism and the synagogue as part of my personal inheritance. As a child, I often accompanied my grandfather to *mincha* services following my afternoon Hebrew school lessons. In the synagogue's small auxiliary sanctuary, I took my place amidst a group of approximately twenty elderly men, unselfconscious as the only female amongst them. I viewed myself as a rightful member of this quorum and naturally answered the prayers with "Amen", confident that my participation was as valid and valuable as that of any other member of the Jewish nation. At Passover seders, I read the Hebrew text of the Haggadah with such conviction that family members prophesied my future as a rabbi, as if it was a perfectly natural vocation for a young girl.

For my peers and me, grade seven was the bar and bat mitzvah year. Almost every weekend, I would go to synagogue with my friends and attend the bar and bat mitzvahs of my classmates. Few distinctions were made in our world between boys and girls in terms of their entry into Jewish adulthood. Some of the girls, like myself, were paired with another classmate for a joint bat mitzvah. The boys were all granted solo performances, and their parties tended to be bigger and more opulent than the girls' receptions. But, on the whole, the girls felt that they were as much part of this celebratory year as the boys, and certainly as much a part of the congregation as any of the Davids, Aarons and Jonathans.

Consistent with most Conservative Jews, the only other time I showed up at synagogue with any regularity, apart from afternoon *mincha* services, was on the High Holidays. Again, I would sit with my grandfather and other family members. It was a very social happening, a time when I would have the opportunity to see friends from summer camp and Jewish kids who attended schools other than my own. But the sense of belonging did not dissipate after I greeted my acquaintances, passed through the front lobby and took my seat inside. I felt a part of the synagogue in every way and that I deserved to be seated near the centre, close to the bimah and the locus of the cantorial action.

I have every confidence that my sons enjoy a similar sense of belonging, and I am pleased that they have a synagogue where they feel at home. But their experience is completely disconnected from my involvement in synagogue life. At this stage in our family's development, only my youngest son visits me in the women's gallery, occasionally to keep me company, but more often to refuel his supply of sugary victuals. My other sons are now too old to enter the women's quarters and truthfully, it is easy to understand why they would be disinclined in any case. Accustomed to the main sanctuary, why would they be willing to settle in the women's section and forgo their privileged vantage point?

At the same time, I believe many of the girls and women at our synagogue share my sons' sense of belonging, even though they do not claim the Torah and prayers as their own. Instead, they are contented with the more nebulous experience of simply being at synagogue. Separated physically and ritually from the practice of public prayer, their experience of belonging is passive. They are socialised from their early childhood to know their place behind the curtain, and feel resigned, even oblivious, to their utter exclusion from the synagogue proceedings.

It is impossible for me to speculate about the relationship my daughters, if I had them, might have with communal prayer. Many girls in my community, raised in the bosom of Orthodoxy, accept their role in the synagogue without question, and attend services regularly, often sitting by their mothers' side. Others express their discontent by boycotting the synagogue, spending their Shabbat mornings sleeping or lounging around the house. Interestingly, there does not seem to be any outcry from the next generation of Orthodox girls, young women whose worlds afford them endless personal and professional opportunities, but no chance of reading from the Torah or leading their congregations in *Shemonah Esrai*. Mostly, cowed by peer pressure, the girls who do dislike the confines of the women's section remain silent, resign themselves to the prayer problem or eventually leave Orthodoxy altogether.

How would I try to usher a daughter of mine into the world of communal prayer and guide her to a satisfactory resolution? I cannot even begin to imagine such a scenario. With my own position on communal prayer so murky, it is unfathomable that I would be able to offer any reasonable solution. Several years ago, my husband and I were part of a valiant but failed effort to create a new *minyan* in our community. We tried to form a more egalitarian model inspired by the prototype of Jerusalem's recently formed Shira Hadasha, a strictly Orthodox congregation that incorporates every halachic opportunity for women to have an active share in the Shabbat services. Then, in the wake of our failure, I initiated a monthly women's *tefilla* group, a forum that enjoyed modest success, but never gained vibrant momentum. Would I do more if I had daughters? Would I feel the need to leave our community and find a place that offered more progressive prayer options? It is possible that if I had daughters they would be impervious to my reservations about synagogue. And, if they were, would I feel compelled to dispel their contentment?

I do not have family in Israel, and my husband's family is divided between Israel and the US. The lack of a nearby web of familial support makes our connection to a synagogue that much more important. Upon making aliyah, we had to create our community from scratch, building social ties with friends, neighbours, acquaintances from work, recreation and synagogue life. Since moving to Israel ten years ago, we have built a community life for ourselves and have done so with a strong concern for what is most comfortable, appealing and inviting for our sons, because they will have to take their place in this community in a very public, conspicuous forum.

I know that my sons, at least my older two, are aware of my misgivings about attending a synagogue with a women's section that I find degrading. And it is indeed important to me that they develop into open-minded, sensitive individuals with the ability to empathise with people's struggles and the wisdom to comprehend when the status quo is unjust. But, as their mother, I cannot sacrifice their experience of synagogue because of my grievances. So I come to synagogue from time to time, and try to ignore the fact that my presence is marginal. I do my best to overlook the offensiveness of the auxiliary room where I am stationed, and the partition meant to keep me and the other women out of sight, removed from the main stage.

So far, I have been able to contain my anger. I remain indifferent, emotionally divorced from my surroundings. I can only hope my disengagement prevails and allows me to attend my son's bar mitzvah with an undivided heart. If not, one of my most joyful moments will be tinged with unforgiving bitterness and a sadness that I will be unlikely to forget.

Mutations

Masha Gessen

I spent the day of August 21, 1992, driving to a moun-
tainous desert town whose name, in the scorching heat
and fine dust, was a seductive mockery: Palm Springs,
California. It was the most Californian of endeavours, an
editorial retreat for the Los Angeles-based magazine
where I worked. I ate dinner with my colleagues at a bland
Mexican restaurant. I had two sour margaritas, talked
more than I usually did, and told a story that left me
vaguely uneasy, as I always feel when I talk about my
mother: I cannot talk about her without telling lies. I don't
remember what I said, but it was something complimen-
tary, even prideful, I think, and though I loved my mother
and was proud of her, talking of her in that way, with all
that had gone wrong between us, was most certainly a lie.

I woke up at four that morning, in the bedroom of a
rental bungalow, with a wave of nausea pushing its way up
to my burning dry throat. I stumbled to the bathroom and
threw cold water inside and on myself, washing my face
and head clumsily, then looked at my bloated face in the
mirror and wondered how two margaritas could have done
this to me. I went back to bed and next opened my eyes at
a few minutes before seven, without a trace of a hangover
but with a sudden wakefulness I could not fight. With
hours to kill before the meetings began, I tried going out
for a walk in the desolation of Palm Springs, considered a
swim in the kidney-shaped pool, and finally went back
inside the bungalow intending to read some magazine
submissions. I spread them out on the coffee table and,
before starting, picked up the phone and dialled my
parents in Boston. I was checking in at least daily back
then and knew they'd be awake — they were three hours

ahead. These considerations were background noise; I'd picked up the phone without pausing to think, and was just getting one of my daily chores out of the way while I was killing time.

A strange male voice answered the phone. "Papa?" I asked, knowing that it wasn't.

"Hold a minute," the man said nervously, and a moment later my father came on the line. My mother was dead. The man answering the phone was a policeman who had come to fill out a report which, as it turned out, is a necessary part of letting someone die at home.

My mother had been diagnosed with breast cancer two years earlier. By the following summer it had already spread to her bones, and six months before she died she was told it may be in her liver — it wasn't then, but it got there and killed her.

My mother had last woken up at seven that morning — four o'clock in California, when I'd first woken up — and asked for ice cream. Her liver was failing. Her throat must have been burning up. She died a few minutes before ten. That was the moment I had bolted awake for the second time, the bizarre toxic symptoms of three hours earlier mysteriously gone, and my inextricable physical relationship to my mother proven to me for the first time in my conscious life at the very moment hers ended.

The second time the physical relationship proved itself was on January 28, 2004, at a coffee bar in Cambridge, Massachusetts — an accidental location I'll avoid in the future, much as I have avoided revisiting Palm Springs. I was sitting at a small square table, trying to fix my ailing laptop, when my cellphone rang and a professionally sensitive woman's voice said, "I am returning your call. Yes, the results of your tests have arrived, And there is a change." She paused. "In the BRCA1 gene, there is a deleterious mutation." She paused. "I'm sorry."

She was calling to say that my mother had passed on the bad gene, the breast cancer gene (that's what BRCA

181

stands for, a scientific abbreviation that is too easy to decipher: breast cancer). I was surprised. I was shocked. I shouldn't have been. I had gone to get tested, I had known enough to know that I was a likely candidate for the mutation, but I was convinced that I was negative. Even if my mother had been a carrier — I couldn't know, because she died two years before the gene was discovered — I had only a fifty per cent chance of having inherited it. That night in Palm Springs had taught me nothing: I was certain I was immune to my mother's physical legacy.

Something had gone wrong between me and my mother, something so profound and so old that I find it difficult to describe. There was no tragic fight, no horrible misunderstanding. For as long as I can remember, we simply felt like strangers, not particularly intimate ones except by virtue of circumstance: we happened to live together. Nothing between us was ever unconditional, even the physical proximity. I left home at fifteen.

Our relationship was a frozen sea, with scattered tiny islands of common ground. She died before we'd had much chance to claim those islands: before I wrote anything she — also a writer and a translator — would have enjoyed reading, before I translated my first book, using what I had learned from watching her work, and before I too became a mother.

When I started writing professionally, she said proudly, "My genes have won out." I remember being surprised, and silently dissenting: I did not doubt my mother's gifts, but I never believed they were also mine. I counted on more — and less. My mother was a more talented writer, a more diligent reader and a more enterprising student. She was also handicapped by a desperate fear of people that could turn routine communication into a feat of heroism. She died at forty-nine, still gifted but not accomplished: even if by external measure she may have been considered successful, she still felt anonymous and overlooked. I think that long-ago conversation with my colleagues in Palm Springs had in fact concerned my mother's career achievements, and this was why it had left me so uneasy. I know the fear too, but of necessity I learned to get out and make my way among people early, and I had always thought that this was why I had done well with barely half of her gifts. I had assumed I was simply better at living than she had been. And even though, like all daughters of mothers who die young, I have a difficult time visualising myself past a certain age, I had always, without really thinking about it, assumed that I would make better of what I had, and for longer, because I am not as afraid. I thought my gifts were my own, making me free from her legacy altogether. Then I found out that I got everything from her, including the flaw that killed her.

Here is the story of my flaw. I carry a genetic mutation that kills women early — earlier and earlier with each generation — through breast and ovarian cancer. Scientists have identified two genes (BRCA1 and BRCA2) as influencing these cancers. If these genes are damaged in certain known ways (two ways are known for BRCA1 and one for BRCA2), a woman's risk of breast and ovarian cancer increases manifold. The hereditary roulette works as follows. All of us have two copies of each and every gene. Those with the mutation have one normal copy and one damaged one. A child inherits one copy of every gene from each parent, so if one parent has a mutation, the child has a fifty per cent chance of getting a damaged copy of the gene. That, in turn, in the case of the BRCA gene means that her lifetime risk of breast cancer may be as high as eighty-five per cent, and the risk of ovarian cancer may go up to fifty per cent. For some reason, probably having to do with the environment or diet or lifestyle, these days women with the mutation are getting the cancers at an earlier age than their mothers' and grandmothers' generations.

From what we know about genes, the bad ones are supposed to get washed out of the population through natural selection. No one knows for certain why some mutations survive, but the theory many scientists subscribe to is that, in addition to causing disease, they serve a protective function against other, more common ailments. The effect of the sickle-cell anaemia gene, for example, is known to be protective against malaria. The Tay-Sachs gene, some believe, may guard against tuberculosis. These genetic mutations can perform their protective function if the carrier has just one copy of the gene with a mutation; they cause disease only if a child inherits the "bad" gene from both mother and father — a twenty-five per cent probability when the parents are carriers. There are critics of these theories, those who say that talk of natural selection in a modern population of humans is highly suspect, but it's a way to understand how genetic mutations get passed on through generations.

The story of the breast-and-ovarian-cancer mutations is more harsh. There is no indication that these mutations have any sort of protective effect. If a foetus inherits two bad copies of a BRCA gene — one from each parent — it will not be viable. A girl baby who is born with only one defective copy of the gene will not develop cancer as long as the other copy is functioning. But when the "good" copy also suffers a mutation — as, it seems, will happen in most cases — cancer will develop, and the disease will be more aggressive than in people without such mutations. A male child with the mutation may also eventually develop breast cancer, but this happens far less frequently. The risk of cancer goes up steadily with age: about twenty per cent by age forty, forty per cent by age fifty. Very rarely do women under thirty develop the cancer, and the chances of cancer pass the fifty per cent mark only around the age of fifty-five. So throughout human history, a woman would most likely become sick after she had given birth to and raised her children. For modern women, particularly western Jewish professional ones who have children later, the mutation may bring cancer before the child-rearing years are past.

Mathematically, women are just as likely to inherit this breast-and-ovarian mutation from their fathers, but they are not as likely to suspect that they have it unless their mothers have been stricken. Because in most countries this sort of genetic testing is not routine (an exception is Israel, where the mutation is relatively common), women who discover they carry the mutation often come from matrimonial cancer dynasties: mothers, grandmothers, great-grandmothers, and sisters in every generation have had the cancers. These women are terrified of having daughters. Some of these women hate their mothers.

That these mutations were discovered first among Jewish women is probably largely, though not entirely, an accident. Jews are an obvious choice for the study of genetics: they make up compact populations certain to share many genetic traits. So do Icelanders, Scandinavians and a large number of other ethnic groups, but they are not as frequently found near large medical-research centres. It may also be that Jewish medical researchers have chosen to study familiar communities.

My generation, making radical and underinformed decisions, may be lucky to be the guinea pigs — or not. In the last ten years a few thousand mostly Jewish, mostly midlife women, mostly in the US and Israel, have gained the kind of knowledge humans are unfamiliar with having. I have had my fortune told by a genetic counsellor at a hi-tech medical centre in Boston.

My daughter was born nine years after my mother died. I gave her my mother's name: Yolka. She has fashioned it into a story of life. "You know," I recently heard her tell a friend of mine. "Before, I used to be a small baby. Then I was born. Now I have grown and become a girl. Before, I used to be Grandmother Yolka, but I died."

The calm simplicity of that story pleases me, but I worry now about what I have passed on. My overconfidence about my own hereditary fortune affected my daughter too: when I gave her my mother's name, I was certain she would take only the best. Women who know they have a cancer-gene mutation are, I have discovered, rarely so cavalier. I have talked to young women who would rather adopt a child with an entirely unknown health history, than risk passing the possibility of breast cancer on to a daughter. I have talked to older women who are wracked with guilt over having passed on the mutation. I have talked to a woman who hates her eighty-four-year-old mother for being cancer-free while she and all her sisters, who inherited the mutation, have developed cancer. They focused their anger on the mother's refusal to be tested for the mutation — as though it would have made a difference — and when she finally relented, and tested positive, they rejoiced in the chance to lay blame.

With a disease as unpredictable as cancer, the opportunity to blame an actual person is an unexpected temptation. Often mutations can be traced through generations, based on the history told by death certificates, obituaries, and fears passed on from mother to daughter. I have talked to women who have seen their mothers, grandmothers, aunts, sisters and cousins struggle with cancer and succumb in a pattern that becomes familiar. My own mutation goes back to my mother, who got it from her father (he was killed in the Second World War at the age of twenty-two, but his sister later developed ovarian cancer, pinpointing their branch of the family as the culprit). My grandfather and great-aunt seem to have got the mutation from my great-grandfather, who died of colon cancer in his early sixties (mutation carriers seem to have a slightly increased risk of colorectal cancer as well). Then the trail gets lost, as it often does, since in chains of mutation-carriers generations seldom overlap by much: most of my other great-grandparents lived to see me born, but this one died years before I came along.

The first time I went to a gathering of women who carry the breast-and-ovarian-cancer mutation, I found myself looking hard into their faces, looking for familiar features. Unlike, say, people with HIV or multiple sclerosis, we share more than a similar condition, parallel concerns and identical hopes: we have common blood. The current mainstream scientific thinking is that mutations like ours do not occur spontaneously at different times in different populations. These mutations are sometimes called "point mutations", to indicate that the sequence of the gene is not scrambled but simply that one allay (the one coding for the 189th protein, in my case) is punched out. These mutations are thought to have what is called a "founder effect" — that is, to go back to one person. The fact that my particular mutation is found among both Ashkenazi and, albeit less often, Sephardic Jews, means the "founder" was a very distant ancestor, someone who lived long before the split into Ashkenazim and Sephardim. It is also one more piece of proof that these two groups have a common root.

That is why one can refer to these mutations as "Jewish" without incurring the wrath of the politically correct, as long as they can make the leap — especially difficult for Americans — to thinking of Jewishness as an ethnicity rather than a religion. That can explain, for example, why a Catholic population in the American southwest that traces its roots to a ship that sailed from Spain in the fifteenth century, has a high incidence of the same mutation that I got from my mother: the sailors were probably Jewish before they became Catholics. The cutting-edge science of the twenty-first century has a way of turning one's thinking about blood, religion and disease positively medieval.

I looked around the room at the women carrying my mutation. They looked nothing like me, but many of them had the thick post-chemo hair, the brittle post-chemo skin and the protruding breast prostheses that reminded me of my mother. The hospital where my mother had her mastectomy and where I now go for my breast MRIs was across the street. But she was not here.

When I learned of my mutation in January 2004, I was thirty-seven, my daughter was two and a half, and her

187

brother — who is adopted — was nearly seven. I had been thinking of having another child. My cumulative risk of breast cancer was roughly fourteen per cent. I was, in the absurd argot of the trade, a "previvor": not yet diagnosed with cancer but with a high risk of getting it. I went to see a genetic counsellor.

Those who learn that they carry a mutation like mine are immediately admitted to the cancer caste. I found myself carrying a cancer centre's patient card, walking past a wig-and-prosthesis shop on my way to see my doctors, and retracing my mother's steps down the hospital corridors — still hoping that in my version, the same genes will add up to a better life, and a longer one.

The genetic counsellor, her head permanently cocked to one side in a show of sympathy, suggested there was only one way out of the cancer ward. She advised me to cut out my ovaries. She said I might also consider removing my breasts. I was still using them to feed and comfort my daughter then. Breast milk had turned out to be the magic potion of motherhood: it nourished my daughter during her frequent illnesses when she was a baby, and it could fix frustration, anxiety or a stubbed toe once she became a toddler.

I spent weeks reading medical studies and doing frantic arithmetic, careening from one option to another. In the end I leaned towards chest surgery, but I decided to proceed slowly. I weaned my daughter. I managed to convince her that big girls do not drink from the breast. It took a couple of weeks and then she took to holding my breasts, which she still does — before she goes to sleep, when she wakes up, or for comfort when she has hurt herself or feels insulted. Every time I cuddle her, I worry: how can I get rid of them when she needs them? The argument that ought to trump them all — that any trauma is worth it if it means having me around — doesn't convince me. What worries me, gnaws at me to the point where I feel a stabbing pain in my chest — my breast — is the fear of losing the physical connection with my daughter that I never remember having with my mother. It was there as sure as the fact that I bolted awake the moment she died three thousand miles away, but I never felt it. Touching her did not give me comfort.

There is a black-and-white picture of me at the age of perhaps two months, my mother holding me. My mother, her lips buried in the black down on my head, has that look of being desperately tired and profoundly in love, a look — or, rather, a state — I recognise. This is the last evidence that we had that connection. When I walked into her hospital room at Boston's Brigham and Women's Hospital in August 1990, she pointed with her chin toward the flatness under her gown and said, "I fed you with that breast." She sounded like she was saying something one said in such situations. I mumbled something non-committal, which is to say, unfeeling: I felt nothing.

In the two years between my mother's operation and her death, we tried, through short phone calls and more-frequent visits, to make up for whatever it was we had lost. Our progress was uncertain, and we both believed the effort was doomed. Six months before my mother's death, I stayed with my parents for a few weeks. As I was leaving, my mother said she had written a letter to her own mother boasting that we had managed to spend all that time together without fighting. That was our accomplishment; intimacy and affection were beyond reach. When we were saying goodbye, my mother hugged me and whispered, "Be happy, my girl." I was giving a talk the next day in the same town, but my mother was too weak to come. I never saw her alive again.

During those two years I developed a habit of thinking of my mother as I got on a plane. After years of little air travel, I started flying a lot soon after my mother was diag-nosed — and discovered I had a paralysing fear of flying. Then I found that when I thought of my mother, imagined her face and voice, the fear abated and a sort of calmness set in: I usually fell asleep just before take-off. The psychobabble in my head said that when I thought of the unexpected calm with which my mother was facing her own death, it made it easier to consider even the possibility of an air crash. I now think the mechanism was simpler: thinking of my mother was enough to calm me because one is never really mortal as long as one has a mother.

When I boarded a small plane in Palm Springs on August 22, 1992, a half-price mourner's ticket across the country in my hand, the old panic grabbed me without warning. I tried to visualise my mother, but the trick did not work. I saw her face, I heard her voice, but the fear only deepened. I no longer had a mother. For perhaps as long as twenty years we had denied each other the affection of a mother and daughter. For ten years I had lived separately. But only then, at the age of twenty-five, boarding a plane to go and bury my mother, did I feel finally untethered and unprotected.

My daughter will go on in the world with feet and eyebrows that are replicas of mine, a stubbornness just like mine, and the habit — my habit — of scrunching up her face when doing something that requires great concentration, such as colouring between the lines. Most importantly, she will carry with her the memory of me, perhaps even the physical sense of me, and maybe that will be enough to make her feel safe even after I am gone. I think about this in the sleepless early mornings, when she presses her hot heels into the small of my back, and I know I am the only thing that protects her from the cold wind of fear and freedom that comes into the room through the open balcony door. Then she taps me on the shoulder and asks me to turn around so she can hold my breasts.

Forging
New Links

A Man of Worth

Elly Stanton

Who can find a man of worth? For his price is far above anything you, or in fact anyone, can afford.

And when thou wert thirteen, didst thou not say that thou wouldst never marry anyone except for a knight in shining armour, which he polisheth himself and hangeth up when he cometh in? And when thou art eighteen, thou shalt get a wave of panic and persuade thyself that no-one shall ever show the slightest interest in thee. And then one day, by some miracle, behold, thou shalt meet someone who is quite nice — not perfect, of course, but who hath some good genes and liketh children, which is basically all thou art bothered about. And thy mother and father shall breathe an heavy sigh of relief, and thy mother shall engage thee in conversation whilst goeth out thy father to inspect his car.

And then shalt thou beget children, and thou shalt rise when it is still night and feed and change them, and thou shalt rise also when it is day, and thy lamp shall never go out at night. And then thou shalt say unto thy husband, "Art thou going to consider that field, plant that vineyard, make thine own coverlet, etc?" And he shall retort tartly, "I am not one of your multi-taskers, you know. Right now I am engaged in keeping up that bank balance, that which you are so fond of spending." And thou shalt reply silently, "And thine ego." And that is basically it.

But then, thinkest thou, he is so good with the children, and thou goest dewy-eyed watching them together. And thou shalt swear unto thyself an oath that thou shalt never spoil the children the way his mother spoiled him. And thou knowest for a fact that thou shalt do even so. Worse, probably.

So, you may go and take that thing off and put on something longer. Just because your friends look silly is no reason for you to. And another thing: don't judge a boy by the size of his car; that's so passé. You might as well know now, 'cos nobody else ain't gonna tell ya, you're responsible for the Jewish gene pool.

Thought you'd be pleased.

Undercover Jewish Mothers

Sibyl Ruth

Here's the shortest story. I'm from a Jewish family. I became a mother when my daughter Hannah was born on 30 August, 1997. QED. I'm a Jewish mother. End of story.

But am I? Did I take care of my two stepchildren as a Jew? Go into labour as a Jew? Has there been something innately Jewish in the way I breastfed Hannah, changed her nappies, took her to playgroup, to nursery, to infants' school? I keep asking myself, and the answer's no. I didn't go to the right kind of classes, read the right manuals or know the right people. Nobody told me.

Does Hannah — at five and a half — know anything, anything at all, about being Jewish? As I consider this, she comes into the room.

"Hannah, I want to ask you something. There's a word, and I want you to tell me if you know what it means."

"Okay."

"The word's *Jewish*."

She thinks for a moment and states, "It's a religion." Then, "Why did you ask me that?"

"Well..." I wish I hadn't started this. "I wasn't sure you knew. I don't think it's something that me and Daddy told you. Perhaps you got it from books. Or school."

"I didn't."

"But you did about Hanukkah. In your nativity."

"We didn't."

Surely she hasn't forgotten the play the whole infants' school did in her reception year, which enacted a whole year of festivals? As ever, Hannah contrives to be both right and wrong, straightforward and mysterious. I decide to leave it. For the time being.

Let me begin again. If not at the beginning, a bit further back.

* * *

My mother was born in Berlin in October 1926, as Hannah Berndt. My maternal grandparents were assimilated Jews. My grandfather had been very much a patriot in his youth, and enlisted at the earliest opportunity when the First World War broke out. He won the Iron Cross, but would never tell anyone what he'd done to be awarded this.

Immediately after the Nazis took power in 1933, the Berlin Jewish community set up an education committee which moved quickly to establish a private elementary school. It was this school that my mother attended when she began her education in April. This meant she was spared the difficulties that Jewish children attending existing schools would have been exposed to. It also helped that the city had a large Jewish community. My mother's written that while her parents explored the possibilities of leaving Germany they "kept their worries to themselves and did their best to protect us from unpleasantness, but they could not shield us from everything that went on around us."

My grandparents were both doctors. My grandmother's field had been skin problems and venereal medicine, but from 1936 to 1937 she studied for a diploma in psychotherapy at the Jung Institute in Zurich. It was this diploma that enabled her to obtain a permit — initially for one year — to reside in the UK, where she could practice as a psychotherapist.

So in September 1937, my maternal grandparents, my mother, my aunt and Lottie, their "home help", came to England and settled in Liverpool. Their emigration must have seemed a risky business, with their future welfare uncertain. Of course, as it turned out, the risks of remaining in Germany were infinitely greater.

Now that I'm a parent, I wonder more and more what it must have been like for my grandparents trying to safeguard their family and plan for the future against a background of rising anti-Semitism and economic uncertainty. Hannah's a year younger than my mother was when the National Socialists came to power. I should like to think that in similar circumstances I would have my grandmother's foresight and courage. Perhaps if my family's safety was threatened I'd be prepared to tear up my roots, make complicated plans in order to leave the country I've always lived in, to safeguard their future. But I can't be sure.

* * *

For a long time I simply thought they were German. My dad's not Jewish. He was brought up as a Baptist in industrial South Wales. His mother died suddenly, before he was two, and after that an aunt and uncle took care of him. He did well at school, went to university and became an academic.

I was born in Belfast because he'd taken a lecturing job there, but we moved to Manchester when I was three. When people asked me where I was from I said, "I was born in Northern Ireland but I'm not Irish. I'm half German and half Welsh."

It never occurred to me that I was Jewish. If I had been, I would be one of the handful of children who stood waiting outside the hall during hymn-singing and prayers at school assemblies. I envied them, laughing and chatting while the rest of us droned our way through "Oh Jesus I Have Promised" and the Lord's Prayer.

The only other representations of being Jewish I encountered — Fagin in the film *Oliver* and Shylock in *The Merchant of Venice* — had no relationship to me. They were fantastic, fictional characters, remote in time and place.

* * *

When I was fifteen we learned some twentieth-century European history at school. I saw there might be a connection between Hitler's rise to power and my mother coming to England, and went home determined to get some information. I remember my mum standing in the bedroom saying "The questions are coming thick and fast, aren't they?" After her answers I knew that the German half of me was a Jewish half as well.

And I remember sitting with her, my dad, my two brothers, all of us watching a TV documentary about the year 1945. Suddenly there was footage taken when the Allied forces liberated Belsen.

Perhaps now, when there's TV coverage of each and every world disaster, when warfare and horror are a staple feature of computer games, young people are less easily upset by what's glimpsed on a screen.

But for me, the world changed with the film taken at the concentration camp. I realised what would have happened to my mother's family if they had not got out of Germany. What *did* happen to their relatives, to friends. Overwhelmed, I ran from the room. My mother didn't follow. I heard my younger brother ask, "Why is she crying?" and her explanation: "She didn't like the nasty pictures." After a few minutes I went back, sat down and watched the rest of the programme. No one brought up the incident again. As if nothing had happened.

* * *

I know now that it is not easy to explain complicated things, upsetting things, bad things, to a child. The journey from innocence to experience is best when it's gentle, gradual. A mother's asked many things and she does her best to respond. Even when she doesn't know. Even when there is no answer.

Stories help. Hannah was introduced to death by *The Story of Babar*. Towards the end of this, the king of the elephants eats a "bad mushroom", turns a very nasty colour and dies; Babar is then chosen as the new king. For some time afterwards, if Hannah overheard a reference to someone's death, she'd state that they too, must have eaten a bad mushroom.

* * *

Grandma died when I was seventeen. Mostly I remember her as a melancholy old lady isolated by deafness. Sometimes she'd start talking German to me, and I'd have to shout, "Grandma, speak in English!"

Her funeral was a routine crematorium job in a Lancashire town I hadn't visited before and haven't since. Someone played Beethoven's *Ode to Joy* on a tinny electric keyboard, and the gathered mourners competed with one another to see who could display the most emotional restraint. I sat hunched in my seat, battling with anger at not having been told about how ill she was, guilt at not having tried harder to talk to her, and grief. Only the strange sing-song of the man who said Kaddish seemed able to bring comfort. Though I had no idea what it meant.

* * *

A single death can be accounted for. But not collective killing, nations' complicity in millions of deaths. How do you begin to explain that? And when? At five? Or fifteen?

Like my mother, I have become a member of the Religious Society of Friends, a Quaker. A central belief of this faith is that "there is that of God in everyone." And in my dealings with others, this is what I try to show, and to look for. I am a fortunate woman. Mostly, that is what I find.

I don't want to bring Hannah up to be frightened, to think of society as dangerous and bad. I want her to be alive to the goodness that is in and around us. I hope to be able to pass on to her whatever strength is in me, for her to double that.

Hannah now knows that people do not usually die from eating bad mushrooms, but because they are old or ill, and doctors cannot make them better. She has not yet judged me, blamed me for misleading her about the evils of the world. But one day she will.

199

My friend Rosamund had a Saturday job at Harry Berger's, a Jewish dry cleaner's. When she was offered work at the library instead, she passed the dry cleaning on to me. I got taught how to fold shirts and jackets, to slide them neatly into carrier bags. I learned something else, too.

Harry didn't seem to like me. So, one quiet afternoon, I attempted to curry favour with him by announcing, "My mother's Jewish. So I'm half Jewish."

"No you're not," said Harry.

"How do you mean?"

"You're all Jewish," he told me. "If your mother's Jewish, then you're Jewish too."

The idea of being all something, complete rather than half-and-half, was strongly appealing. Even if my sense of Judaism was now inextricably mixed with safety-pinning numbered pink strips into the flies of smelly trousers.

I did some research about what being all Jewish might mean, questioning Malcolm and Jonathan, two of the boys at school who missed assembly. They told me about Friday night being family night, with candles, everyone sharing conversation, good things to eat, laughter. It sounded like Christmas once a week. With different food.

My father believed that well-behaved children were both inaudible and invisible, and saw the dinner table as a place for swift, silent refuelling. My mother believed mainly in keeping my father happy. I was used to being shushed and frowned at during meals. Clearly I was missing out on my birthright.

Perhaps if I made a different choice from my mother's, found a Jewish boy to fall in love with me, I'd be able to hook into that sense of family, community, that Jonathan and Malcolm took for granted.

* * *

Simon was a third-year undergraduate when I was in my first year, and he seemed to fit the bill pretty well. A talented classicist, chair of the college student union, and a member of the football team, he had succeeded in making himself at home in WASP-ish Cambridge. But he had a prayer shawl and phylacteries in his chest of drawers. His mother sent him matzos every Passover and his family lived in a part of London where my grandparents nearly ended up. I was overcome with gratitude when he ditched his economist girlfriend and set about seducing me.

Student life was an enticing but treacherous beach. Great on the surface, but before you knew it you were stepping into quicksand. Twenty-one-year-old Simon might lend me his body, a little mental companionship, but wanting him to give me roots, a firm identity? It was a tall order.

One evening we were talking about parents, and he said, "It doesn't seem to mean much to you." He meant being Jewish.

And by his standards, it was true. After a term we split up. After seven years he married the daughter of a rabbi and a psychoanalyst, became a father.

* * *

I could not imagine wanting or having children. My image of motherhood was tied up with suburbia in the 1960s — a rejected universe of Avon ladies, coffee mornings, Kenwood mixers, dinner for the man of the house when he came back from his important work.

I was moving around north London from one short-life rented flat to another. I tried different jobs and didn't settle to any of them. In between I claimed benefit. No big deal. Sooner or later, I'd find out what I should be doing. I went out with different people and they finished with me, or I with them. None of it mattered.

One of the flats was near Stamford Hill. I kept passing Hasidic women, modestly dressed, their heads covered. If they weren't pushing prams, they were heavily pregnant, holding the hands of tottering children. They were my age, but they seemed decades older. Often they walked a step or two behind their husbands, who had hats, untrimmed beards, and wore black suits. Sometimes my glance would veer towards the women's faces. I wondered if they were happy. I imagined they knew where they belonged and what the future held for them. Their eyes never met mine. We were neighbours and yet we were living in different countries.

I could not imagine a life centred around taking care of other human beings. It was hard enough taking care of myself.

* * *

I was thirty-five when I met Alan. For different reasons, neither of us was sure we wanted to go out with anyone. But we sat in a Black Country pub, on a date, drinking our half-pints and making conversation. We'd got as far as discovering that he was a lawyer and I was an advice worker, that we'd had a similar education and both liked eating fish, when he said, "Of course, my mother's Jewish."

I said, "That's a coincidence. So's mine."

Then I felt an unseen door closing. Or opening. I could choose to run away, or I could stay and see what happened. It was frightening.

* * *

Alan soon introduced me to his daughter, who was nearly six, and his seven-year-old son. In one day, without signing my name on the line, I became committed. At our first meeting, my stepson began calling me "Sibyl-mummy". It was as if the pair of them consciously, successfully, set out to charm me. They showed me teddy bears, held my hand, clamoured to sit next to me, climbed onto my knee. We went swimming, kite-flying, sledging, bike-riding. I taught them to make pancakes.

Starting to look after my stepchildren was hard. I was utterly unused to children, and I had to learn everything. The way children do not go straight to bed, but keep coming downstairs. They're frightened of the dark. They bounce into your bed first thing in the morning, before you're awake. They don't want to do what they're asked. They fight. They expect you to know how to mend things that they have broken. They love garlic bread. They hate garlic bread and they always have done. Their tummies hurt. They want ice cream. They keep asking why. They're starving. They're full up. They've had an accident and now the bed sheets need changing.

If there are negative Jewish mother stereotypes, they're nothing compared to the stuff about stepmothers. It is imperative that you prove the fairy tales have got it wrong. You sacrifice your space and your time, you're not yourself, and you try to work out how your life arrived at this point.

* * *

Once upon a time my mother told me that she was proud to be a Jew.

But it can't have been easy to feel that pride living in England, as a refugee from Germany, with the two countries at war. She spent the early 1940s in a boarding school, playing hockey and netball. I imagine her Jewish identity falling away, a relic of that long-ago life, in which she'd attended Theodore Herzl Schule and nearly all the family friends had been Jews.

Later, when she went to university, Jewish fellow students, tried — and failed — to get her to join their Society. She told me, "They were all Zionists, and we argued about Israel. They got quite angry I didn't want to join."

She met my father when they were both lecturing at Aberystwyth. I used to think the bond between them was based on a shared sense of being on the outside, un-English. It could be more than that. My mum carries the knowledge of her family's good fortune in getting out of Germany together. My dad's childhood was marked by the loss of his mother, and by being sent away from his widowed father. He grew up with a sense of displacement, similar to that of children sent here on the kindertransports.

When my mother was a young woman, her first name was uncommon, positively foreign. So she chose to Anglicise it, change it to Hazel Ann. When she got married, she became Mrs H A Lewis, leaving no outward trace of the girl she used to be.

From the moment my pregnancy was confirmed, I knew that a girl would be called Hannah. It would be an act of reclamation.

* * *

I was in a ward at the Women's Hospital, putting my two-day-old child back into her cot. The African man, who studied at a nearby missionary college, paused en route to his wife, at the end of the bay.

"You have a beautiful baby."

"Her name's Hannah."

"That's a lovely name. Do you know her story? In the Old Testament?"

"I — I think so."

"See you later."

I tried to remember about the biblical Hannah. I was pretty sure she was Samuel's mother.

"I brought you this."

The student was back. With a Bible.

"Oh. Thank you."

"Look. I marked the place."

Out of politeness, while present-day Hannah slept, I read how long-ago Hannah had to wait and wait to have a child. Eventually, crushed in spirit after years of not having a baby, she goes to the temple and prays, promising that if she does have a son, the boy will be dedicated to serving God. Eli the priest says that her prayer will be answered.

Hannah gives birth to Samuel, and once he's old enough, she takes him to the temple. Again she prays:

God knows what's going on.
He takes the measure of everything that happens.
The weapons of the strong are smashed to pieces,
while the weak are infused with fresh strength.
The well-fed are out begging in the streets for crusts,
while the hungry are getting second helpings.
The barren woman has a houseful of children,
while the mother of many is bereft.

God brings death and God brings life,
brings down to the grave and raises up.
God brings poverty and God brings wealth;
he lowers, he also lifts up.
He puts poor people on their feet again;
he rekindles burned-out lives with fresh hope,
Restoring dignity and respect to their lives —

"That's a good story," I said, handing the Bible back.

The student glanced over at Hannah, smiled. "May she be fruitful," he said.

It was a blessing.

A Mother Who
Chooses to Be Jewish

Anne Harris

When I was asked to put my thoughts down in writing
about what it meant to be a "Jewish mother", it alerted
me to the fact that, yes, I am a Jewish mother. This may
sound very obvious. As a convert to Judaism, I think of
myself as Jewish. Having a son of fifteen months, I clearly
think of myself as a mother. But a *Jewish mother*? I wasn't
so sure of this.

I think this is because my idea of a "Jewish mother" has
mostly been formed by some of the women we see on the
television, such as Beattie, the character made famous by
Maureen Lipman in the British Telecom commercial.

Most Jewish mothers, however, wouldn't immediately
look to these characters to define what is meant by a
"Jewish mother". They would look at their own mother or
grandmother. As a convert to Judaism, I don't have
Jewish mother, or a Jewish grandmother. However, I do
have Jewish friends, and some of them are also mothers,
so I do have real examples to look at and see what a Jewish
mother really "looks like".

The reality is that Jewish mothers are as varied as
mothers of any culture are. There are some people I know
who do loosely fit the image of a Jewish mother, and
others who don't fit any image at all. The one thing they
have in common is that they are all Jewish and all appear
to be very good mothers.

Possibly more important to me than how I feel about
being a Jewish mother is how I feel about my son being a
"Jewish son". This area is more complicated. My father
isn't Jewish, obviously my brother isn't Jewish, and my
partner isn't Jewish. I didn't grow up as a Jew. We decided

206

not to have my son circumcised because of all these reasons. Circumcision felt very tribal (which of course it is) and not necessary for someone's faith. In addition, I didn't want him to be different from his father, and in any case, the whole operation felt quite barbaric (although I'm sure it isn't) and I didn't want him hurt at all. As I didn't grow up in a Jewish household, the non-circumcision was not an issue for me at all, although I do know Jewish friends who have deliberated over this and worried deeply about it.

Since my son isn't circumcised, is he really Jewish? In Orthodox circles, I think the answer would be no — he cannot be Jewish. However, even if he was circumcised I don't think they'd accept him as Jewish, as I converted into Liberal Judaism.

Another area of concern is how will he feel if he attends the King David School, a Jewish school in Birmingham, where we live? And how will he feel at cheder when he realises he is different from the other Jewish boys?

Another part of me worries that I have introduced my son to potential problems at school that I never had, in that he may be labelled as Jewish by his teachers and by other children. In a culturally diverse city like ours, being a different faith from others may not be an issue. But where I come from in the northeast of England, children who were different were often the targets of bullies. I don't think people really knew any Jewish people and therefore their idea of "Jews" was very much based on media images or the ultra-Orthodox community living in Gateshead.

As I have already said, my family isn't Jewish and neither is my partner's. They are not overtly Christian, but they do celebrate Christmas and give presents at Easter. I would not really want to prevent my son from participating in things that I enjoyed as a child. In addition I have observed that since I've become a mother, I do many things that my own mother did, and sometimes trying to be too "Jewish" feels forced. It has made me realise that converting to Judaism as an individual is fine, but it is more complicated when you have your own family.

My partner is an atheist and although he agreed when I converted that our children would be Jewish, the reality is that now that we have a child, he doesn't feel entirely comfortable with this.

We have both agreed that we will celebrate some of the "Christian"/secular festivals as we did when we were children, although we will try to explain that we are not commemorating the life of Christ but enjoying festivals that have been held for thousands of years and began long before Christ. We will also celebrate Jewish festivals, and I will take Samuel to *shul* whenever possible, particularly to children's services. I will take him to cheder when he is older, but will probably send him to a mixed-faith school.

So will this make him a Jewish son? Possibly not in the traditional sense, but then we aren't Jewish in the traditional sense. I think it makes him our son — Samuel, who happens to have a mother who chooses to be Jewish.

The Same, but Different:
Jewish Adoptive Motherhood

Ann Joseph

Jewish motherhood for me has meant Jewish adoptive motherhood.

I am one of those incredibly lucky few who achieved Jewish motherhood via the adoption route.

As I am a Liberal Jew, my children do not have to be halachically Jewish. Any child brought up as a Liberal Jews is accepted. My husband, perhaps wiser, or less driven by his hormones, felt unable to offer a home to the severely disabled Jewish children we were first offered, but shared my view that being halachically Jewish was not of prime importance.

Amazingly — and to my secret, inner joy — both our children have Jewish birth mothers. Perhaps the wise social workers saw through my earnest assurances that I did not mind; perhaps they believed, as I do, that an adopted child has enough to cope with without the imposition of a different, minority religion.

So we had our son, who arrived with his *tallit* bag and Jewish name. Circumcision was down to us, and we chose to wait until the adoption was complete. Perhaps we could have done it earlier, but the complications of getting consent seemed too great. Because of the lateness and because we are Liberals, we preferred to have the circumcision undertaken in the local hospital.

However, the possibility that our son might one day want to marry an Orthodox girl led us down the route of wishing to register the adoption with the Beth Din. We were summoned to visit a group of rabbis in Golders Green, who duly inspected the circumcision and declared it kosher. For me, this was a very strange experience and the nearest I will ever get to the feeling I've heard many women express about the circumcision ritual, that of being excluded from my child.

For most of my son's upbringing, his adoptive status has made no difference to his Jewish progress through religion school and bar mitzvah. Only for me, during the bar mitzvah ceremony, did it make a difference. As I sat on the bimah, like any proud mother, willing him to get through it, I became obsessed with the idea that his birth mother would come bursting through the doors, like the bad fairy at Sleeping Beauty's christening. Of course it never happened; it was only something in my own head; but it is these fantasies that make adoptive motherhood so different from doing it the normal way.

My daughter's arrival was both sudden and delightful. It involved a long drive to collect her from a roomful of tiny babies. We were not there to choose the one we liked best — that only happens in fiction — but I knew instantly which one she was by her "Jewish nose". Instant bonding with a nose seems as good a way to start as any.

No awful circumcision dilemmas, but I felt the need to register her with the Beth Din, for future marriage prospects. Our religion visits the sins of the parents upon the children. She is a *mamzer*. Now I know why I am a Liberal Jew.

My anxieties at my daughter's bat mitzvah, that the bad fairy might appear, were much less. Perhaps it is because she was a girl, and there would be less certainty from the birth family that she was having a ceremony. Perhaps it was because it was the second time around, and I had survived the potential spell the first time. Or maybe it was because her personal history made their sudden appearance less likely than at my son's ceremony.

Is Jewish adoptive motherhood very different from any other form of motherhood? I do not think so. Being Jewish is different. Being an adoptive mother is different. All of us deal with motherhood in different ways, but for me, being given the chance by my children's birth mothers to enjoy this experience is a matter for enormous gratitude. I hope they believe they did the right thing. I would love to be able to tell them so — but whether they did the right thing is something only my children can decide.

The Mezuzah

Lisa Saffron

I am a ceramic box, bold and solid. My cylindrical front is emblazoned with the Hebrew letter *shin*, black against a stone-coloured frame. The *shin* is curved and boat-shaped, like a sailboat with one upright passenger, journeying forth undaunted. Above and below the *shin*, I am decorated with turquoise and brown triangular stripes and symmetrically aligned gouges. I am handsome in a primitive, folky way. I am larger than most mezuzah cases, standing 14cm tall and 4cm wide. There are two nail holes on the rectangular base on which I perch. I should be on a doorpost, strongly affixed, and positioned at a slight angle. But I have been hanging around, languishing in cupboards, neglected amongst forgotten trinkets and holiday souvenirs. I should have been enthroned on the doorpost with due ceremony within thirty days of moving in. But I have been waiting for years, more years than I care to recount. Still, I am patient. I cannot be banished forever, and no matter how hidden and forgotten I may be at times, I always re-emerge.

In 1985, I gave birth to a daughter. I named her Dena. I made a deliberate decision to become a mother. As soon as I made the decision, I knew that I had to be open to whatever happened. Every step of the journey was out of my control. I had no control over conception — all I could do was introduce my eggs to the sperm and hope for the best (fortunately it was love at first sight). I had no control over the survival of the foetus, as I discovered when I had previously miscarried. I had no control over the labour and delivery — my home birth dragged on and on until I dragged myself into hospital. I had no control over the health of the baby, how much she cried, at what age she started walking, what words came out of her mouth or what thoughts she had in her little head. What I did have

212

some control over was me — I could create myself as a mother, the kind of mother who gives her child the space to create herself. I was fascinated to see what kind of person she would create.

But when, at the age of eighteen months, she began creating herself in opposition to me, my openness clogged up. I skidded straight into the classic parent-child power struggle, the kind where the child wins and the parent loses. I slipped into judging myself, acting as if doing it right would make me and my child all right. Any problems she had, any kind of misbehaviour — it was my fault. I worried constantly whether I was a good enough mother. Only when my daughter hit adolescence with a bang was I forced to give up wanting her to be a certain way. Only when I couldn't figure out how to control her did I remember that it was me I was supposed to be controlling. Only then did I stop blaming my mother.

Among her many other wonderful qualities, my mother is impulsive, emotional, energetic, positive, generous and lax on boundaries. These days I appreciate her, now that I am a mother myself to an eighteen-year-old daughter, now that I know just how hard it is to parent with integrity. But for many years I was angry with her. I was annoyed that she wanted to fix problems, that she couldn't listen to me without recommending a book or a therapist or a group that had the answer to whatever problem I was grappling with. I got irritated with her consumerism and the endless supply of gifts with and without strings attached. I was frustrated by her continual changes of mind. I wanted to become a different kind of mother.

At the age of thirty-two, I figured I was ready to become that different kind of mother. I had passed through a ten-year heterosexual phase and emerged with a stable lesbian identity. I was established in a job with good maternity benefits. I owned my own flat, had a solid friendship network and felt part of a lesbian community. Although reluctantly single, I knew from the experience of friends that it wouldn't be wise to wait until circumstances were ideal before I started trying to get pregnant. I was very conscious of my age and my conspicuous lack of success in finding a woman partner.

I conceived by self-insemination — a rather cumbersome procedure for avoiding sexual relations with a man. I actively sought and found a gay Jewish man willing to donate his sperm to me. The gay connection gave us a sense of solidarity. The Jewish connection gave me the illusion that he was less of a stranger than he was. Initially we agreed to have no further involvement once I was pregnant. He signed up as a donor, not as a daddy. In fact we became good friends and saw a lot of each other, but he never took on any parental responsibility.

Having a baby was wonderful, incredible. But for the next five years, I was on my own with her — and I have to admit, that wasn't so wonderful. I did learn some valuable lessons, in particular that self-pity and depression are a waste of time, and that I can't afford the luxury of a negative thought. I learned that I can do anything on a good night's sleep. I learned how to be happy. I learned that things don't stay bad forever.

When the desperation of singledom eventually eased with the help of psychotherapy and Buddhist meditation, Maria appeared in my life as if by magic. It seemed a perfect fit. Maria brought an end to my loneliness and my single parenthood. Dena and I provided Maria with a ready-made family, one she could slot right into as a parent. We enthusiastically set up home together. We told Dena she had two mummies. We didn't read the step-family advice books. If we had, we might have had a smoother ride.

We had and still have fundamental differences in parenting style and household management. I am impulsive, emotional, energetic, positive, generous and lax on boundaries. I change my plans frequently. I give advice freely and I recommend growth books to all and sundry (sound familiar?). Maria, on the other hand, is sensible, reserved, thoughtful, organised and firm on boundaries.

She likes to know what's happening from moment to moment. She won't take advice and she hates growth books. When Maria moved in with us, she used to roll her eyes a lot and tut. She taught me to make shopping lists. Some day, I'll learn to bring the shopping list to the shop — and to buy only what I've written down on the list.

Given all our differences, I guess it's amazing that we hit it off in the first place and managed to set up home together. Even more amazing, we're still together thirteen years later. I attribute our relationship's longevity to our shared values, an important one being a love of food. What I learned from Maria is that couple parenting in a step-family is a lot harder than single parenthood. It's definitely not the cure-all I had thought it would be when I was a single mother.

When Dena was in her most difficult teenage phase, Maria and I decided to apply to become foster carers to children with even more difficult behaviour than Dena could ever dream up. "So, what's with the fostering?" our friends wanted to know, having seen us tearing our hair out with worry over Dena's behaviour. We weren't coping at all well. We were fighting with each other and failing completely to provide Dena with the clear boundaries she needed. My parenting skills were not up to the task, and Maria's stepparenting role prevented her from forming a warm relationship with Dena. Our family was not a happy one.

Yet fostering has been good for us as a family. Dena enthusiastically stepped into the role of big sister, gallantly leading the fourteen-year-old girl into bad teenage habits like lounging on the settee in front of the TV all day, watching anything from cartoons to horror films. Once, irritated by their laziness, I managed to stop myself from telling them off when I saw this girl, the girl who doesn't do hugs, lying with her head on my daughter's shoulder.

For me and Maria, this has been a joint project. We have experienced equality in our caring for the girls, something

215

we could never achieve in the stepfamily situation with Dena. We've also had the opportunity to learn how to deal with sibling rivalry — an opportunity sadly missed by those of us with single children. We have had some great outings, going places and doing things no self-respecting teenager would be caught dead doing with their parents.

Fostering didn't solve our problems, but it certainly put them into perspective. When I saw firsthand the consequences of seriously bad parenting and the long-term damage this does to children, I stopped worrying about whether I was a good mother. I also became even less tolerant of prejudice against lesbian and gay parents (not that I was that keen on it beforehand).

So where does being Jewish fit into my mothering? Ever since a trip to Israel in 1968, when I was fifteen, I had avoided everything Jewish. I didn't deny that I was Jewish. I just took no interest in it. In my usual all-or-nothing fashion, I had thrown the baby out with the bath water. But when I decided to become a mother, I found I wanted that baby back. I wanted something distinctly Jewish to share with my daughter.

The Jewishness I wanted was a sense of belonging to a clan, to be part of something bigger than the lonely single mother/single child family unit I had formed. I wanted the comfort of familiarity, the warm glow I associated with Jewish food, humour, music and gatherings.

I enrolled three-year-old Dena in the Jewish nursery school in north London where I was living at the time. First I had to produce proof of our Jewishness. My single parenthood eliminated one source of evidence — a Jewish marriage contract. But all was not lost. They would accept my mother's.

I called her in America. "Mom, I need your *ketubah*. Can you dig it out for me?"

"I should know what a *ketubah* is?" she snapped anxiously. "I've never been into that Jewish stuff, not like you when you were thirteen." She was still mad that I stopped her eating bacon during my adolescent religious

216

phase. Nevertheless, she dug up some sort of document that did the trick.

During the two years that Dena was at the Jewish nursery, she made friends with a girl from an Orthodox family. One Saturday, Dena was at her house playing and I joined the family for the havdalah service marking the end of the Sabbath. We gathered round the table and said the blessings. Hungry to belong and to be accepted, I wished with all my heart that I could be warmed by the glow of the braided candle, the scent of the spices and the taste of the sweet wine.

Before dinner, while chatting to the girl's mother, I had come out for the first time and discovered how different were the worlds we each inhabited. She had just heard about a Jewish child at the nursery who had been sexually abused by her stepfather. She was shocked, and had babbled at length about the dangers of stepfathers, expressing concern about Dena's safety. Seeking to reassure her, I said I had no intention of bringing a stepfather into our family.

"But surely one day you will meet a man and marry him," she'd said. "I know you're single now, but that won't last forever. And then how will you protect Dena? Any man could be an abuser."

"I'm a lesbian," I said, in my strongest proud-to-be-gay voice. However, it came out as a high-pitched squeak, not at all conveying my true meaning.

If she had been shocked by sexual abuse, she was doubly shocked by lesbian motherhood. "But, but…" she stammered, "Dena will never have a father. She will never grow up to know what men are like."

I knew then that I could never belong to that narrow segment of the Jewish community.

I had come across this kind of doublethink before and had always found it mystifying. I didn't learn what men are like from my father. I only learned what my father was like. Although he has similarities to some men, he is a unique individual. There is no one else just like him. Dena learned what her father was like because she spent time with him. Sadly, he died when she was nine, before she got to know him as well as she would have liked. Nevertheless, knowing her father didn't teach her what men are like. They're not all the same.

I couldn't help thinking that my lesbianism informed my mothering in a profoundly positive way. By accepting myself as I was, I showed both self-acceptance and acceptance of diversity. I demonstrated to my daughter that women can be independent of men. I gave her a framework for understanding prejudice and oppression and people's shared humanity. I taught her to be an individual with respect for her own authority. I didn't get the impression that any of these values were rated very highly in the Orthodox Jewish community of north London.

Two years at the nursery was enough to convince me that this wasn't a community where Dena and I could be accepted for who we were. I sent Dena to the local state school, renowned for its multicultural population and its celebration of diversity. As a child of a lesbian mother, Dena was right at home. So was I.

Over the following years, we went to a few Passover seders, lit a few Shabbat candles and had one or two Hanukkah parties — but I felt a hypocrite saying the blessings and praising a God I didn't believe in. Dena didn't know what she was missing, but Maria was disappointed. As an anti-religious ex-Catholic, she loved the Jewish ritual and encouraged me to do more.

My need for belonging and for spiritual expression was not satisfied by these sporadic forays into Judaism. Curiously enough, it was my exploration of Buddhism that eventually brought me back to Judaism. When Dena was two, I found in Buddhism a spiritual path that was accessible and meaningful to me. Ever faithful to the Jewish commandments, I began teaching this path diligently to my daughter. I talked of it when I sat in my house, when I walked by the way, when I lay down and when I rose up.

Only after I learned the Buddhist practices of mindfulness and loving-kindness did the Jewish kabbalistic creation story resonate with me and bring me back to my Jewishness.

As I understand it, the story starts with the world in an undifferentiated wholeness which shatters into an infinite number of sparks. These divine sparks are hidden deep in everyone and everything. The task of each person, indeed the very purpose of human life, is to extract the divine sparks, to raise and spiritualise them and by so doing, restore the harmony of the opposites and redeem the world. We repair the world through our loving-kindness and compassion. As we journey through life, every one of us encounters those people, events and things that contain those divine sparks that we are meant to redeem. Each encounter and life event, no matter how great or how small, is an opportunity to raise a spark of holy light or to plunge the world even further into chaos. This "raising of the sparks" is the process of *tikkun olam*, the restoration or repair of the world.

My first conscious act of *tikkun olam* was to go to the Israeli-occupied West Bank and raise the divine sparks with the people committed to the Jewish values I've always held dear. These people are Christians, Muslims and Jews. They are Palestinians and Israelis. They believe in peace with justice.

> I am the case that holds the essence of Judaism, the central truths condensed on a tiny scrap of parchment and symbolised by the letter *shin* for Shaddai, the Almighty. On the parchment scroll is written two chapters from the Torah, both from the book of Deuteronomy. But the parchment scroll is gone. It has been wrenched out, torn apart. Now I am empty, waiting. I am nothing more than a pretty box. I am curious to see what comes to fill the vacuum.

When I return from my trip to Palestine, I am ready to put the mezuzah up on my doorpost. In my mezuzah, I place the divine sparks I've raised from the Torah:

219

Pursue justice, only justice. (DEUT 16:20)

You shall not oppress a stranger, for you know the heart of a stranger, as you were slaves in the land of Egypt. (EX 23:9).

You shall love your neighbour as yourself. (LEV 19:18)

In my mezuzah, I place the divine sparks I've raised from the Talmud:

> "On three things the world stands: on justice, on truth, and on peace." Rabban Shim'on ben Gamli'el said while Rav Muna carried on arguing, "These three are one thing: Where justice is done, truth is done and peace is made."
> Rabbi Hillel says, "What is hateful unto you, don't do unto your neighbour. If not I for myself, who then? And being for myself, what am I? And if not now, when?"

In my mezuzah, I place the divine sparks I raised from a teardrop that pierced my heart in the Garden of Gethsemane overlooking Jerusalem, where long ago another Jew of conscience wept, his heart broken with sorrow, over the suffering of an oppressed people.

In my mezuzah, I place the divine sparks I've raised from the community of people of conscience, Jews and non-Jews, Israelis and Palestinians, who refuse silence rather than complicity with injustice.

In my mezuzah, I place the divine sparks I've raised from my daughter when she tells me she wants to come with me next year to Jerusalem.

Choices in Israel

The Conservative Revolution: Mothers and the Kibbutz

Rakefet Zohar

The thing I remember most about arriving home from hospital with my firstborn is my disorientation. I remember laying the baby on the double bed, pulling myself up and wondering — what now? Am I supposed to know what to do with it? Why can't I just take it to the baby house, where someone who knows what to do with babies can look after it? Sure, I'll visit, I'll even breastfeed if I'm told to, but at this very moment, I would gladly go to sleep for a while, and don't anyone disturb me, thank you.

My husband, full of confidence in me, glanced at us briefly and went to park the car. The baby started to cry and I wondered if there was something wrong with me. Rather than feeling concern for his crying, I felt guilty for not caring very much. Do all first-time mothers feel like that? Or was it something in my upbringing? I grew up as a kibbutz child, slept in a children's house together with sixteen other children under the care of very dedicated nannies, none of whom was my mother. Is it possible that my maternal instincts had been destroyed?

A few moments later Kushit, the experienced baby *metapelet* (nanny), arrived. She took the baby and soothed him and changed his nappy, and everything was fine. The baby was fed, bathed, put to sleep, and was cared for just the way babies ought to be, and eventually he grew into a child, then a youth, a brother to three younger boys, none of whom suffer from negligence of any kind, and everybody seems happy and content. Except for me, still puzzled by the very same questions about motherhood and the kibbutz and where I fit into it all.

223

The first kibbutzniks were Jewish pioneers who made aliyah from Europe to Palestine some hundred years ago, with the dream of creating a new and just society in the land of Israel. They established kibbutzim, small settlements of a few dozen people (mainly young men at the beginning), and based their lives on the socialist principles of equality, cooperation and solidarity.

Sworn socialists and ardent students of European psychology, the kibbutzniks regarded the typical bourgeois family as a living manifestation of many social ills. They saw the family as an agent of exploitation, in which working-class women were not paid for housework or for the care they provided to support the worker. In addition, the capitalist male exploited his own wife as a vessel for sexual services and production of the male heir to whom he could pass on his capital.

From Freud the young pioneers learned about the neurotic bourgeois family as the origin of all pathologies. Most of them were at the impressionable age when youngsters usually leave their families and experience independent lives with their peers (at university or in the army, for instance). Bearing this in mind, we can better understand why the first kibbutzniks wanted to replace the family with a co-operative community based upon ties of brotherhood rather than those of the family unit.

Soon love affairs occurred, and the group learned to tolerate the formation of couples. But when the first babies were born the dilemma was unavoidable: if there is no family and no housewife, who will take care of the children?

The answer was: we, the commune, are responsible for the children. They are *our* children, *our* future, therefore it is our duty to care for them and to enable our women comrades who gave birth to them to take part in greater missions, such as building the kibbutz and the nation. The children will be a part of the group. They will have their own house, where they will experience communal life with other children. They will live there, play there, eat there and later study there. Their "parents" will be all the kibbutz members; their caretaker, or *metapelet*, will be appointed by the group. Biological mothers will breastfeed at the baby house, but apart from that will have no other duties regarding the child. After work they will be given a few hours to spend what would now be called "quality time" with the child. The idea was that women would be freed of their role as mothers and that their relationship with their children would be based solely upon pure, mutual love. This is how "communal education" was formed. What a wonderful idea. Or was it?

Thinking of my own family, I believe that without the communal system there is only a slim chance that my mother would have been able to raise three daughters in a small, remote village and become a prominent leader in the kibbutz movement, as well as manage a large factory and head a local university. One of the main reasons she was able to build a career was that she was neither a housewife nor a traditional mother.

My two sisters and I grew up in the communal education system. We lived in our own children's house together with our age group and a very dedicated crew of teachers and *metapelot* who met most of our needs. Every afternoon we would go to our parents' home for about three hours, and then go back to sleep in *our* home — the children's house. To this day, the children I grew up with are as close to me as family members. This is less true of the *metapelot*, who moved from one group of children to the next.

I was happy to grow up on a kibbutz, and as an adult I wanted to stay a kibbutz member and to bring up my children in exactly the same way. Later I left the kibbutz for a year in London and to study at Tel Aviv University, and I acquired a feminist outlook. As a feminist I considered myself even more lucky to be a kibbutznik — a member of an enlightened community, where women have not only equal rights but also economic equality. I believed that the communal education system was the only way to free women from their biological destiny and to allow them to grow as whole individuals.

So when my first son was about to be born I was calm and confident, because I knew the kibbutz would take care of everything. I would return from the hospital and pass the baby on to the baby house, where he would be taken care of by good and experienced *metapelot*, and I would go back to my normal life: writing, teaching, an active member of society. Oh, yes, and I would also have a son...

There were a few signs that I was slightly out of touch with reality. For example, halfway through my pregnancy I was asked to work at the baby house a few times a week, in order to learn how to take care of babies. As an outspoken feminist I announced that if taking care of babies is a skill to be learned rather than a mother's God-given talent, there is no reason why the father-to-be should not learn it as well. My husband succumbed to my whim and spent one painful day at the baby house. That was the end of the experiment on his part. *He* is a problem, I concluded to myself, and said nothing.

How little did I know. My husband was one problem, to be sure, but society around us soon proved a much greater problem. I believed that since the biological mother had so little to do, it should be not be too hard to modify things a bit more so that my husband could share the few duties left to us. But I was wrong. Mothers around me fought for their right to exercise the few maternal duties still left to them, quite unwilling to dilute them further by sharing them with the fathers. In the meantime, the kibbutz, as a community, had never even acknowledged fatherhood as a legitimate social role. For example, a mother's workday consisted of seven instead of eight hours, and she was expected to visit each of her children for about an hour a day. Fathers were expected to love their children too, but had no additional responsibilities or rights. Therefore, when I asked my husband to take half my maternal leave, I had to deal not just with his resentment, but also the complaints of his boss at work and the scorn of other mothers. I was very disappointed. Where was the equality I was promised?

Things only got worse when, at my husband's insistence, we moved to his kibbutz for a time. A couple of years earlier, this kibbutz had changed the children's sleeping arrangements from communal (the children sleeping at children's houses) to familial (sleeping with parents). My husband couldn't wait to have our son sleeping at home with us. I tried to conceal my disapproval and told myself it was only for a short while.

But it wasn't. We still live on that kibbutz, raising four boys who excel in waking up every night as many times as they possibly can, usually in order to move from their bed to ours... to my space. I quickly learned that complaints about your own children were taboo among the women on my new kibbutz. Women here celebrated their motherhood. They were proud of their success in abolishing the communal sleeping arrangements and felt victorious and emancipated. They struggled to prolong maternity leave and to work fewer hours in order to spend more time with their children. They talked about children nearly all the time; the rest of the time they talked about housekeeping, menus, shopping and dieting. The boldest talked about husbands. Work was considered a boring subject and politics, even kibbutz politics, were completely irrelevant.

At first I was terrified. What could I possibly have in common with these women? But they embraced me despite my bizarre feminist ideas, and I accepted their hug. Still, inside myself I kept asking for an explanation: what had happened to these women? Why had they turned themselves from relatively free and equal women into caricatures of housewives from the 1950s? Why had they renounced their right to develop careers and contented themselves with work in the kitchen, the launderette or the children's houses? Why did they avoid public office and settle for social marginality? And above all — why were they so pleased with themselves?

227

The most common answer was, of course, biology. Women had to obey the laws of nature. Regardless of ideology, the only role they felt comfortable with is that of mother. If that was true, where did it leave me? Why did I not feel comfortable with the role of mother? Was I a freak? Was my sister, the production manager in the plastics factory of my former kibbutz, also a freak? And what about my mother — was she not a role model but actually a product of twisted ideology? Somehow that didn't seem reasonable.

Many people around me (women as well as men) believed that women are simply lazy, using motherhood as an excuse to work fewer hours, to avoid social responsibilities, to take a daily siesta — in short, to enjoy themselves. An answer like that, I thought, could only be given by someone who does not understand the amount of work involved in motherhood. Someone who does not know that when women finish work at two o'clock, they start their second job at home: cleaning the house, folding the clothes, taking their offspring to the doctor... No, this couldn't be the answer either.

So maybe it was a classic case of the "flight from freedom", I thought. Erich Fromm once said that most people fly from freedom because of the responsibility it carries. To be responsible for your own life is heavy-duty stuff. Maybe women on the kibbutz had built their own little women's world and preferred to avoid public and social responsibility? But if that was the case, why hadn't the men run away from freedom too? And why did the kibbutz allow women to escape from doing their share?

Then one day it dawned on me that I wasn't asking the right question. Women on the kibbutz had not given up their freedom — they had never been free. They had never been free of the gender concepts of "woman", "wife" and "mother". Therefore, their social inferiority was not an outcome of their retreat to conservative motherhood. On the contrary, they had chosen to concentrate on their role of mother in the hope that it would compensate for their social insignificance.

228

This idea took me by surprise, as it contradicted my firm belief that we kibbutz women had one of the best deals in the world. Like most people, I thought feminism was totally unnecessary in Israel, a country with female soldiers and kibbutzniks. It took me a long time, and numerous conversations with first- and second-generation kibbutz women, to understand how wrong I was.

In the beginning the kibbutz, as I said earlier, collectivised the burden of motherhood and regarded caring for children as a joint effort that should be shared by all members of the community. In practice, however, who would actually be given the job? The answer had been painfully easy: women.

One or two women would mind everyone's children. But who would cook for the children? And who would mend their clothes and do their laundry? And, while we're at it, who would do all these things for the adult kibbutz members — who would be *our* mothers? The answer was the same — the women would be our mothers and our housewives. They would do it not just for their own children and husbands, but for the community as a whole. This would be their share in the building of a revolutionary socialist society.

The women rebelled against this idea. They said to the men, we are just like you. We came to Israel to till the soil, to be productive workers, to free ourselves from old ideas and traditional roles — yet here we are, stuck in our mothers' shoes.

They fought, but they lost the battle. First, because they were outnumbered by the men. Second, because socialism was considered a greater priority than feminism. This meant that the ambitions of the few, the women, had to give way to the good of the collective. And most important, because they were better qualified for the job of housewife.

Since childhood, these women had been trained in their native countries to cook, wash and mend clothes, and to look after baby brothers and sisters. So when the first kibbutz babies were born, everybody (including the mothers) preferred to have them looked after by people who knew what they were doing. No one was willing to take more risks than they had already taken by having babies in such harsh and dangerous conditions.

The same went for food. At the end of a long day in the fields, everyone wanted a tasty meal, not a burnt one. Thus kibbutz women found themselves trapped in the traditional role of housewife — only now they were communal housewives.

It wouldn't have been so bad if this role had been accorded the appreciation it deserved. After all, women undertook a vital role that no one else could fill. They were also as (un)able as the men to work the land, since in Europe these men had studied religious and academic subjects and had never done manual labour or agricultural work. The role could have been shared. Working the land, however, was considered the jewel in the crown of these new pioneers, and the men coveted, caught and kept it for themselves, justifying it by saying that the women were needed elsewhere.

Within about twenty years, gender relations in the kibbutz very much resembled those of a traditional middle-class family: the "collective husband" provided and ruled; the "collective wife" served and obeyed. The men worked in the fields (and later in factories owned by the kibbutz), held the majority of managerial offices inside the kibbutz and represented the kibbutz in the public sphere. The women divided among themselves the many roles of a traditional housewife: one cooked for everybody, another did everybody's laundry and another looked after all the babies.

The most dramatic aspect of the new way of life that kibbutz represented was communal baby care, which rapidly became one of the kibbutz trademarks. It touched on one of most intimate of human bonds, and as such was considered proof of the depth and sincerity of kibbutz solidarity. But was it really?

When I came to live on my husband's kibbutz I worked in the kitchen with a veteran woman who was about eighty years old. She once told me of an experience she had had as a young mother. She came to the baby house to breastfeed her baby, and the *metapelet* told her to feed another baby first, because his mother's milk had dried up. So her own hungry son screamed in the next room while she breastfed the other baby and cried her heart out. Sixty years later, her eyes were still wet when she told me that story.

Such stories are typical of the early days of the kibbutz, when ideology was fierce and collective discipline was strict and uncontested. It illustrates two main problems of the communal education system: it was not voluntary, and it was based on hierarchy rather than on collaboration.

The most problematic aspect of the communal education system was that it was mandatory. The principles of collectivism and equality demanded that everybody abide by the same rules, whether they liked it or not, whether they were friends with the *metapelet* or hated her guts, whether their child was easygoing or ill-tempered. The suppression of free will in such delicate and intimate matters was devastating.

Second, in the spirit of Bolshevism, the kibbutzniks talked about democracy and equality but believed in a clear hierarchy that sets the representatives of the collective over the individual. In the field of childcare, it meant that the *metapelot* had authority over the biological parents. They supposedly held the wider and more professional perspective while the parents represented only narrow personal interests. So rather than offering the mothers joint parenthood, what the kibbutz actually did was nationalise parenthood. The more a kibbutz had a strict hierarchy and discipline, the more it was determined to keep the parents out of the picture.

But even good, harmonious relationships with the establishment did not make up for parents' needing a more intimate relationship with their children. While the kibbutz cared for their children's everyday needs, parents found themselves stripped of ways to express their love and caring. In the attempt to free women from the "labours of love", mothers were deprived of many of the joys of love. Take food, for example, a delicate matter in many Jewish families. Feeding one's young is without doubt a basic manifestation of a parent's love and care. Kibbutz parents could not express their care in this way because the children ate all their meals separately. Still, I cannot forget the king-size five o'clock "compensation tea" my parents used to prepare for me and my sisters every day. It was a wholehearted effort to gather the family around the table even if no one was actually hungry. This may explain why for many years kibbutz women were obsessed with baking cakes — an extracurricular food into which they could put their hearts.

Along with the many emotional problems that arose from the communal education system, the family-like division of labour also had some major social consequences. The concentration of women in the departments of infants' education and of services such as kitchen or laundry duties, kept them from the centres of economic and political power. As in the traditional family, women sustained the family's emotional and physical needs, subservient to the power and prestige of the "collective fathers".

At the same time, this division of labour based on gender created a feminine subculture well known in some rural societies. My mother, for example, occasionally talks of the camaraderie among the women who established the kibbutz. A small group of first-time mothers along with very young but dedicated *metapelot*, crowding inside the warm baby house during the cold winters on the tiny, windswept kibbutz they had just started. By feeding the babies side by side, bathing them, playing with them and helping and comforting each other, kibbutz women fulfilled for each other the roles of mothers, grandmothers and older sisters left behind hundreds of miles away.

Less emotional, but still important, were the relationships among women in the workplaces allotted to them. There the women learned to work together, to develop expertise and to exercise their power within their protected, all-female surroundings.

Thus the conditions for a revolution were created: frustration, an underprivileged group with strong emotional ties and a framework in which to develop organisational skills and taste the flavour of power.

So where did the revolution go? What happened to all that anger and frustration?

Again, this is not the right question. The revolution happened big-time, only it was not the one I had expected. Instead of saying "We won't be housewives any more!" kibbutz women said, "We'll be housewives in our own houses! No more collective responsibility over children, clothes and food. From now on we will only take care of our own family." And they got what they wanted.

What a disappointment. How little it took to appease my frustrated sisters. From my highbrow feminist point of view, I took them for fools. Or worse — traitors. How could they throw away all this energy and settle for the degrading role of a traditional housewife once again?

There is no point in patronising. One should try and understand why women made this choice. Sure, they wanted a bigger role in their children's lives. But why take all the housewifery with it?

First, in order to separate the housewife from the mother, one needs a feminist paradigm, and kibbutz women were complete strangers to feminism. Women's liberation was recognised as a part of national liberation (Zionism) and class liberation (socialism), never as an independent agenda. In practice, women were required to postpone their feminist aspirations and support the men whose self-proclaimed mission was to establish the state and the kibbutz. This attitude became even more predominant after the state of Israel was established and the revolutionary talk was replaced by a masculine talk of "force", "construction" and "establishment". Minority rights were unthinkable issues. In the new situation, women's main mission was to have sons and raise them as

233

warriors, builders and heirs to the state of Israel and the kibbutz movement. In other words, a woman's primary duty was to be a mother.

Such a political climate was deadly to feminist thinking. Martha Freedman, an American feminist who ran for the Knesset in the 1960s, was considered a joke. The only way women could exercise their power was through their one legitimate role — motherhood. Kibbutz women did revolt against socialism, but they bypassed the feminist faith in their eagerness to enrol in the religion of motherhood and the family. Moreover, in manner typical of the newly reformed, they took their new role in the most conservative and traditional direction.

Now it is clear to me why I could not find allies in my battle for maternity leave for fathers. Kibbutz women certainly fought for "a room of their own", but paradoxically it was not a room in which to write quietly, but rather a room for a quiet breastfeed.

Another reason for their choice was a demographic one. The majority of second-generation kibbutz women were not born on the kibbutz, nor did they join it for ideological reasons. Most of them simply married kibbutz-born men, so their priorities lay with their family rather than with the commune. Again, it seems unrealistic to expect individual newcomers with no strong social ties to the community to embark upon a battle championing reclassification of gender roles on a political level.

Instead of fighting men, *their* men, kibbutz women launched an all-women contest between mothers and *metapelot*. The latter, themselves frustrated mothers, did not put up much of a fight, and during the 1980s and 90s communal sleeping arrangements were abolished from all the kibbutzim in Israel. But the mothers did not stop there. They moved on to demand control of the household budgets for clothes, food, and furniture, which had formerly been controlled by the community. Instead of the money being used to provide daily meals in the communal dining room, they wanted to be able to decide what to do with it. This move is usually called privatisation, but here it was really "familisation". Women worked to increase family budgets as much as possible, because this was the only budget they were in charge of.

The rise of the family led to the decline of communal services such as kitchen and laundry duties. This inevitably meant the redundancy of many women workers, which only emphasised the misogynistic stereotype of the lazy and socially marginalised woman. It is no wonder that women increasingly took refuge at home, gradually making the family — where they were in charge and empowered — the major social unit of the kibbutz. From their own point of view, it was the first time ever that kibbutz women had any significant social standing and influence.[1]

So here I was, a young mother in my thirties, waltzing into my new kibbutz, eager to share the light with my new sisters. No wonder the crash was painful. For me, arriving in this ultradomestic society was like arriving at a penitential institution: cooking, cleaning, endless petty and tedious tasks that I had never had to deal with before (nor had I seen my mother deal with them), and for which I had no inclination or talent, let alone motivation. I suffered while everybody expected me to rejoice. I was angry with my husband and angry with the women on my new

---

[1]It is interesting to note the reaction of kibbutz men to these developments, which I would describe as acceptance. Although they perceived the "familisation" process as undermining the principles of communal sharing, eventually they put gender interests before socialist interests, and were willing to succumb to the demands of their wives as long as they didn't interfere in the masculine domains of economic and public affairs. Eventually the effect of familisation went far beyond the private sphere of the family. With the growing emphasis on the family as an economic unit, the men felt an increased need to provide, and a shift from an equal-wage system to a differential salary system was instigated. Many regard this shift as the last nail in the kibbutz's coffin.

kibbutz who had thrown away a historic chance to become real pioneers. And most of all I could not stand their smugness.

More then ten years have gone by, and I have learned not only to stand them but to like and appreciate kibbutz women. I have also learned that it takes more than equal rights, and more than economic equality, to liberate women. The kibbutz, although a socialist and egalitarian community, had still managed to dominate women through the very principles of socialism and most potently through the collectivisation of motherhood. As long as gender roles and stereotypes are not contested, no real change can prevail.

Today kibbutz women and mothers are not liberated from these roles, but they are much freer than before from communal tyranny, and more confident in their own powers. I hope we can learn to turn this personal, unfulfilled resource into actual social action. I want that to happen not only for the women of the kibbutz but for the kibbutz itself. I believe that the principle that stands at the heart of kibbutz life is that of human solidarity, and that the realisation of this principle requires skills such as co-operation, communication, empathy and a preference for compromise and mediation. Are not women the champions of exactly these skills? Today, even more than before, I believe that the kibbutz can benefit from the empowerment of its women members no less than the women can benefit from it.

Some Complexities of Raising Jewish Israeli Boys

Ayala Ronen Samuels

By the time I had the first of my three sons, at age thirty-two, I was already a very involved, knowledgeable and caring Jew. Becoming a mother gave me new ways to be Jewish, and new avenues for exploring my Jewish identity.

From the beginning, I have experienced motherhood as a Jewish Israeli woman. However, the attempt to separate the Jewish part of my motherhood from other, more universal parts of it is artificial and challenging at the same time. Also, I am not alone in raising my children. Being married, I share the laughs and tensions, policy-making and rule-enforcement, hopes and fears, with my husband (though I do take the lion's share of it all). The following examination of my role as a Jewish mother is the result of what felt like breaking down the big picture into the puzzle pieces that must have been there initially.

What is the essence of Jewish motherhood? In what ways do national, religious or cultural factors affect my motherhood? The invitation to write for this book has raised these questions and forced me to ponder them.

My response is that being Jewish, I am offered, or forced, to maintain a delicate and dynamic balance of pros and cons. The Jewish part of my motherhood is at times a privilege and other times a liability. Sometimes it is an obligation, and at other times it is a very heavy burden. In the stories below, I try to illustrate the complicated and rich fabric of what it feels like to be a Jewish mother.

Preparing for the birth of our first son, my husband Ami and I were not particularly concerned with Jewish issues. We were like all not-so-young couples, getting ready for the huge event of becoming a family. However, the issues

237

presented themselves very quickly. When the baby was born, he needed a name and a *brit*. A name we found, but the *brit* had to be planned way too fast, in a time that was personally most chaotic and challenging.

We lived in Manhattan, New York, at that time, in student housing, away from family and an organised social network. I was soon to discover that raising a baby in a young, urban, academic environment means improvising and learning as you go, with no role models and very little help. But we managed to put together a *brit*. We found a *mohel*, and a friend helped me buy some good Jewish food at Zabar's, the great New York delicatessen. Another friend searched and found that Peleg, our son's name, was also the name of Abraham's grandfather. I remember myself sitting, struggling with breastfeeding a wobbly baby, and reading through Psalms to find the exact quotation where the word *peleg* — a brook — is associated with eternal peace on earth. We did not choose the name Peleg for Jewish reasons, but finding that it does have deep roots in our cultural history became significant, as we were about to welcome the baby into the covenant of God with Abraham.

The *brit* is a very difficult event for parents, and especially for mothers. I hated the ceremony, particularly the act of cutting and then the crying of my baby, when I was not allowed to hold him. I had not had much sleep for more than a week by then, and hardly had time to take a shower, not to mention eat breakfast, before the event. I didn't know what to wear, as my maternity clothes were too bulky and my pre-maternity clothes too tight. There was only one moment during the whole event that made me feel good and a part of it — when I was asked to say the blessing *Gomayl Hasadim Tovim*, thanking God for having survived the delivery. I was surprised that "they" knew how difficult and scary "it" was, and that "they" had inserted a tiny role in the ceremony for the mother.

After having gone through three *brit* ceremonies with my sons, I suspect that my silent co-operation with this

238

ritual was due to my weak, confused and overwhelmed state of mind and body during the first week after giving birth. It is not impossible that a more relaxed, thorough and rational thinking process would result in altering this tradition. Why didn't I use the nine months before giving birth to debate this question? Well, for eight and half of them I was busy denying the fact that a pregnancy is bound to end with delivery. In the last two to four weeks, I was too frightened of delivery to think about anything else.

Choosing names for our other two sons was more complicated, and became a meaningful part of our family story. When our second son was born, right on the due date, we did not have a name prepared for him. We just could not find one that both of us liked. The baby made his entrance to the world early in the morning on Thanksgiving Day. Later that day, Ami took Peleg to New Jersey for a holiday dinner with relatives, an older couple. As the hostess served the turkey and stuffing, she gently asked if we were going to name the baby after Ami's grandfather, who had passed away a year earlier. Later, my husband came to see me and asked what I thought of the name Amos. Then he called his father, to confirm that Amos really had been his grandfather's Hebrew name. A week later, in his blessing for the baby, at the *brit*, my father-in-law said that this moment, that question, was for him an "I — Thou" encounter. He was referring to the term coined by Martin Buber, the twentieth-century Jewish philosopher, who defined revelation as a rare moment when a person engages in an I — Thou dialogue with God. Apparently, the name Amos was offered to the late grandfather by his son, my father-in-law, when he came from Texas to Israel to celebrate Ami's bar mitzvah and decided to be bar mitzvah (be called to read from the Torah) for the first time in his life.

Naming our son Amos enabled us to connect to my husband's family chain. The naming story reminds us how giving a name is a way to emphasise this chain and offer the child meaningful history to ponder upon in maturity. Ami's father suggested the name Amos to his own father because Amos was the prophet whose philosophy was the foundation for the way he lived his life, and it suited his liberal understanding of Judaism. We chose it because we liked the sound of it and because of the loving memory it brought us. For the liberal Texan grandfather, Amos was a second, added, for-religious-uses-only name. For the young Israeli boy, it is his name, sounding different in Hebrew than in English, but still easy to travel the world with.

When I was four months into my third pregnancy, my own father became very sick. We were back in Israel by then. As my father's condition worsened, the doctors forbade me to visit the hospital for fear of endangering the foetus. I was afraid that my father would die and not even meet this new grandson. Privately, I started examining alternative ways to name my son after my father. It was then that I woke up from a vivid dream in which the baby came out of my body and told me, loud and clear: "Shalom, I am Gilad."

I was surprised and bothered by the dream. My husband tried to wave it away. However, five months later, when the baby was born, crying like any normal baby, we named him Gilad. Calling from the maternity ward, I told my father, who was still recovering from his illness, that his new grandson, his thirteenth, was named Gilad.

"A very nice name you have chosen," said he, "and an interesting one. It was my own cover name all the years I served in the Palmach.[1] When I left the army, a friend suggested that I adopt the name as a family name, but I did not do so because of my brother, who got killed in that

[1]The Palmach was the Jewish Zionist underground in Israel prior to its war of independence. When the state of Israel was established, the Palmach served as a basis and infrastructure for the Israeli Defence Forces.

war..." Even my mother did not know about the old cover name. As to me, if I knew about it, the knowledge came to me via unrecognised channels.

There is no record of how and why my father, who has since passed away, chose the cover name Gilad. For me, telling my young son the naming story is an incentive to remember his grandfather and at the same time to understand his active Zionist legacy. Naming children after deceased relatives gives parents an opportunity to pass on their family stories — in our case Jewish stories — to their children. I used to think that naming a child after someone, especially after a soldier who was tragically killed in a war, places an unfair burden on the boy's shoulders. Now, I see it more as a standing invitation to remember and enrich one's life with a beloved story from the past.

The naming stories bring warm memories. Like our holiday stories or the historical anecdotes I tell my sons as we travel in Israel and elsewhere, they give me opportunities to construct and enrich their Jewish identity. I want them to have a clear and strong sense and understanding of Judaism. I also want them to be proud to be Jews. But how should I prepare them for the price they may have to pay for being born to a Jewish mother?

Raising our children to be Jewish is a lifelong endeavour. It has to do with the way we celebrate holidays, our weekly Shabbat ceremony, and our life-cycle events — *brit*, bar mitzvah, eventually wedding, I hope. Moreover, it influences the way we explain the world to them. Sometimes, however, it is a two-way road, when children's questions force us to examine our own beliefs, values and logic, and our ability to pass these on. Here is an example of such a process.

My husband and I decided long ago not to eat pork. Our decision was a conscious one, made for Jewish reasons rather than because of our family traditions. Neither of our families refrains from eating pork. We do not see our decision not to eat pork as part of observance of the laws of kashrut, although one may argue that it is a remnant of a long continuum of kashrut observance. Even though I grew up in an extremely secular environment, I felt as if I had inherited some physical aversion to this meat.

For thousands of years Jews would not touch pork. Many preferred to die rather than eat it; they chose to reveal their Jewish identity in a hostile environment and not give in on this. It was called "other", or "different" meat. I see pork as a symbol, not just meat.

In Israel, not eating pork comes naturally and easily. There, one has to make an effort to find and eat pork. However, upon leaving our homeland, pork becomes an issue. When we go out with family members in the United States, our sons watch in dismay and envy as others order anything on the menu. The questions spill out, first in a whisper, then as an argument: are they not Jewish? Are we Orthodox? You don't mind if I eat seafood, but pork is outlawed, so where is the line? Who draws the line?

When we were living in Luxembourg, the pork issue became even more challenging than I had expected. In Luxembourg, pork is a basic ingredient of the local menu. It appears at breakfast, lunch and dinner. Our boys attended the local International School, and pork was a very common hot lunch plate there. Their determination to avoid pork distinguished them from the other children and publicly identified them as Jews. The boys checked the ingredients of everything they ate in order to make sure they didn't eat pork by mistake. My older boys often shared their food with their younger brother to help him avoid pork.

At one point Amos became a target of jokes and mockery by other boys. They told him everything was made of pork and the juice he drank was really pigs' blood. The taunts eventually stopped, thanks to an informed educational process, but my son was left with the feeling of being marked out and a possible target because he is Jewish.

Is it good or bad that I put my sons through this? Life would be easier for them without the need to think about what they eat. It is my own guideline that separates pork from shellfish, which does not have the same symbolic associations for me as pork. In fact, by drawing this line, I am separating my family both from Orthodox Jews — for them we are not kosher enough — and from Liberal Jews — for them we are too kosher.

My sons' questions and difficulties forced me to rethink the issue — and to conclude that yes, pork is a powerful symbol. Not eating it does help one to remember that he or she is Jewish. The laws of kashrut are smart in this sense, and eventually we may adopt more of them and make the distinction between our Jewish home and other eating places. While the food awareness sometimes frustrates them, the boys take pride in their ability to do the right thing and help each other in the process. A while ago, after an encounter with a classmate who gave him a "Heil Hitler" salute and passed him a note with a swastika on it, Peleg told me he wants to wear a Magen David necklace or even a *kipah*. I find it a strong, defiant, and definitely typically Israeli reaction: we are not afraid of being recognised as Jews. We are proud to be Jewish and are ready to bear the not-always-pleasant consequences.

Hesitantly, I approach one of the worst aspects of being a Jewish mother, and in particular an Israeli one. Having given birth to three boys, I have been acutely aware, from the moment their sex was announced in the delivery room, that they might become soldiers one day. It is very hard trying to explain feelings that are not to be discussed in public, anxieties that we, Israeli parents, share but are reluctant to verbalise. Every parent in the world fears for his or her child's well-being and prays for his or her safety. We Israeli parents are burdened with a much heavier load: we raise children, notably boys, to become soldiers, who will probably need to fight to protect their country. How can I articulate this, when merely writing these words, I am overcome with tears?

Perhaps a few anecdotes will help me navigate through these stormy waters. A vivid memory: 3rd

243

September, 1993, New York. I sit in the living room, watching, on television, Rabin shaking hands with Arafat on the White House lawn. A baby is in my arms. I hug him really hard and, crying, I tell him: "See? Peace is coming! You will not have to fight, you will not be forced to kill in order to survive, and you will not be killed in a war..." How distant and illusory this hope seems now!

A couple of years ago I was sitting in a restaurant in Israel with two dear friends. Our three firstborn sons are very close to each other. The boys were all about to be bar mitzvah, and we mothers were enjoying exchanging tips, hopes, and laughs relating to the big events.

Then one of us sighed and said, "Isn't it great, how they are growing up? Remember how it felt when they started school?"

Silence fell around the table. We couldn't talk about it, but my friends' eyes told me they were thinking the same thing: one day, and it will come much too soon, we will be talking about the army.

A year earlier, I was talking about this issue with a friend who was a week from taking his second son to enlist in the army. For days before our conversation I had watched him, and had seen in his eyes Abraham preparing to go to Mount Moriah.[2]

"How can you stand it?" I asked.

"I can't," was his response. "If it was up to me he would not have done it. It is he who is now ready and willing to go."

"My sons are pacifists," I said apologetically, shielding myself at the same time.

"I know," he said. "Mine was too... It is an amazing process which happens when they get close to finishing

[2]"And He said: 'Take now thy son, thine only son, whom thou lovest, even Isaac, and get thee into the land of Moriah; and offer him there for a burnt-offering upon one of the mountains which I will tell thee of.'" (GEN 22:2)

school, when they turn from pacifists to fighting-unit volunteers."

Often, during discussions at home, I can see how the values and ideas I offer my sons may become, one day, the breeding ground for this willingness to fight for their country. For instance, they recently read a book by Janusz Korczak and I told them about how he bravely escorted the orphaned children he loved so much to the train that took them all to the gas chambers. The boys cried, devastated by the thought that the best this teacher could have done for the children was to die with them.

"Today, this cannot happen," I promised, in an effort to lift their spirits. "Now we have the state of Israel to protect every Jew in the world and make sure that the suffering of Jews will not be ignored again by the world."

"Precisely," said my older son. "And can you believe that there are young Israelis who will not join the army? Who do they expect to protect their country and their people?"

I could only respond to this with a hug that was aimed mostly to hide my eyes from his.

The thought of my sons becoming soldiers in the Israeli Defence Forces is inherently connected to the issue of the Holocaust — the Shoah. What role does the memory of the Shoah play in my deepest self, in the well from which I drink my mothering water? I constantly suppress and hide the fears, but cannot get rid of them: will my children be persecuted? Will they be deported and victimised? If history does repeat itself, am I preparing them well enough to survive its worst? Over and over again, Jews were mistreated and killed only because they were Jews. Often, the survivors of yet another wave of anti-Semitism were saved merely because they emigrated and fled the disaster area in time. The lesson of this history is a heavy burden on me. When all is well, when it is easy to be Jewish, we can pretend that this lesson is a legend of the past, irrelevant to our life. But these days, some Palestinians openly express a desire to kill every

Jew and destroy the Jewish state, denying us the very basic right of life. Strong winds of anti-Semitism sweep through Europe again, allied with extreme and fanatical Islamic fundamentalism. I cannot avoid these doubts: are my children in danger because they are Jews? Am I putting their lives under threat as a result of my decision to live in Israel?

On the other hand, by leaving Israel, I might deny my sons the opportunity to live the fullest and richest Jewish life and take a part in the greatest Jewish adventure of all: creating a humanist Zionist Jewish society in the Jewish state. Furthermore, perhaps it is a genetic Zionist default in me, but I feel that leaving Israel now borders on treason. So what should I do? Will I be making the best Jewish choice by escaping the coming tragedy or by facing it and joining the front line in preventing it?

Making these enormous life-shaping decisions, I find inspiration and spiritual guidance in this quote from the Avot chapter of the Mishnah: "You are not required to complete the task, but neither are you at liberty to abstain from it."

This is probably true regarding my sons as well as my country. While it is my duty to teach the boys all I can and create for them the best living conditions possible, my efforts are just one factor in the end result. The same goes for Israel. While I should do my best to help Israel improve its society and future, and shouldn't exempt myself from it, I cannot complete the task.

In teaching my sons to be Jews, as well as in choosing a homeland for them, I am repeatedly torn by the huge swings of Jewish motherhood, elevated by pride in my enormous heritage and overwhelmed with the fears it plants in me. From the excitement and exhilaration of naming a newborn, to the hopefully never-ending task of teaching him about his people, culture, and religion. From studying his bar mitzvah portion with him, to backing him up when he feels threatened as a Jew, "Jewish" questions are, for me, a prominent part of motherhood.

In essence, being a Jewish mother is an enormous responsibility. As a Jewish mother I need to pass on the story, the tradition, and the commitment. Above all, I have to pass on the willingness to pay the price, knowing that the price may be unbearable.

Pioneers

Batya Jacobs

Mattityahu, my *yishuv* (settlement), my home, my eleventh child — I suppose. When we arrived here, you were a scarred and wounded mountain top. Some of your houses were already topped with their quaint red roofs. Others had only walls, and yet others just had a floor plan. Poor, lonely Mattityahu — nary a tree, nary a bird, nary a footpath between the few houses that were "ready" for habitation.

We watched you grow, Mattityahu, I and my growing family watched you grow. We watched the kindergarten playground arise from the dust, we watched the intricate mesh of electricity lines and telephone cables threaded over wooden poles till they became a man-made spider's web. We heard a brokenhearted mother cat howling for her kittens that had been covered with a tractor-shovel's worth of rubble. My sadly abandoned children played, dug and burrowed in the builders' sand with their equally abandoned friends.

It takes a long long time to build a *yishuv*. It takes hours of doing, it takes hours of saying and, because everybody's ideas and dreams are so different, it takes compromise, in fighting, politics and pain. All to build a *yishuv*.

Now I sit at my computer and use electricity without worrying when the generator will be turned off to "have a rest." Now on this sweltering summer day I take an ice-cube-filled drink without going to the neighbourhood fridge (the generator could only carry one fridge per group of houses). I see my rather English-y cottage garden in full bloom and recall when the lorries came and dumped the topsoil on our barren, stony grounds.

We were really idealists, the group of people, the "seed", as our beloved Ivrit calls it, that clawed our settlement out of smashed-down mountain top. We were trying to build a religious *moshav shitufi* — a partnership. Partners in the workforce, partners in the earnings, partners in the day-to-day running. But we did have our own kitchens! More independence than in a kibbutz, yet more interdependence than a plain old place to live. Socialist in origin, we paid the stipend according to family size and not according to the worth of the job. The smaller families grizzled as the summer soft-fruit rations let you buy one peach for the small families and three for the big ones. There was no incentive to work apart from the love of our *yishuv*, the love of our fellows. We worked, we talked, we tried and tried and we were so, so, tired.

My other children lost out. My Mattityahu child, like an unwieldy, insatiable cuckoo, devoured my strength, devoured all our strength, and our other children — "the children of the sand piles" — played as they waited and waited for us parents to be free.

How could I have made such a mistake? How could I have lost sight of my true path, my real children? How could I have expended such effort to try to hold up and concretise such an unwieldy, unworkable, way of existence?

I am a product of the sixties, with its stress on justice, on fairness, on non-materialism, on sharing wealth. Oh, how I did believe in it! Oh, how I still do believe in it! *But* — I was also a member of the pram-pushing little girls' brigade. I was enchanted with my dollies until I was shamed out of it by my older sister. I continued my motheringness in my relationships with my friends, always being the "auntie" figure, the nurturer.

I nurtured Mattityahu as I nurtured my children, giving it time and thought and action. I did not totally neglect my kids. Far from it. I was in the forefront of the fight to stop women's work from being compulsory. I never really had even a part-time job until my youngest started nursery

249

school. Is it my Jewish mothering that made me want to stay at home with my children, or is it just me?

I gave my heart to Mattityahu, but many of its deities turned out to be false. My idealism wasn't shared by the next generation. They hadn't seen the first traces of building on a snuggly mountain top bathed in the effervescent red-pink glow of the setting sun, with only the braying of the guard duty Bedouin's donkey to fill the empty hours of the night. They had not marvelled at the first bird or sung and watched the men dancing as the first lawn was laid at the end of a long workday. They hadn't spent some sleep-deprived years trying to keep Mattityahu afloat.

> Oh Mattityahu,
> Dear Mattityahu,
> Just you wait,
> Sweet Mattityahu,
> Tomorrow you will be!

I wrote as I dreamed, wrote as I nurtured, wrote as I gave.

If I could have it over again, I would be much clearer about my boundaries, much clearer about what sort of socialism is possible to live by in a group of normal human beings. If my knowledge had been more informed by Torah values, I would have avoided some almost fanatical following of false trails, of non-natural "goodness".

One of my married children lives on Mattityahu. The other three live close by. One of them is often the *ba'al koreh* (reader) for Mattityahu's *shul*. I think they all have some attachment to the place. I also think that the older ones did suffer from a very diluted "Lord of the Flies" syndrome. They made their community rules — the laws of the sand piles — while we were making our community rules — the minutes of our weekly general meetings.

A Jewish mother follows her Jewish husband, with their Jewish children, to a Jewish land. There they build and develop a Jewish settlement with Jewish values (with a few hiccups on the way). The Jewish mother, as true Jewish mothers really know how to do, opens her arms wide, wide, and embraces the whole bunch — Mattityahu and all — and gives them a big, big cuddle (and a bowl of apocryphal chicken soup). And they all live happily ever after!

A State of Intimacy
A Jewish Mother in Israel

Shirly Eran
Translated by Ayelet Porat

When I was asked to write an article for this book, I
wondered how qualified I was, for I do not see myself
primarily as a "Jewish mother". I define myself as a
"woman" and an "Israeli". Of course, things aren't that
simple. Sociologically, I may be defined as a left-wing,
secular, Ashkenazi Jewish, Israeli woman. My identity,
like anyone's, has been shaped by the values I grew up
with, personal experiences, and the choices I made — one
of them to become a mother with a parenthood partner
(not a romantic one), another being the choice to pursue
human rights.

What is Jewish about my motherhood? I don't know. My
Judaism is in many ways something I take for granted. I
was born into a Jewish family, grew up within a Jewish
society and during my teenage years took an interest in
Jewish traditions and issues. Besides all that, the shadow
of the Holocaust is ever-present. The Holocaust was
pumped into my veins as a child, with talk at home about
family members left behind, with school programmes and
with books I read, like *The Diary of Anne Frank* and *The
Children of Mapu Street*.[1]

The reality of my life as a Jewish woman in Israel,
where Jews are the "lords of the land", contrasts strongly
with the constant presence of the Holocaust and the

---

[1] A novel by Sarah Neshamit, published in 1977. It is a fictional
account of the Holocaust experiences of a group of children who
played together in a courtyard on Mapu Street in Kovno,
Lithuania.

perception of the Jew as victim. The Holocaust makes me think of helplessness in the face of authority and the unlimited evil of which of humankind is capable. As a mother, this has made me want to raise children incapable of such acts. I don't want them to grow up thinking that there's only one right side that has all the right answers. I don't want them to be able to stand aside and ignore the suffering of others, or to join those causing that suffering. Others may view matters differently, and try to raise their children so they won't become victims — they want them to know how to fight so they won't let anyone trample all over them. I don't believe it's possible. Proud and strong people can also become the victims of evil regimes.

In Israeli society being a mother gives you a very comfortable status — a status that makes you part of the consensus, even if you were once on the fringes of society, or outside it altogether. Even though being a mother is only part of my identity, it is a dominant part, because it more or less dictates the course of my life, for better or for worse.

Now, that I am a mother of two — yes, a very comfortable definition — it's easy to see the complexity of matters. Did I want these children for selfish reasons? Yes, of course. I think that I perceive motherhood as being a necessary phase of development, perhaps even more important than the phase I skipped in not being part of a couple. In this sense, although the way I chose to have a family seems to go against the mainstream, I believe I chose the traditional path. In Israeli society, the easy way is to be a mother. A mother has validity, a right to exist, and she serves important national goals. Israeli society sanctifies motherhood and embraces it with love and encouragement. Behind that embrace is an ideological goal: expanding the Jewish population, as a whole and in Israel in particular.

For me, motherhood is first and foremost a state of intimacy — that closeness to a new human being in his or her formative stages that is mostly so wonderful, but sometimes wearying and difficult in its intensity.

This intimacy, which I so longed for, is a lot more complex than I anticipated. Juggling the children's wants and needs with my own expectations, abilities and wishes is the essence of motherhood. The first thing about being a mother is taking part in the creation of something so wonderful that it is beyond the imagination. Next comes the attempt to let that new person develop in his or her own way, moving between the need to accept the child as s/he is and the wish to shape him/her, and between the child's true self and my expectations.

There's also a lot of self-mending in motherhood. As a girl who grew up in a very protective environment, I nonetheless experienced a lot of rejection that in a way formed my personality. As a mother I try to protect my children from such painful experiences, and I know that in doing so I'm often trying to protect myself as well, from reliving those experiences though my children. I try to make my children's world secure and to remove from their path any obstacles resembling those I blame for problems in my personality. One of my greatest challenges is to try and differentiate between my inner world and my children's reality, between the fears based on my experiences in the past, and how I handled them, and my children's experiences and ways of handling things.

Sometimes I'm aware that I view my children in accordance with social conventions, and I'm bothered when they diverge, even if it doesn't hurt a soul.

One of the more difficult aspects of motherhood is the obsessive engagement with the question "Am I a 'good enough' mother?" and the endless attempt to give more, to do more. These attempts are often unnecessary and even harmful, and come at the expense of calm and serenity. This might be a stereotypical element of the tireless "Jewish mother". The guilty feelings are related not only to the care of my children but also work commitments, household chores, the extended family, and more.

What does it mean to be such a mother? For me it means that my life revolves mostly around my children. They are the centre of my emotional world. This can be attributed to many causes, some personal and some more general: the lack of a spouse; Israeli society, in which parenthood is the only legitimate way of life; and the model of the Jewish mother who runs her children's lives. All this aside, for better or for worse, my motherhood experience is dominant.

As I examine my expectations of my children, I try to differentiate those based on my needs from those more essential to their development as human beings. I relate to social aspects of these expectations: in my opinion, one of the most important roles in motherhood, in parenthood in general, is to help the person I helped create become useful to himself and others.

A part of the self-mending in raising children, for me, is the attempt to keep them from becoming prejudiced. Yes, I do have my prejudices. These sometimes raise their ugly heads and remind me of that part of my personality. It is easy to say that we're all human beings, but it's not that easy for me to relate to people I consider different — I have a hard enough time relating to those I consider similar to me. It's important to me that my children grow up open-minded, sensitive to other people, to animals and to nature around them — or what is left of it.

One of my experiences as a mother is the continuous search for the right message to give to my children — how to behave with other people and face other people and how to avoid hypocrisy. It is hard, since I myself don't always act that way: sometimes I express impatience, ignorance, spite and aggressiveness. I try to make my children understand how important they are to me, and how much good and potential they possess.

Simultaneously, I strive for them to become sensitive to others, beginning with their relationship with each other, and moving out to their friendships and their relationships with other individuals and groups we live with.

The trauma of terrorist attacks is present in our lives. On the day I gave birth to my first son, casualties from such an attack were brought into the same hospital. The day after we came home, another serious attack took place, and yet another occurred a few days later. Since then the fear of these attacks is also a part of my motherhood, and it has been integrated into my natural tendency to overworry.

In this endless bloodshed we live with, I don't want my children to grow up believing that in order to live here they must always fight the enemy, an idea that stands at the core of Israeli education. I want them to believe that in order to live here, as anywhere else, they have to be tolerant and open-minded to people who are different, and ready to give of themselves. Some people might claim that I'm naive and unrealistic, that if you want to live here you must fight, since there's nowhere else for us to go. For me, however, living here is a matter of fact and not some kind of idealistic goal, so I don't think it justifies the fighting. I don't want my kids to think that stepping on others is legitimate self-defence. For me it is more legitimate to give up a homeland than to step on other people in order to live there.

My partner and I chose to send our children to a Jewish-Arab school. It was an attempt to fulfil a dream — a personal dream, not of coexistence, but of openness of mind, the ability to see beyond colour, garment or custom. A dream about the ability not to categorise people because they're different. We are Jewish. For me, that is not a matter of choice or belief. It is a fact: we belong to a certain group that shares a past and traditions. My older son is eight years old, and he knows about his roots. The fact that he has Arab friends does not interfere with his identity — on the contrary, it helps him to understand that his identity exists alongside many others. I think he knows that a different identity does not make you better or worse than others. I hope we are providing our children with the tools necessary for coping with a difficult reality.

Identity in
the Diaspora

Nativity

A short story by
Mandy Ross

Naomi detested Christmas. For as long as she could remember, from October to January she braced herself for the annual assault of tinsel, flashing lights, school projects and performances, Christmas stamps, snowy advertisements for mechanical dolls that cry real tears (batteries not included), Christmas cards to be sent and received, trilling carols in all the shops, extended shopping hours, crazed shoppers, traffic jams, obligations, enforced jollity and heavy drinking. Ho, ho, ho! All this to celebrate the birth of the son of someone else's God.

With eight candles and just one song, Hanukkah, the minor Jewish festival at midwinter, struggled to compete. Across the land, every Jewish family (including Naomi's), with very little open discussion of the subject, privately found their own level of accommodation. Some ostentatiously ignored Christmas, eating scrambled egg on toast on December 25. Some joined in guiltily, with low-level family festivities. Others gave presents for all the eight days of Hanukkah *and* Christmas Day too. Some went the whole hog, with kosher turkey, presents and even a Christmas tree, so that the children wouldn't feel left out. Last year, Naomi had seen ads in the local shops for halal turkey, so she assumed that Muslim families, and those of other non-Christian faiths, must face the same dilemma.

The effect was cumulative. Each year, Naomi found it harder to shrug off the onslaught of compulsory Christmas. Against her will she found herself humming "We Three Kings", or "Away in a Manger", though she switched immediately to "Ma'oz Tsur", the Hanukkah song, as soon as she became conscious of it. As December progressed and the days grew miserably short, Naomi grew cross and sour and misanthropic. Which she hated.

"Could it be SAD — you know, Seasonal Affective Disorder?" ventured her friend Susie.

"So that's what they mean when they put 'Season's Greetings' in their cards," spat Naomi, planning a winter solstice ritual for December 21 to try to turn the tide.

* * *

And then, one spring…

"A Christmas baby! How lovely!" said her GP, midwife, colleagues, neighbours, and all her non-Jewish friends.

"Yes, if it's a boy we're going to call him Jesus," she took to snorting under her breath after a while.

"A Hanukkah baby! How wonderful!" chorused her parents and in-laws, sister, cousins, the rabbi, the rabbi's wife, and all her Jewish friends. "Now you'll have some-thing to celebrate!"

* * *

Naomi and her husband, Michael, had been trying to conceive for years. After all the tears she had shed, month after month, Naomi wept for joy as she saw the faint blue line emerging and then shining out from the pregnancy test wand. At last! Every particle of her existence sang at the prospect of pregnancy, a baby, a child… except for the Christmas birthday. Should they have waited just one more month?

She vomited throughout the late spring, but sailed through the long, hot summer. By September, she was satisfyingly rounded. In October, when the first carols were playing in the shops, she was putting her feet up in the evenings. By November, when the municipal lights were switched on, she couldn't imagine how she would get any bigger. But she did.

On December 1, her last day at work, Naomi wore Michael's big red jumper with her red maternity trousers, and she found a wide black belt long enough to meet around her belly.

"Ho, ho, ho!" she growled as deeply as she could. "Look what Santa's bringing this year."

* * *

After she left work, Naomi sank onto the sofa and left it only to haul herself upstairs to the bathroom more and more frequently as the baby settled over her bladder. Staying home from the tinsel-larded shops, she sent off for baby clothes by mail order, and watched videos to avoid the Christmas programmes on every TV channel.

One afternoon when Naomi was putting the rubbish out, the little boy next door waved to her.

"I've started opening my advent calendar," he called. "Only twenty-two days to go. I'm counting down."

"Me too," snarled Naomi. "I'm hoping it might come early..."

"What?" frowned Christopher.

"... or late," she said, and slammed the door.

* * *

The rabbi's wife came to visit, bringing homemade apple *kuchen*.

"Oy, yoy, yoy, *mazel tov*, darling, you're huge!" she cried when Naomi opened the front door. "It's a good sign. Big belly, healthy baby. Are you eating properly?" she asked, making her way towards the kitchen. "It's a mitzvah, in your condition. Come on, have some cake. I'll make a pot of tea. Getting excited? I know your mum is."

"There was something I wanted to ask," said Naomi when the rabbi's wife paused for breath. "Are there any blessings for when I go into labour, and when the baby's born?"

The rabbi's wife frowned, rubbing her chin.

261

"I don't remember anything when I had my babies," she said. "I'll ask Solly."

* * *

A week later, short of breath and too tired to do anything but lie on the sofa and phone people, Naomi rang the rabbi's house.

"I'm sorry, darling," said the rabbi's wife. "I didn't get back to you. I did ask Solly, but he said there's not much specifically. There's the *Shehechianu*, of course, and..." She tailed off.

"Oh," said Naomi. "Well. Thanks for asking him."

"God bless, darling," said the rabbi's wife. "We'll be thinking of you."

Naomi and Michael waited. Every day, Naomi hoped the baby would come early. As the days passed, she switched to hoping it would come late.

"Never mind," said Michael. "Does it matter what date it comes?"

"Yes, it bloody does," shouted Naomi, extreme pregnancy adding to her seasonal bad temper.

* * *

And then, early in the morning of Christmas Eve, the pains started. She wasn't sure at first, just an odd, recurring sensation that made her want to lie down, even though she was lying down anyway.

"Bang on time," she muttered between sensations. "Just my luck. Oh well, surely it'll come before midnight. I'll just have to push hard."

Later she didn't care what time it was or when the baby was born, as long as it did get born, and soon. She was adrift in the timeless endurance of labour, hanging her head, howling and groaning and pushing when she was told, forever and ever and ever.

And then suddenly, there was a bleeping monitor, and a gathering of strange faces looking down at her, all talking in calm, fiercely urgent voices. She was lifted onto a trolley and sped along corridors, people explaining incomprehensibly in her ear and holding a board for her to sign her name. She shivered uncontrollably. Michael ran beside the trolley, holding her hand for as long as he could, calling out to her after the theatre doors swung shut.

* * *

When she woke, the baby was lying in the crook of her arm. Michael grinned at her from a chair beside the bed.

"Congratulations!" whispered the midwife. "It's a beautiful boy. I'm just helping him latch on." She adjusted the baby's position and moved Naomi's arm to support him. "Happy Christmas," she said. "He was born just after midnight."

Naomi couldn't speak. She craned her neck to look down at the baby now clamped to her breast, his eyes and fists tight shut as he sucked. Eventually he finished, or fell asleep, or both, and as he loosed his grip, his head tipped back a little, his face beaming up at her.

Then she remembered her conversation with the rabbi's wife, and silently she recited the *Shehechianu*: "We praise you, Eternal God, Sovereign of the universe, that you have kept us alive, and enabled us to reach this season."

* * *

Even as she struggled through the next painful days of wound-dressing, engorged breasts, rasped nipples and raging hormones, Naomi felt she understood something new. Suddenly the Christmas story, familiar through inescapable repetition over the years, seemed only an appropriate response to the birth of a baby, any baby — her baby. He was a miracle, a wonder, a joy, a mystery, a human. The stars shone over his hospital cot; her family and friends travelled to see him and bring gifts; she was sure that animals would turn their faces to gaze at him.

From then on, Christmas was different for Naomi. She still avoided the garish, gaudy shops and swore at the hideous ads on the TV. She put Danny's birthday cards in front of the Christmas cards from friends, neighbours and colleagues. But she smiled at the municipal decorations and lights put up for his birthday. And every year she imagined pagan, cave-dwelling, nomadic mothers resting after their babies' miraculous births, whose celebrations had borne the Christmas story and other myths we tell today.

Voilà, Motherhood

Susie Kaufman

My husband married in by accident, not design. He was brought up without any Jewish education. I often think that, at some crucial window of development, the spiritual lobe of his brain remained unstimulated. When we met we discovered our differences. Both of us were Jewish, but from very different backgrounds and with different beliefs. He had little interest in religious rituals, customs, laws or *yomtovs*. The only Jewish people he knew were his family and the one or two other Jewish pupils at his secondary school. I had been to a Jewish primary school and had socialised almost entirely within the community. One-third of my secondary-school class was Jewish. He had no need of Jewish community life, joining any club, or seeking friends from within the community. I enjoyed community life, wanted to be part of a club and to find like friends. I wanted my future to be a continuation of my childhood. And so did he of his. We stopped going out.

We went out again. We compromised. We got married.

He has always kept kosher in our home. We live away from our home town and in the early years I returned home for the *yomtovs*. Why didn't I join the Orthodox community? I found it too hard. I was shy, and there seemed to be such established friendship and family units that I felt unequal to the task of making a place for myself. Growing up, I had always been somebody's daughter or sister or grandchild, niece or cousin; here I felt that I had no history, no status, no place.

I became pregnant with our first child. I joined the National Childbirth Trust relaxation classes. And there I met a Jewish girl. Our son was born. We arranged for the *bris* (a continuation of my husband's infant experience!). I stayed friendly with the Jewish girl and we began to socialise. Through her I met many young Jewish marrieds with young children. My husband became friendly with a Jewish man where he worked. This man belonged to the Reform *shul*, and he introduced us to it. My family began to express concern about our son's Jewish education. There was no way my husband would attend the Orthodox *shul*. He couldn't read Hebrew and he couldn't sit with me. We joined the Reform *shul*. It was a compromise for both of us.

I found that making a place there for myself was not difficult. We mixed with people whose partners were not Jewish or not interested. This felt comfortable for my husband, and he was prepared to join in.

Our daughter was born. I tried to guide our children spiritually and religiously with a consistent approach. But my childhood had been steeped in Orthodoxy, and I didn't know the Reform ideology. I learned as I guided, and probably gave out many mixed messages. However, it seemed to work, and our son was bar mitzvah there and our daughter bat mitzvah. We have made good friends and enjoyed the Jewish life it offered, for which I am enormously grateful.

Whenever I could I have gone with the children to be with my extended family for *yomtovs*, and so they have experienced both types of service and family life. Our life has been a mixture of Reform and Orthodox; Reform by name and subscription, we have felt the guilt of the Orthodox, knowing we were bending the laws.

When our son went away to university he chose the Orthodox *shul*. When he has travelled he has chosen to visit Orthodox *shuls*. Recently, after the wedding of a close relative, both of our children said that they intended to marry in an Orthodox *shul*. Somehow, both of the children have come to perceive the Orthodox as being what they want. Perhaps it's the market atmosphere and joke sessions, the camaraderie in the men's section that enticed my son. Perhaps it's the fashion and the sense of sisterhood that draws my daughter. No — I feel that for them, it is not just a matter of practicalities or of choosing a particular club, but a tug from the soul. Perhaps singing them to sleep with *shul* songs when they were babies did more for their spiritual awakening than I realised.

And so my husband and I began again to have the same kind of discussion that marked the early years of our marriage. But this time, instead of projecting into the future about what kind of family life we would have, we have been dealing with facts and personalities. He does not want to join the Orthodox *shul*. He still feels no need to be affiliated. Our children, however, do. And so I have taken the step of joining the Orthodox *shul* with the children, while still maintaining our family Reform membership. We joined Reform to create a cohesive family unit. I have joined the Orthodox for my children's future, and I return as if from exile.

And our future? My husband does not believe in an afterlife, nor in religion, and does not want an Orthodox burial. The time will undoubtedly come when I have to choose only one membership and we will have to complete the discussion on which *shul* and which burial board.

And where have I found the courage to do in middle age what I couldn't do when younger? Undoubtedly from my children. I am able to do for my children something I was unable to do for myself. *Voilà*, motherhood.

Did I Do Right?

Marlena Schmool

It is about twelve noon on a cold February day. It is snowing. I am standing and looking from the hospital window across to the Houses of Parliament with a small bundle in my arms, wrapped in a blue blanket. He is about a day old and I am looking down at him, asking him — and myself — out loud how I can do my best for him. He is my firstborn, and I remember very vividly at a distance of over thirty-four years how intensely I wondered what would become of him, and how aware I was that I would be responsible for who he would become. For my generation, I was old to be a first-time mother. I hadn't had much to do with babies since I left home for college, but I had read some child psychology as a student. Thanks to John Bowlby's *Child Care and the Growth of Love*, I was very aware of how formative the mother-child bond was meant to be.

Fast-forward three years four months. My daughter was born accommodatingly at 6.55am, giving my husband time to get back home to tell firstborn about his baby sister, then get him dressed, fed and taken to nursery school. There was no philosophical questioning this time. Experience had taught me that I wasn't the only influence in my child's life, and I was more relaxed. I am still more relaxed with my daughter than with my son. I think that original internal questioning in some way set the tone of our relationship.

I have never thought of myself as "the Jewish mother"; I probably tried very hard to avoid nearing the stereotype. I'd certainly avoided it with marriage. Ashkenazi northern British, I'd married a Sephardi Israeli immigrant. If I was affected at all by the comic cliché of a Jewish mother, it was by our joint reaction to it. While we were certain that we wanted our children to have a sound academic education and to succeed in what they undertook, we didn't see ourselves as having "my son the doctor". And I definitely was not going to wash his socks forever.

Within eighteen months of my son's birth I was very aware of how bored I was, just being at home with the baby. Bowlby — and by now Dr Spock — notwithstanding, I really needed something to keep my mind working. I did some committee work and research to keep my hand in. Then, when our daughter was less than three months old, my husband asked me how I felt about helping him in the business he was thinking of setting up. There was only one answer.

The small spare room became the office. I juggled last-minute letters with 6pm feeds. I also made especially small gefilte fish balls to give to the insurance company inspectors who visited on Friday morning. We had a cottage industry set-up. If there was any Jewish precedent, it was my great-grandmother running the front-room store in Belfast in the 1920s and 30s. I was also to some extent following my own mother's example. Although my father had a factory with the full range of staff, my mother also worked for him from home. I regularly came home from school to see her bookkeeping on the morning-room table. The example I witnessed was working as a family, independently. There are reams of learned papers to show that Jews like to be self-employed, and as a family we followed that lead. In that respect my children have certainly followed a Jewish pattern. My son is a musician — self-employed. My daughter is an actor — self-employed.

As you can see, my feelings about being a mother are inextricably woven with those about being part of a family. The Ashkenazi-Sephardi mix in ours was complicated by the Diaspora/Israel balance. I am third-generation British; my grandparents were part of the late-nineteenth-century immigration that I frequently refer to when lecturing on the demographic history of British Jewry. My husband was fifth-generation Israeli-born but, by dint of his family's Gibraltarian antecedents, could trace his British links back to the eighteenth century. As he would remind me, he was more British than I am.

In bringing up our children, all this meant that we spoke both Hebrew and English at home; we chose a primary school where this could be reinforced; and then, because I felt very strongly that children had to know about being Jewish in a non-Jewish society, we also sent them to cheder when they moved to secondary schools. We went as a family to the Spanish and Portuguese Jews' Congregation, because it was the only synagogue where my husband felt at home. We lit candles and said *kiddush* on Shabbat and festivals. But we were a mixed family. Both traditions were equally respected. We started the Passover seder with the Sephardi practice of lifting and circling the seder plate, we had both *suvganiot* and *latkes* at Hanukkah, and ate homemade aubergine salad in the days before you could get it in the supermarket.

Just writing this reminds me of the different strands the children had to deal with. My pleasure in seeing them as adults is that they are honest, hardworking, creative, sensitive and think for themselves. Maybe having had to work through what would nowadays be seen as a multi-cultural background has helped them towards this last characteristic. When I look into myself, this is what I am most proud of.

However, for a person who has spent so much time examining Jewish identity and continuity, this raises many questions about cultural transmission and the future of Judaism. All the practices we followed were supposed to pass on Judaism to our children. But I didn't do enough. Jewishly, my children are secular and unaffili-ated, part of the group that my profession has called the missing generation. (Personal note: I hate the term and always think of it as "hidden", not "missing".) Yet they both have a strong sense of community, which comes out in their lives and work. As to what they think, I certainly

270

don't go around with an attitude questionnaire, although there are times when I'd like to.

Over the years I have frequently asked myself what more I could have done that would have rung true to myself — or, more exactly, that would have rung true to *ourselves*, because fathers and mothers both influence their children. Anything that had rung false would have been impossible. I suppose my major mistake — or misreading (and it was mine, because my husband was willing to follow my lead as to what would be an appropriate Jewish education outside of Israel) — was not to consider how quickly the world might change and how much more educated and committed my children would need to be to feel part of the Jewish world. I thought that providing my children with more or less the same type and level of Jewish education that I had had would equip them to stay committed in a wider society that was more welcoming than it had been to my generation. We made sure that they went to cheder regularly — no missing for something more interesting, and not just up to bar/bat mitzvah age — and they were taught well. This was Jewish education as I understood it, backed up by home practices and synagogue attendance. When we had to make choices about secondary-school education, I was not prepared to send them to a school that I felt *then* was a "school for Jews" rather than a "Jewish school". I wanted them to be Jews, but to be part of the world beyond the Jewish boundaries — as I had wanted for myself. Also, neither my husband nor I was a strong enough believer to become more observant. Had we been so, our children would have seen a different example and might have made all kinds of different choices.

So, what do I feel I have passed on to them that is Jewish? Well — a commitment to social justice, intellectual autonomy, knowing right from wrong, and understanding that financial reward and individual success are not the only yardsticks for judging a person. I remember when my son was at his senior school, he was extremely put off by the materialistic standards and behaviour of many of the other Jewish boys. Perhaps if he had been at a Jewish school he would have seen a counterbalance and would not have equated that approach with his religion. My daughter does not see the world in such black-and-white terms but still feels more at home in more open groups.

If young Jews today have to choose between the very Jewish tensions created by the universal and particular strands in the Jewish heritage, then my son and daughter have clearly chosen universal. By that I mean that they have absorbed those Jewish teachings about how people should behave towards each other rather than the teachings about how to relate to God. We don't talk about these matters, so I can only go by how they live their lives, infrequent comments and the way they make their adult judgments. The exception to this is some conversations that have shown me that my daughter has thought out very carefully where Judaism stands in her life. About that I am glad. One point both my husband and I were clear on — we wanted our children to think for themselves. Having brought them up with this attitude, it would be hypocritical of me now to turn round and say that they should believe what I tell them just because I'm not always comfortable with their views.

Their choices have not always led to quietude at home. My father, *z'l*, was of the old school. Although he never said anything directly, we could see from his grim face that he was unhappy about our children's choices of friends as they were growing up. Mothers maybe are different. Neither my mother nor my mother-in-law ever judged. Beyond that, as grandparents, they were all proud of how the children grew up. I am getting to the stage where I would welcome grandchildren and the large family gatherings that I grew up with at festivals — but I also remember how tense they could be. Maybe more than anything else, I transmitted that ambivalence.

Letting Go

Anna Sullivan

"You taught me how to be a mother," said my daughter. I thought that I had just muddled through as best I could. I had all my three children by the time I was twenty-four. Six years later I was on my own, and we lived as a single-parent family after that.

My father was a gentile and a communist, my mother was the Jewish wife of a communist. There was no religion in our house, not even from my mother's family, and so I was brought up with no real sense of being Jewish.

I was six years old when the Second World War ended. My generation grew up with the images of the Holocaust flickering on the screens of local cinemas. Then a collective amnesia descended, a silence, a desperation to put such unpleasant things behind us. My father had fought at Cable Street, and my mother had organised summer camps for Spanish children, refugees from Franco's Spain, and yet they never talked about the Holocaust or its meaning for our family.

What has this to do with Jewish motherhood? Nothing on the face of it, but I believe that somewhere among the muddle and emotional cacophony of my mother's family, I learned that children were everything and that they had to come first at all times. I learned about sacrifice from my own mother.

Once I cried in despair at all three of my selfish teenaged children, "Everyone in this house has complete freedom except me!" For me, this was all part of being a good mother. They should be allowed to spread their wings, and if they behaved badly it was my fault. Well, wasn't it? Is being a Jewish mother about unconditional love? Is that not the case for all mothers? Or is it also, for my generation, because as Jews we have more to fear for our children? When the silence surrounding the Shoah was finally broken and the memories and stories were revealed, did we see, in all those lost children, our own?

Just as my love for my children is all-consuming — you could say that they are the love of my life — so I know that sometimes I can be a bit invasive. Recently I went to check on my eldest daughter's house while she and her family were on holiday. I spent at least an hour and a half cleaning her fridge. I would not dream of poking around in anyone else's fridge, or of cleaning it. It would seem a terrible cheek, a comment on their hygiene. I felt no such inhibition in my daughter's house, yet I know it probably drives her mad.

My own mother would voice her opinions on all aspects of my life, including my mothering skills, but she was always at my door when I most needed her. Perhaps that's why our children can stand such overbearing love. In the end we are always there.

My biggest challenge came when my younger daughter became religious. She had been living on a kibbutz for some time. Then she went to a girls' religious college in Jerusalem and became a changed person. How did she get from the young woman in shorts, pruning trees in an orchard, to a woman who when married would cover her hair and most of her body, and who would no longer eat in my house? I felt totally rejected. It seemed that she had turned her back on me and all my values. What had I done to deserve such treatment?

I know now that what happened was not to do with me but with her and the path in life that she chose. Eventually I realised that children are not an extension of their parents, but it was a painful transition for me. I also had to deal with the alienation that my other two children felt from their sister's life.

When she met the man who is now her husband, my daughter had not yet changed her life. He was a nice boy from Ilford who drove an MG sports car and went on skiing holidays with his mates. When she became religious, so did he.

I found it much easier to discuss the differences in our philosophies with him than I did with my daughter, who just got angry with me. I have worked much of my life as a teacher, have been very involved in community politics and have always considered myself a socialist. For me this means having an attitude to life that encompasses respect for other people and helping those in need when times are hard, sharing your good fortune. My father said to me that as far as he was concerned, socialism was no use without love, and that is about how I see it too. I had hoped that I'd passed this on to my children. But I felt that my daughter's return to the religious life of Judaism was a criticism of my beliefs.

I had always had a close relationship with my daughter, and in fact with all my children. Now we could not even have lunch together. I knew that if I didn't want to lose her, I had to stop thinking about my own feelings and instead look at her new life in a different way.

Slowly I began to see how happy she was. That she lived in a community where people really did help each other. That the teachings of the Torah echoed many of my own beliefs. I began to realise that what I saw as withdrawing from the modern world was for her a new freedom. My daughter taught me the beauty and strength of Judaism. In a way, she helped me to discover the roots that I had lost.

When she made aliyah to Israel several years ago, I thought I would die of grief. Half of me understood why they were going, as I love Israel, but the other half could not bear parting from my beloved child. But another thing I have learned about being a mother is that to keep your children by you, you have to let them go with good grace. Then they will always come back. They will always be with you, in spirit if not in body.

Through my new understanding of the rich and diverse world of Judaism, I have become closer to my daughter. When our children are young we love them and guide them, but when they grow we also have much to learn from them. A hard journey to travel.

Breaking the Chains:
On Being a Secular
Jewish Mother

Julia Bard

I turned up at the rabbinical court, to receive my religious divorce, wearing jeans. My father was very cross, but I told him that it was because I was there under duress. Despite his own traditional background (and mine), he understood why I was protesting. Jewish law states that, without a religious divorce, or *get*, any children you have subsequently will be considered the offspring of an adulteress. This is the only definition of a bastard (*mamzer*) in Jewish law. But while bastards have lost their stigma in the secular world, in the mainstream of our community they are outcasts. They are not accepted as real Jews and, crucially, may only marry other bastards — or converts! Not only that, according to the rabbis, "The stigma of *mamzerut* lasts forever. All the descendants of a *mamzer*, male or female, carry the *mamzer* stigma until the end of time."

If my divorce did not have the rabbis' blessing, so to speak, any subsequent relationships would be adulterous according to strict Jewish law, therefore any children of those relationships would be bastards or *mamzerim*. All of which sounded to me then, and still sounds now, like superstition designed to confine and control women's sexuality. Nevertheless, I was caught up in it. I didn't have children then, but I had to make a decision as a potential Jewish mother.

Even though I thought the law was both iniquitous and nonsense, could I decide that any children and grandchildren I might have would be driven out of Jewish life "until the end of time"? I couldn't, so I went to the Beth Din (rabbinical court) so the rabbis could rubber-stamp my first husband's permission for the marriage to end. The jeans were my token two fingers to the power of the religious authorities over women and children.

Six years later I married a Jewish man. Like me, he was an atheist, a secularist and a socialist (personal convictions, unlike arcane details of your mother's divorce, do not affect your status as a Jew). When I was expecting my twin sons, I did a course in modern Jewish history. Although I knew my biblical history from years of attending Hebrew classes as a child (as well as from my Church of England primary school — things were different then), and was well informed about the Holocaust and the Zionist interpretation of history from my years in a socialist Zionist youth movement, this gave me a totally new perspective on the centuries between the destruction of the Second Temple and the establishment of the state of Israel.

From the Golden Age in Spain and the medieval Jewish communities of Europe to the Enlightenment, this was an exciting opportunity to explore how varied and vibrant Jewish life across the world had been. When the course finished, I started to read more about Jews I'd known very little about, from the flourishing communities of Arabic and Indian Jews to the isolated community in Ethiopia. Having always been taught that the exile of the Jewish people from Judea in AD70/70CE was an unmitigated tragedy that had led to nothing but persecution, discrimination and, finally, genocide, I was learning that, while there had, of course, been periods when the Jews had suffered, our culture had developed over the centuries in such a way that to be a minority was natural for us. We had strong relationships with the surrounding societies without being assimilated into them. We had our own languages, customs, food and traditions, but wherever we lived we incorporated large elements of the surrounding culture and language into our own; we were creative, adaptable and diverse.

278

Most significantly, I started to realise that there were conflict, dissent, and diverse perspectives *within* each group of Jews. Though the religious authorities claimed that Jews had survived because we were united by a single set of beliefs and stuck rigidly to its rules, in fact Jews had survived by being adaptable. The power of the rabbis was, and continues to be, challenged, both overtly and by people simply walking away from their influence. The borders of our community have never been hermetically sealed, and its leaders have always adapted their injunctions to local conditions. Adulteresses are no longer stoned to death and, I now knew, even the rabbinical courts had, and continued to, turn a blind eye to the inhumane laws of *mamzerut*.

I was beginning to see how I might be able to bring children up with a sense and knowledge of Jewishness that was not in conflict with my commitment to human rights, equality and progressive politics.

Our twin sons were born the following year and, despite being enveloped in a fog of exhaustion, we were very happy. Having children threw up unexpected feelings and ideas. Their birth had been difficult — traumatic, even — and in a different era, one or both of the babies could easily have died. Their vulnerability and absolute dependence not only made me think about how generations of women had cared for and protected their children, but also brought the question of Jewish continuity to the surface of my mind. I wasn't obsessed, but when they were tiny I realised why some societies see twins as a blessing while others see them as a curse. If we'd been in danger, as so many Jews had been only one generation before, it would have been impossible for me to pick them up and run away.

I was also amazed by how different they were from each other, right from the moment they were born. Their personalities were so strong: they looked different and sounded different; they felt different when I picked them up; they responded differently to being hungry and to

279

being fed, to being tired and to waking up. They might not have been able to walk or talk, but these were fully fledged individuals, and my partner and I were committed to nurturing that individuality.

Our families assumed that Jacob and Reuben would be circumcised. For us this was far from an assumption. It was a difficult dilemma. Without going through all the arguments, as we did at the time and have done many times since, we could not justify to ourselves deliberately injuring a healthy, contented baby unless there was some overwhelming benefit to be derived from it.

Just as it had done with my divorce, the weight of family and community bore down on us. There *was* an overwhelming benefit, they said: "Without circumcision they can't have a bar mitzvah or get married in a synagogue." This, we discovered later, was not true. Unlike the stigma of *mamzerut*, possession of a foreskin does not exclude males from being part of the Jewish people. We were told "It's healthier for boys to be circumcised." When we looked later, we found no medical evidence for this claim. "It's a perfectly safe procedure," we were assured. Here there *was* plenty of evidence — of postoperative infection and accidental damage.

We were worn down by the pressure that preyed on our heightened emotions. For me, the most difficult thing to withstand was the burden of "three thousand years of unbroken tradition". Like a chain letter, you know it's a sham and that you shouldn't collude by participating in it, but when you're tired, fragile and emotionally vulnerable, as I was in the first few days of my children's life, you often don't have the nerve to take a chance on bringing bad luck.

I was excluded from the room where the "ceremony" in which the men "welcomed" my sons into the community was carried out, but my partner describes how powerless and horrified he felt by the procedure. When he emerged from the room he said, "We shouldn't have done it. It's like witchcraft." When the babies were handed back to me, screaming, blue in the face, and with a drop of wine on their lips, I knew I'd betrayed them. I vowed then that I would never lie to Jacob and Reuben as I had been lied to. Neither would I ever again compromise my children's right to be protected from violence and coercion, and to grow up free to work out and live by their own values.

I wrote about these experiences in *Jewish Socialist* magazine and participated in several meetings and television discussions about circumcision. There was an immediate response from mothers faced with the same decision. Even now, eighteen years later, I occasionally receive a phone call from a woman whose pregnancy is being overshadowed by the dilemma. There are no easy answers. Each family is different and not everyone shares my analysis and way of identifying with the Jewish community. I'm sure that if I had been faced with the situation again, I would have made a different decision. The important thing is that it should be a *decision*, not blind obedience to an injunction. My responsibility as a mother should have been to make an *informed* choice on behalf of my babies, not to cave in to propaganda.

Later on we discussed these events with them and they couldn't work out why we had agreed to let them be circumcised. "You don't smack us," they said. "You've always argued against violence against children, so how could you agree to it?" In a way, being forced to confront those questions has strengthened our commitment to bring them up without trying to force them into the mould of respectability and religious conformity that I see when I look back at my childhood in the 1950s and 60s.

Of course, they haven't grown up in a vacuum. They have confronted the same constraints and conflicts that face everyone else, along with the additional pressures and rewards that come with belonging to a minority. Being a Jewish mother, for me, as a campaigner — a secularist, a socialist and a feminist — has meant working out with the children ways of inhabiting the territory where Jewish and non-Jewish life overlap; of forging significant and organic relationships not only with other Jews but with the whole range of people they work and play amongst in their everyday lives. This is a contrast to the traditional/Orthodox-ish background I came from, where the boundaries between Jewish and non-Jewish life were rigorously policed in case, God forbid, we should want to "marry out".

When it was time for the boys to move from primary to secondary school, we lived close to the Jewish Free School (at that time still located in the inner city) and many people, both Jewish and non-Jewish, assumed they would go there. But neither we nor our sons thought it was right for Jewish (or any other) children to be segregated. A critical part of their education, we believe, has been for them to grow up in and of the local community, on equal terms with everyone else.

I was also a member of Women Against Fundamentalism, a group of women from many different backgrounds — Jewish, Christian, Hindu, Muslim and more — who were challenging male religious domination of their own communities and were campaigning against the religious takeover of community schools. I am as opposed to Catholic or Muslim schools as I am to Jewish schools and don't think the educational needs, rights and freedoms of young people are best served (or served at all) by religious agendas.

I was glad that my sons did not want to be in a school where they were privileged either as boys or as Jews. Jacob and Reuben went to the mixed comprehensive nearby, which, like most inner-city schools, ignored the legal obligation to perform a daily act of worship of a mainly Christian character. There are some Jewish children in the school, but a significant proportion of them have been marginalised in some way by the mainstream Jewish community, some because they have a non-Jewish parent, others because their families are politically dissident. It's a pity, socially and politically, that our local school is missing so much of this element of the local population, and a pity, too, that so many Jewish children are segregated from their non-Jewish peers.

However, as a Jewish mother, I was less subject to the pressures to conform to the expectations of mainstream Jewish life than were the mothers of students at the Jewish school. I was not a member of a synagogue, for instance, and nor were my children or partner. We discussed the implications of this together.

We talked at length to the boys about whether they wanted to have a bar mitzvah — the ceremony that marks the transition from childhood to adulthood for Jewish boys at the age of thirteen — and, if so, what that would entail including study, preparation and attendance at synagogue. When I was thirteen — in the days before bat mitzvah (the girls' version of the bar mitzvah) was de rigueur — the thought of standing up and performing in front a congregation was so appalling to me that I was thankful not to be a boy. So I was somewhat astonished when they both said that they did want a bar mitzvah. They were prepared to study, but it was to be a secular ceremony. They definitely did not want to join a synagogue. They were already knowledgeable about Jewish history and particularly about progressive Jewish traditions, and both felt very positive and assertive about their Jewish identity. Our involvement in the Jewish Socialists' Group (JSG) meant they had had a communal context — adults and children — in which to develop their perspective, and support when they broke the conventions. Other women in the JSG had also been hugely supportive to me over the circumcision issue.

Their bar mitzvah included music, and readings in Yiddish, Hebrew and English, reflecting the traditions into which they had been born. They chose the content from a wide range of material. There was Hebrew poetry from the Golden Age in Spain, prose by the "non-Jewish Jew" Isaac Deutscher, Yiddish songs of the nineteenth century and the immigrant experience. Thirteen close friends and relatives gave them a wish for each year of their lives, and the whole event was officiated by a dear friend, the author Michael Rosen.

Looking back at the speech I made, I found this:

> Of course, there are plenty of people who will try and tell you what's best, from your parents and grandparents to Tony Blair and Rupert Murdoch. Believe me, I know how tempting it can be to tell Jacob and Reuben what *I* think they should do, what *I* think they should say, what *I* think they should think. Growing up in a minority culture where guilt is woven through the fabric of family life, it often takes superhuman strength *not* to pull out all the emotional weapons a Jewish mother has at her disposal. But when I fail to convince them by rational argument and I do resort to emotional blackmail, they resist it; they argue back and refuse to conform. And they're right, because they understand that people only use those tactics when they can't justify what they're demanding.

Now they are eighteen and about to leave home. Life will pose all kinds of challenges for them, and they will have difficult judgments to make. They are confident and assertive about their Jewish identity and understand a lot about the complex issues it throws up for them. There will be those who try to convince them that they should "return to the fold" and find safety within the firm boundaries of Orthodoxy. There will be others who are hostile to anything Jewish. And there will be all kinds of possibilities in between.

I know that I have come in for criticism — from relatives distant and close, and from other members of the Jewish community — for the stances I have taken. A proper Jewish mother is supposed to use her unique position of influence to teach her children the ancient traditions, to "protect" them from the temptations of the gentile world and to hold in her power responsibility for the continuity of the Jewish people. I see it differently. I hope I have given my children the freedom and emotional resources to make their own choices about how they identify themselves and whom they relate to. Chairman Mao (of whom

I'm not usually a fan) said in a speech to young people: "The world is yours as well as ours, but in the last analysis it's yours."

My hope for my sons is that they will face their world with integrity, be true to themselves and continue to promote the rights of others, even when that seems to be more difficult than falling in with the expectations of the people around them.

The Lunch

A short story by
Anne Sebba

"I'm writing a story about my experience of being a Jewish mother," I told the Palestinian writer friend I was having lunch with.

"But why you? You're not *really* Jewish," she said. She seemed genuinely puzzled. Silence.

We had only just started studying the menu, and she forgot about her corner of bread now left soaking in the dish of fancy olive oil. Of course, she knew I was Jewish. Really Jewish. But I don't live in Golders Green, don't go to synagogue more than three times a year and don't always support Israel. Okay, I don't look Jewish, either, which other people often find disturbing. Since they can't categorise me, they seem to think I'm somehow being deliberately evasive. What I am, though, is totally absorbed in my children's lives. That makes me a fairly Jewish mother. Come to think of it, my friend is fairly absorbed in hers, too.

Nonetheless, how extraordinary that this remark should burst onto the surface so spontaneously, when I had always assumed that one of the reasons we both enjoyed meeting from time to time to discuss work in progress (or, more usually, work we wished was in progress) was the gentle arguments we had about the Israeli-Palestinian conflict. I presumed that my Jewishness was an intrinsic part of this banter, so she could tell her friends genuinely that "some of my best friends…" We swapped cuttings, contacts and prejudices.

And me? I was always stimulated to hear a fact-filled contrary view, argued with enormous emotional intensity, instead of the ones filtered through my usual social gatherings. Dinner parties these days, now that our children were in their twenties, often ended with a discussion of whether or not we dared tell them that if they "married out" we would mind, even though we prided ourselves on having as many non-Jewish as Jewish friends. We boasted about how we had come such a long way from our parents, who threatened dire consequences such as sitting *shiva* or having nothing further to do with us if we "married out". What on earth did this mean? Out from what?

On Friday nights we often invited non-Jewish friends along with the Jewish ones — see how homogenised we were — and, while I was happy to give public thanks for the bread, the wine and the light, and private thanks for my wonderful children, I cringed at hearing about God choosing us above all other people. Why did we continue to think we were the in crowd and everyone else was out?

"I'm not the only one they've asked," I explained. "The idea is to collect as wide a variety as possible of Jewish women's experiences of being a mother."

Again, she just couldn't get it. "But your experience of being a mother is probably exactly the same as mine. We both live in the same town, buy our food from the same supermarket. I've even seen you in the same doctor's waiting room. Come off it, our children even went to the same school, and we both complained about the same lousy English teacher. Don't tell me you encountered anti-Semitism at Southwood."

By the time she had finished we were engaged on the starter. I have never before welcomed a plate of *insalata tricolore* so gratefully. It gave me time to ponder.

No, of course I hadn't. The teachers had bent over backward to let Sarah make Hanukkah cards while the other children made Christmas cards. I laughed at the memory. At the time I'd been cross that they had singled her out, drawn attention to her. Couldn't they just have let her do what the others were doing? But Sarah had been to Israel in her gap year; an attempt by her Jewish parents to make her understand her roots, or an attempt to help her find a nice Jewish boyfriend? Anyway, it was too early to tell if that particular experiment had worked. My friend's daughter had been to India, she told me. No search for roots here. No need to seek cultural identity, just an interesting trip, meeting new people and making new discoveries. I remembered how relaxed about it my friend had been before departure, and how terrified I had been about the dangers my daughter would be facing.

The rise of anti-Semitism was another regular dinner-party topic, linked to the fear of marrying out. "You might think the man she's marrying is wonderful and tolerant and that they have so much in common. But when it comes to arguments over Israel, he won't support her there, you'll see," was pretty much the usual line.

My friend's daughter had just moved into a flat with a new boyfriend. It seemed ridiculous to ask what religion he was. He was English, and he worked for a small independent film production company. "He's lovely," she told me. "We hope they'll get married eventually." She was utterly at ease with the relationship. Again, how envious I was. I wondered what right being a mother gave me to care about the religion of my children's friends or lovers. Weren't mothers meant to worry about whether their children would be made happy? It was not evident to me that religion was what did the trick.

I saw the justification of Israel, historically and emotionally, in terms of the Holocaust. If this tragedy was never to happen again, then Jews must have a national homeland. But my Palestinian friend had often told me I was being naive. That was what Jews said in the postwar world, but Israel had been created as a pragmatic solution to what had been going on long before the Holocaust, as European statesmen carved up the region in the nineteenth century for geopolitical reasons when the Ottoman Empire fell apart. Zionism had been hard at work long before Hitler, she insisted, and its raison d'être was economic and political reality, not social concern for elderly east European Jews. And anyway, the proportion of Jews in Israel who had come because of the Holocaust was tiny these days. "It's filled with right-wing American zealots and Russian criminals, who have only a tenuous connection to Judaism. Did you know that one in four Israeli soldiers is Russian? That's why the kibbutzim are dying out. Why should the Palestinians give up their homeland for these people? You know, our children have a right to a homeland, too," she said.

Yes, I said, but...

"But the real iniquity is that you'd have more right to go there" — she could not say the word Israel, almost choking on the one occasion I had heard her try to utter the name — "than me. Yet for generations my family, right up until my father's time, had a house, and some land, in Safed."

This time I was saved by the fettucine. We turned our discussion briefly to the ubiquity of Italian — or what passed for Italian — food. This after all was meant to be a Lebanese restaurant, but it had become Lebanese-Italian. "You should eat in a proper Arab restaurant, in Jericho or Cairo or Beirut," she told me. "The food is wonderful and spicy, not this European mishmash of tastes." I knew what she meant, as she was a wonderful cook and had once treated us in their home to Middle Eastern dishes that only someone who grew up knowing how tahina and tabbouleh were meant to taste could possibly re-create.

Gently, she brought the conversation back to the Middle East. She told me about her favourite Arab restaurant in Jerusalem, where she had been as a child when her grandmother was still alive. I already knew about her father, who had come to England to study at London University in the late 1930s and, caught by the war, had stayed. But by then he'd fallen in love with an English girl he'd met at university, married her, and after the war, found work as a journalist on a specialist Middle East paper. His wife became a teacher and, once they had children, the family did not want to live anywhere else, even if they had been able to go back. But my friend's grandmother, a widow by this time, had stayed on in Palestine — as her family never stopped calling it — alone, when the rest of her family had fled, living in a small flat with some distant cousins when she became infirm. My friend had not seen her grand-mother in her final years, since her father refused to visit after 1967. We had, at previous lunches, already travelled down the bumpy road of who started and who responded in that fateful year, and the right to a nation's self-defence, let alone existence. But all those discussions seemed a long time ago in the present mood of suicide bomb-induced crisis.

Finally we got onto the subject of other work in progress. She told me she had just been to Gaza to write a story about the appalling lack of medical facilities, supplies and personnel there and how the Red Crescent was only just managing. It was a sort of hell, she said. She was, I thought, about to say that therefore she could understand why the suicide bombers did as they did, since one hell was pretty much like another. But she didn't. She was just as opposed to violence as I was and instead felt a terrible sadness. As I did.

I told her about some articles I was writing, which I suddenly felt were weak and pointless, about good people, full of optimism, trying out various low-level initiatives for peace and dialogue — but where would any of these lead? There was even a story I had wanted to write for International Midwives Day about an initiative started by Israeli and Diaspora Jewish midwives to link hands metaphorically and start a movement for peace with their Palestinian counterparts. The slogan was "Every baby has a right to be born in peace." Privately, many of the Arab midwives welcomed the idea, but publicly none of them would commit for fear they would be branded as traitors.

I was just telling her about this failure when the waiter brought the bill. As usual, we fought politely over it, pretending it was so long since we had last met we couldn't remember whose turn it was. We hadn't exactly had a row; all our lunches had some sort of heated, usually political, exchange — more like a tennis match than a Paxman savaging — but this one was different because it had become so personal. I felt she thought she had hurt me; more seriously, she thought I had failed to understand her. She was both proud — Arabs had once had a noble culture when they had been explorers, mathematicians and poets — and also felt the pain of victimhood with a sense that Jews did not equate her sense of displacement with their own. Because so many Palestinians today were uneducated and turned to violence, many people forgot their centuries-old achievements. She often reminded me of them.

"When you write your story about being a Jewish mother, will you discuss your guilt — your famous Jewish guilt — about how Jews have made innocent Palestinian babies suffer because they are held up at roadblocks when they need emergency aid, denied access to decent hospitals let alone enough food to help pregnant mothers, or adequate jobs for their fathers so that they can raise their children? Will you write about what it feels like to live under a curfew or to see your children despair of having enough water to drink when the Jewish family next door has so much it can luxuriate in a swimming pool? Or will you only write about being a Jewish mother in the comfortable UK and fretting about your children doing well in exams and getting a good job? Palestinian mothers have to worry about how to prevent their children becoming martyrs."

Clearly, she didn't expect an answer to all this. She was in full flow now, describing the appalling diet and lack of medical equipment that made the very act of becoming a mother in the occupied territories highly dangerous. It was not difficult for me, though, to think of Jewish mothers fleeing in other times, not so long ago, giving birth at roadblocks in occupied Europe. Surely we could all stretch our imaginations a little?

At the very least, I wanted to stretch out and touch her hand perhaps, but she would have considered that a patronising gesture, all I could resort to since moral right was so clearly on her side. Instead, I told her I'd send her a copy, for her suggestions, if I ever wrote the story. I left the restaurant knowing I never could.

I don't meet my Palestinian writer friend for lunch any more. She moved away. I miss all those missed opportunities to understand another displaced culture so close to our own. I read in *The Times* last month that one of the latest child suicide bombers was called Sami. Like my friend's son. Only the surname was different. But the chill down my spine came from contemplating what might have been. There is a Sami in lots of families I know.

On Not Having
Children

Crowning Elizabeth

A short story by
Sidura Ludwig

Becky was rushing, which is why when the phone rang she dropped her keys and left the front door open, and anyone who was walking past her mother's home in the North End of Winnipeg at that moment would have witnessed her receiving her news. When she picked up the phone she was thinking about how she needed to get to her sister's so that she could listen to the coronation of the new English queen, and how moments in history always happened on time and if you missed them, then you missed out, and it was as if you didn't exist right then. While she tried to reach her keys, lying on the hall floor, she held the phone receiver on her shoulder and thought how heavy it was and how silly that the cord wasn't long enough to reach almost anything. And then her doctor's voice made her stop on her hands and knees, on the floor.

"When you came in for your checkup last week, we did a test," he said. "You're going to have a baby in seven months. You need to come and see me."

She sat up against the wall. She found her hand on her stomach, over her white blouse with the blue embroidery. A baby. In there.

"Becky," the doctor said. He had known her a long time. From the time she was a girl and her mother brought her to see him because Becky was slow. He said then that there was nothing wrong with her. And Becky thought it was funny that he said it again now. "You're a big girl, Becky," he said. "There's nothing wrong with you."

Becky held the phone for a long time after he hung up. Long enough to forget about the keys on the floor and, for the moment, about her sister Goldie, who didn't care

295

anything about the new queen but was waiting for Becky to come look after the baby, Beth, so that she could do the shopping.

A baby.

Becky did love babies. Her niece's ears were her most favourite thing in the world. She loved the way they folded in at the top and how her lobes were so soft they looked like rose petals. When she baby-sat Beth, she would spend what felt like hours examining her face, her toes, her fingers, and imagining what she would look like in ten years' time. Or thirty. Becky's greatest joy was making Beth laugh. Throwing her up in the air and catching her as she fell back into her arms.

She felt her stomach flutter as if she herself were flying, and she wondered if perhaps her baby was practising.

When Becky was a little girl, she had had a skin condition on her scalp. Her head was itchy a lot and she lost patches of hair. Sometimes she would wake up and handfuls would be left on her pillow. The doctor told her mother to cut her hair short.

And so she did — in the kitchen, where it was easy to sweep the floor. She sat Becky on a chair away from the table. The chair had one leg shorter than the other and as her mother cut her hair, and it fell like piles of feathers to the floor, the chair rocked to one side. Becky worried she would be lopsided.

"Mummah," she said in a whisper, more like thinking than saying it, "isn't that enough?"

Her Yiddish mother, with thick, fleshy arms, the skin and fat hanging down off the bone, brushing the side of Becky's face. She cut and cut and Becky thought she hadn't heard her, until her mother said, "You can't be with disease."

And so she kept cutting, and Becky cried just a little because she never realised how much hair she'd had.

After her mother cut it short, it never grew back properly. At school they teased her and called her stupid, and they wouldn't touch her in case all of their hair fell out as well. The girls told her she would never get married because men only liked women with long hair. The boys tried to look up her dress to see if she wore girls' or boys' underpants. Becky took to sitting on the school steps during recess, by the monitoring teacher, with her dress wrapped tightly around her legs and her knees held firmly together. No one bugged her when she sat there. In fact, after a while, they failed to notice her at all, she had folded herself up so well.

She stopped volunteering to read out loud in class because whenever attention was on her, she could feel the kids laughing. She hated her hair so much that she imagined it away. She was so good at imagining things that she actually believed she had thick, golden hair in long braids beside her ears.

It was around this time that she began to collect newspaper articles about the princesses, Elizabeth and Margaret. She kept them in a shoe box under her bed, in her room, and at night she wrote long letters to the girls, offering to become a lady-in-waiting and look after their every need. She imagined that one day she would be summoned by the royal court to take her place amongst the royal family. She imagined a royal subject calling her out of class because her presence was urgently needed in London. She imagined her family's pride when they realised what an important role their daughter was meant to take. And how her mother would cry when she left, and how she would brag to all of her friends about Becky's special relationship with the princess, surely one of the only Jewish girls that close to the royals. Her classmates would stare in envy as she left the school, and Becky thought of each of them ashamed of how they had treated her, and running after her to apologise once they realised her importance. Her imagination really helped when the kids bugged her, because then she just pretended they were laughing at someone else.

* * *

On her walk to Goldie's (only five minutes along Main Street) Becky didn't think of Union Jacks, fur capes or royal jewels, but instead of baby clothes and knitting sweaters and bootees. She had made five pairs for Beth, who had already grown out of them. Becky was very good at knitting and sewing (she worked part-time at a clothing factory), and she was always working on frilly dresses for Beth, with lacy sashes and yellow polka-dot patterns.

She tried to concentrate hard; she even stopped walking and leaned against a tree to see if she could feel the baby's sex. She had decided that she wanted a girl because she just wouldn't know what to do with a boy. Besides, a boy needed a father.

* * *

"Did you get lost?" Goldie asked her, not without sarcasm, when she arrived.

Becky unbuttoned her spring jacket and, humming, went to look for Beth.

"No, I'm fine," she said. Fine. She wanted to laugh out loud! She was so much more than fine, but somehow there was even more joy in keeping it a secret. At least for a little while. Instead, she said to Goldie, "It's lovely out."

Beth was in her playpen in the front room of the apartment. She cooed when Becky picked her up and threw her in the air.

"You've missed half the coronation," Goldie said. "You could have been here on time if it was so important to you."

Beth laughed as she fell into Becky's arms. Becky threw her up again.

"Becky," Goldie said, "please don't. She just ate. It will upset her stomach."

When I have my own baby, Becky thought, *no one will tell me how to look after it.*

"I'll be back soon," Goldie said, putting on her coat, reaching for her white summer purse, always by the door.

"That is, I'll have to be, now that you've made me late."

But Becky didn't hear her. She held Beth close to her chest and ran her fingers through the baby's downy, honey hair. From the radio, the journalist reported that the new Queen Elizabeth sat on her throne, her long, velvety cape trailing on the floor around her, her ladies-in-waiting standing with their arms straight by their sides, and their white gloves well past their elbows. Becky hardly listened.

"Have a good time!" she called, and she made Beth's hand wave as they watched Goldie walking down the block to the bus stop. Then, as soon as she was out of sight, Becky threw Beth up into the air again. She wasn't sick — she just laughed and laughed and laughed.

* * *

When she put Beth down for her nap, Becky made some promises to the baby growing inside her.

I will always tell you how beautiful you are.

I will always tell you how smart you are.

I will never take you to the doctor just because you are quiet.

And she decided she would call her daughter Elizabeth Rose, because of the new queen, and because as her stomach fluttered again she felt as if a red flower was growing from her belly up throughout the rest of her body.

These kinds of things — the baby's name, her beautiful hair, promises — were all things Becky could think about easily. What she didn't think about, what she wouldn't let herself, what she imagined had happened to someone else, was her baby's father and how he came to be that way. Becky didn't think about how he had called her "beautiful" and "princess" and how that had made her stomach melt. She didn't think about the back seat of his car, or his hands on her wrists, or her thighs, or the stickiness between her legs after it was all done, like warm syrup. She didn't think about how he had wiped his brow and his upper lip with his handkerchief, and how he hadn't offered it to her. And she certainly didn't think about how she had taken a bath that night, washing away his little stains, and then cried as the water went down the drain. It's not even that she imagined those details away, it's that sitting in Goldie's living room, watching Beth sleep in her playpen, Becky did not even remember those things happening to her.

That night Becky had dinner with her family — with Goldie, Saul and Beth, with her younger sister Sarah, who was only ten, and with her mother. They all sat in her mother's dining room and they all spoke at once, which made the table seem even smaller than it was. Becky was usually quiet; in fact, the family expected her to be. She thought, as she took sips of her chicken soup, as the schmaltz coated her lips, that the family would all fall silent if she said anything right there and then. Her voice was so unaccustomed to being heard with all of theirs, it would be like a stubborn French horn interrupting a beautifully tuned orchestra.

She finished her soup and sucked on the chicken foot she'd served herself. None of the other family members liked chicken feet, but Becky always ended her bowl of soup by sucking on a bone from the foot, rolling it in her mouth with her tongue. As she did this, she imagined telling everyone her news. She played over the scene in her head — Becky helping Goldie serve the roasted chicken, smelling of garlic and paprika, how she would bring the platter to the table and say, *I just want you all to know that I'm going to have a baby*. She would say it just like that, like she had decided to change jobs (well, hadn't she?). And she imagined them all silent as the news hung above them, and then the burst of voices, laughter, screams, hugs and of course tears, because which one of them ever thought Becky would be a mother. The part that made Becky want to cry was the image of her mother, those fleshy arms wrapped tight around her, her mother's thick Russian voice telling her how lucky this baby would be.

* * *

Becky went to the doctor the next week. She went on her lunch break, none of the other women letting on that they suspected anything. Why would they? Becky had never had a boyfriend, and behind her back, they all said what a shame it was that she probably wouldn't ever have one — she being so simple and all. The one who worked closest to her, Edna, said that at least Becky had a trade; she was so good with her hands and the clothes she made really were beautiful. Very well put together. Yes, they agreed, at least she had that. A woman needed something like that in her life if she wasn't going to have a family.

To the other women they said things like:

"Shirley, enough's enough. When are you going to get yourself a man?"

"Karen, you can't go on like this. You're not getting any younger."

They said these things across Becky's lap, to the single women who sat beside her at their own machines. They said them as though they didn't notice that Becky sat there without a ring on her finger, or a watch from Simpson's, obviously given to her by someone special. When they spoke to Becky, they asked how her mother was, or they told her that the shirt she had just finished was really beautiful. They said that they wished they could sew like she could.

All the way to the doctor's, she imagined telling her boss that she wouldn't be able to work any more, that she had a baby to take care of now. No, she thought. That's not what would happen. Instead, she imagined him coming into the factory and announcing to the women in her unit that Becky wouldn't be working there any more.

Our Becky's going to be a mother, he would say, with his arm around her. The women would squeal. Even as she walked, Becky could feel his arm tightening around her shoulder. As if to say, *It's all right. I'll look after you. This is just the way things are.*

301

Dr Berman's office had small windows, and Becky always felt as if the sun was fighting to get through. She had been seeing him since she was small, since she had that skin problem. It occurred to her that she probably shouldn't like Dr Berman — he was the one who had told her mother to cut off all her hair. But he was also the one who gave Becky a book to read when her mother wondered if she had become dumb, and after she read a whole page without mistakes, he took the book out of her hand and said, "Mrs Rosen, I think you have a perfectly normal, delightful daughter."

(That day, on the bus home from the doctor's, Becky's mother had said to her, "You know, other children speak. I don't feed you enough? You have to swallow your own words?" Becky hadn't responded. She had looked out the window, which was steaming up from the rain outside and the heat inside. She had, though, put her hand on top of her mother's, rubbing the flesh with her fingers, playing with it like dough.)

"Becky," the doctor said now, when she sat on his examining table. Dr Berman placed his hands on top of hers and took a breath. "How are you feeling, dear?"

He always had kind eyes — the kind of pale blue that babies have when they are born, before they change colour. His hands were warm and like a blanket over her own. She had begun to get nervous, and his touch helped her heart to slow down.

"I'm feeling fine," she told him. And then she remembered that he knew, and so she laughed out loud. "I feel terrific. I've never felt so good."

Dr Berman smiled with his eyes, but not his mouth. "Did you listen to the coronation?" he asked. He had her lay down on the table and he massaged his hands over her stomach.

"Oh. Yes. But I could hardly concentrate. I mean, it hardly feels important now."

302

"You used to want to be a princess," the doctor reminded her.

She didn't want to think about back then. "Now I want to be a mother," she said.

"You're excited about this, then," he said.

"I want to have a baby girl," she told him, and this made him laugh.

"That's not something we can choose, Becky."

Her heart started to race again. "I know. It's just what I want."

The doctor sat back down in his chair. He didn't open his chart, or put on his glasses. He sat forward with his elbows on his knees and his hands clasped together.

"What have you told your mother?"

Becky didn't answer him right away. She put her hand on her belly and tried to feel it swollen. She desperately wanted to feel a bump.

"Nothing. Yet."

"She may not have to know," he said. "Some girls go away until after the baby is born. I could help you with that."

She tried imagining her baby, wisps of hair held off her face with ribbon. The image was fading, and she closed her eyes to hold on to it.

"Becky?"

"If I have a baby girl, I want to name her Elizabeth Rose."

The doctor got up and stood beside her, resting slightly on the table. "How will you look after this baby, Becky?"

She opened her eyes and looked straight at him. "I know how to look after a baby."

He turned away and looked out the window. Becky followed his eyes and saw the way the sun made the late spring grass glow as if it were made of wax. He turned back to her.

"Who's the father, Becky?"

"There isn't one," she said. "I'm not married."

He didn't smile at that. Instead, Becky noticed, he sighed.

"I know, dear. But there has to be a father. I need to know who he is."

That's when the pictures of Elizabeth Rose faded away completely, and all Becky could think of were steamy car windows and hot breath, like fried onions. And the grunting, rhythmic in her ear.

"It's nobody nice," she said quietly, looking at her hands, trying to remember what it was like just to be a seamstress who made beautiful clothes for other people.

Dr Berman stopped asking her questions then. He told her that if she liked, he would call in her sister Goldie, who would help her make some decisions. He also said that there was a nice lady at social services whom Becky should see about options and what would happen to the baby once it was born. There are a lot of couples, he said, who would love to have a baby boy or girl. Isn't it nice that you will be able to help them out? Isn't it nice, he said, although Becky was only half listening, that something good can come out of all this?

The reason Becky was only half listening was because she had found her picture of Elizabeth Rose again. Sometime while the doctor was speaking, Elizabeth came back into her head, a perfect baby girl, with wiggly arms and legs, almost like a beetle on its back. Becky had this feeling, like she could feel the baby sleeping against her chest, her nose and mouth pressed into the space where Becky's neck and shoulders met. Her baby had a pudgy, wet mouth, and while she slept, she left a sweet kiss on Becky's skin. And then, in her head, when someone took the baby away from her, she could still feel the little wet mark for a long time after she was gone.

A Woman Unsown

Berta Freistadt

I am sixty-two years old, unmarried, no children, and often wonder what it would be like to have some fine young (ish) fruit of my loins phone me up for a chat, ask my advice, take me out for a meal. I also often wonder how I never got pregnant. Contraception was not easy in the 1960s — was I infertile or just lucky? I used to think that if I ever got pregnant I'd have the child, but then I also used to think that I protected my unborn children by not conceiving them in the first place.

When I first thought about the subject of this book, I really thought being Jewish had no bearing whatsoever on my decision not to have children. I thought it was entirely to do with my mother and the example of motherhood she'd given me. But then I was encouraged to think again, and of course things began to unravel in my mind and I began to see how very complicated my decision had been. Or rather, how complicated all those influences were, woven and compounded, that led me to what, at the time, was a confident certainty that I would never have children.

I am the only child of a mixed marriage between a British non-Jewish woman in her forties and a Jewish refugee from Czechoslovakia. When I was old enough to understand such things, I could see that it was a difficult marriage, that neither of them seemed very happy. It was a marriage of incompatibility. She had already been married twice before and survived the deaths of both those men. She was dynamic, assured, perhaps bossy, and had, as a young working-class woman, given up a scholarship in 1916 to help look after her father's sweet shop. She had survived the Depression in the 1930s by scrubbing floors and sweeping up in a hairdresser's. She had no time for self-pity, either in herself or others, and had finally married my nervous, gentle, depressed father. He had survived emigration in the late 1930s, leaving loved ones behind, only to suffer regular nightmares of what had or might have happened, and to endure the guilt that is the inheritance of all survivors. A favourite memory is of him is sitting by the radio in the corner of the room, eyes closed, listening to Mozart.

At the beginning, affection and sexual attraction must have been enough, but either something happened (and what that was, I can only conjecture), or things simply deteriorated. I can only surmise these things, for he never spoke to me of them. All I know of him came from my mother, and much later I learned how she embroidered truth and filled in gaps. Truth is what you remember, and I remember the dreadful rows. I remember her frustration and bitterness, and I remember his misery. It was catching.

"Put a smile on your face," she'd say to me. "You're just like your father."

My mother was a brilliant pianist, but as a woman of her particular class and time was unable to develop as she deserved. And so, frustrated that her musical talents were wasted, she focused her attention on me. Her single-minded, determined and entire attention. I would get away with nothing until I became something. Something big, something special, something that would please her. My mother never taught me to cook or, for that matter, how to flirt. I wasn't to be like everyone else — I was going to do something different. I don't think I ever quite managed it, but marriage was never on the cards, nor were children.

Now, of course, I'm not the only one to have had a diffi-cult time of growing up, and with such influences and examples you always have a choice — to go with it or to rebel. As I see it, to rebel would have meant finding a man and having hordes of children and making a happy marriage. But I went with it, with the example of unhappiness in marriage, with the expectation of otherness.

And I'm afraid there's something else. I was brought up ugly. When I was about twelve she once said to me, "Well, of course, when you're forty you won't have anything to worry about — you've no looks to lose."

So there in my head forever after was the idea of my ugliness, and ugly people don't marry, do they?

I realise now that my father had married an anti-Semite. Not a paid-up Hitler-was-right type — on the contrary, she would often tell stories showing her delight at discomfiting real anti-Semites. She was, like many of that period (has anything really changed?), just an ordinary, everyday, Jews-are-good-with-money-and-have-big-noses anti-Semite. Now, in my sixties, I look at photos of myself in my twenties and I see how lovely I was. Shining brown hair, gorgeous figure, a lovely smile, a cute Jewish nose. If we had mixed in Jewish circles I'm sure I'd have been snapped up, despite my dubious status. So then I must ask, why didn't we move in those circles? It must have been to protect me — if I wasn't Jewish, no one could persecute me. Or was it his socialist, anti-religious background? In Bratislava or Vienna you could be a Jew without a synagogue, you could have a community without a rabbi — and I suppose Jewish-looking daughters could be pretty and attractive and marriageable just by walking down the street. But in SW19 in 1952 I inhabited a very Christian, blond-perm, small-nosed world where nasty girls at school told me mine was too big and needed an operation, so I knew my mother was right.

Or was it the fault of the synagogue that we didn't belong? Perhaps mixed marriages were even more taboo then than they are now. In fact, I didn't even know that there was a synagogue in Wimbledon, where we lived. But I do have a treasured and magical memory of going hand-in-hand somewhere with my father when I was very young, and standing next to him behind a crowd of darkly silhouetted men who towered above me, and seeing beyond them something bright that glittered and shone like a sun in the distance. Twice he took me, that's all. The idea was that I could choose for myself. So I did. First I chose not to have children, and then, thirty years later, I chose to follow him to my own synagogue, where I stand next to him in services though he's dead now forty years.

I expect people are feeling sorry for me. Poor thing, you're thinking. No husband, no children, she must be lonely. But how could I be lonely, with the dozens of children in my life? My cousin's grandchildren Keneret and Shafir, my young cousins Delisa and Benny, friends' children, the children from over the road who knock on my door nearly every day and even give me presents on Mother's Day. And then of course there's the child I co-parented in my forties, now with children of her own.

Perhaps this arrangement deserves some explanation. In the 1980s one of my friends was a busy working single woman (BWSW) with an eight-year-old daughter and four very close (child-free) friends. One of those friends sadly had no womb, and the BWSW, partly motivated by the demands of being at the bottom of a new career ladder, offered her a way of sharing her daughter by spending time with the child. This arrangement was soon extended to the rest of us and became a way in which we could put some of our then radical-feminist ideals into practice — something we could do to share parenting a little, and a concrete way of helping our friend by giving her a break or the chance to work late. So once a week for about three years, when she was between the ages of eight and eleven, I would collect the girl from school, occupy her till supper-time, feed her and occupy her afterwards until her mother collected her. Sometimes it happened at my house, sometimes at her own. The group was also responsible for sending her to summer camp on a couple of occasions, for helping with decisions about secondary school and, on rare occasions, for discipline. Her mother did everything in her power not to interfere and to allow us to retain autonomy in this delicate arrangement. For a woman like myself, who was a fully paid-up member of the no-child brigade, it was a salutary, educating and enthralling experience.

The girl is now a woman with two children of her own. I don't often see her — though I wore my best hat to her wedding and was first in line with advice about ginger for morning sickness — but when I do we have instant, affectionate rapport, based I believe on those Wednesday-night dinners, the games and dancing, the secret jokes about her mother, arguments about manners and frequent cuddles as she struggled from childhood towards her teens. It's something I once did that I'm very proud of — but I was always pleased to give her back to her mother. The responsibility for anything more would have finished me.

But other than these real children (and I must say, noting how readily my own mother comes to my lips when I'm with them, I believe that choice not to have children was the right one), there are the substitute children I've cared for. I've been trying to calculate how many children I taught between 1968 and 1976. It must be four figures. And now adult students — teaching for seventeen years an average of three classes a week, and about ten students per class, that's over five hundred students. These are people I prepare for, look after, help, criticise, praise, listen to, laugh with, console, encourage, watch grow and develop, arrange parties for and finally send out into the world. Ring any bells? None of them has ever called me mother, though. Reverend mother, but never mother.

Then, dare I mention the cats? Not baby substitutes. I prefer to think of mine more as furry companions who don't argue (not much, anyway) and rarely need their bottoms cleaned. I have a simple contract with any who decide to live with me. I promise to feed, love, brush, play on demand whenever is reasonable, and not to make a fuss when there's something dead on the mat. They, in return, should be very, very nice to me most of the time, and meet me at the door when I come home. Is that a good deal, or what? Who needs children!

Cats in the wild have an adult persona. When they let us feed them and give them a lap they revert to kitten mode in many respects. One furry friend, the late lamented Dracula (if you'd seen his teeth you wouldn't ask), would produce the most heart-rending baby mew to bring me back to pet him five, six, seven times before he'd let me go.

But this is a secret. I'm a grown-up, I can't be seen to baby my cats, can I? Any more than I dare let it be known that I love my students. The established view of love and parenting is neither of those things. People with children, people with spouses have rules for dependency, love and what they claim is normality. I have neither one nor the other. Neither husband nor child.

In the 150th Anniversary edition of *Roget's Thesaurus,* the word "childless" comes associated with such gems as "disused", "unsown", "unmanured", "unharvested" and "impotent". As someone who is interested in if not to say nit-picky about language, I must say that "disused" rather than "unused" seems somewhat in conflict with the section's general feeling of sterile virginity. Nowhere do I find the term "child-free".

Mama and the Handbag

Rebecca Bender

Every few weeks the charities round here hand out plastic bags. You fill them up with unwanted things and put them out for collection on a prearranged day. I am by nature a saver of things, but I have been trying harder to get rid of my clutter and I have been slowly getting through piles of things I have not used or looked at for years. I figure somebody else might want them, I need the space, and it all goes to one good cause or another.

Several times now I have put in the brown leather Italian handbag that Mama brought back for me sometime in the 1960s on her one and only trip to Italy. Memory plays tricks with us, and the heavy significance of this handbag when it was given (and shunned by me) has now been lost in the decades. Was this the bag that Mama actually brought home for me (and why did I dislike it so much at the time)? Or is this the bag that I traded with my sister because we each wanted the bag that the other one had been bought? There is also a faint memory of the clasp having to be changed, but the one on this handbag looks as if it has always been there. Whose handbag is this? Where did it come from? Why has it crossed the Atlantic several times now, from my mother to me and from me to my mother? Why is it impossible for either one of us to keep it and use it or to let it go?

I put this ancient brown leather handbag determinedly into the PDSA bag and put the bag out in the street. There, I think. That is it. I do not have to keep this. I never use it. It is not to my taste. It is the wrong size for me. It is too small. When I fill it with my things, the sides gape and things spill out. It is not safe. It cannot contain everything I need to put into it.

But I cannot let it go. Mama dragged it all the way home from Italy for me. For years she tried to make me take it. For years I refused. When she moved from New York to Florida last year and had to throw out most of the things she had collected over her lifetime, all of which were precious to her, she asked me if I wanted her to send it to me. I said no, and the question kept getting repeated. Each time I said, "No, give it away, leave it behind," but she was unable to do this. So the handbag went down to Florida with her, along with a vast collection of unworn shoes that would have made Imelda Marcos envious, old towels, hundreds of unused handbags, scarves, belts, blouses (all bought on sale). It was one of the many things she found impossible to let go of. Despite everything I had said about not wanting it, despite maintaining this position for almost forty years, she still thought that I might want it.

I visited recently and found my eighty-four-year-old mother in her new, much smaller, home surrounded by the things she could not part with, and I could not refuse her. I took the handbag with as much good grace as I could muster and brought it back to England, where I could dispose of it as I saw fit. But it rankled. I schlepped this ancient and battered bag grudgingly across the Atlantic yet again, alternating between brief moments of feeling like a good girl and more frequent moments of irritation. I had given in, yet again, to this insatiable, demanding woman, this woman who never, ever listened to me or respected any decision I made. But once I got to England, it would be okay. England is my place, it is where I live, and I am in charge of my life here. I felt angry with her, but also moved by her plight as she sat surrounded by all the things she would never use, lost in her world of discounts and unmet desires. I will be generous, I thought, and I will take it back with me and then when I am back home I will give it away to a charity.

Except that I cannot. I cannot let go of this handbag. I cannot use it, but I cannot let it go. And this time it is not

Mama who is not listening to me. This time it is not Mama who is stopping me from giving it away.

* * *

When my grandmother, aged fourteen, left her home in Belarus, first to go to England and then to the United States, she had nothing with her but the clothes she wore and a picture of her mother. I have this picture. It is another thing that I brought back with me from my last trip to the States. It has a hole burnt in it, and on the back there are some words in a strange language. Written over it, in my mother's handwriting, are the words "Mama's Mama". This old peasant woman stares at me across the generations, though it occurs to me that she was probably younger than I am now when this picture was taken. She looks sad and old and tired but, somehow, expectant. "So, tell me, big shot," she says, looking straight into my eyes, "how many babies did you have?"

And I am ashamed. Because I have not had any babies. I am a Jewish woman without babies. Great-Grandma had nothing and Grandma had nothing and Mama had very little when she was a girl. I have a great deal, and not just in the way of material things. But I do not have babies. And I have failed to use or have thrown away some wonderful chances and opportunities in my life because I did not know how to use them.

I think of the frightened, courageous women who came before me, crossing continents with nothing but the clothes on their backs. What they gave to one another and to their ancestors were the children they bore, the children who carried the names and the bloodlines, the children who carried the hope, always the hope, of something better.

* * *

Sheepishly, I head out in my slippers, undo the plastic bag, and retrieve the handbag. It is quite a pretty thing, really.

And it is not unlike one that I might choose for myself now, though I have a vague memory of being furious with my mother thirty-five years ago for choosing something that demonstrated, yet again, that she had absolutely no understanding of me or who I was. Now I look at this handbag, this rather plain, inoffensive, understated handbag, and I wonder which of us had the more flawed understanding. I look at this handbag, which I can neither use nor turn away, and I begin to have a vague sense of why I have never been able to conceive a child of my own. I have a whole host of adored nieces and nephews and great-nieces and -nephews. I adore children and I spent many years working with them. But except for a brief period in my thirties when I got slightly broody, I have never really felt driven to have a child. I have felt only moderately and occasionally envious of friends and family with children but have also felt genuinely relieved that I have been able to live what most often feels like an interesting and varied and occasionally useful life. And besides... I did not think that I could be a very good mother, and I was not prepared to be a bad one.

But there has been considerable pain about being childless when it comes to my relationship with my mother. In the little *shtetl*-like neighbourhood in Brooklyn where I grew up, everyone was either a mother or would one day become one. It was unthinkable that one would not produce children. Only women too ugly to get a man might have this terrible fate befall them, and they were either tragic figures or figures of fun. A woman who did not have children, for whatever reason, was a very rare being and one to be pitied. A nice Jewish girl might one day be a teacher or a nurse or a secretary or even, if she was very very bright, a doctor (but better still she should marry a doctor and be a teacher, because teachers had school holidays off). But she would also be a mother. First and foremost, she would be a mother. You could not be a Jewish woman, a real Jewish woman, without children.

When my sister and I were growing up, it was clear that my mother both needed to be a mother and hated being one. She found us difficult and irritating and endlessly disappointing. She was also, simply, not good at it. Once she was able to return to work, she felt alive again, and all her gifts for getting on with people came to the fore. But she was wracked with guilt because she felt her identity was so connected with this thing of being a mother. It was unthinkable to be Jewish and a mother and not to really enjoy it. So she pretended masterfully. She behaved, externally, like the quintessential Jewish mother. There was not a woman in Flatbush who could "Oy vey" more consistently and effectively than my mother. From Ocean Avenue to Coney Island Avenue and all the way to Cookie's Diner on Avenue M, there was not another mother who could worry more vocally or ostentatiously than my mother. She worried and worried and worried because that was what she thought mothers were supposed to do. She waved her hands about and worried more. But she did not really like being a mother. She was never really easy with it or with what she really was and longed to be.

Without knowing it, my sister and I have managed, between us, to act out the unlived parts of my mother. My sister became a woman who loves being a mother and who is exceedingly good at it. I seem to have carried her split-off, hidden, secret longing to be different, to escape, to challenge the limiting orthodoxies of her impoverished, unhappy childhood. It is hard sometimes to remember that these are both legitimate choices, that we are both okay, that we have both done well in our own ways.

* * *

My mother is a much better grandma and great-grandma than she was ever a mother, though she is still better at talking about it than at being emotionally present with anyone. Her conversation is entirely about her grandchil-

315

dren and her great-grandchildren. They give her enormous pleasure, and there is no doubt that they have helped to keep her alive and engaged with the world. Each new great-grandchild brings forth a fresh wave of hopes and expectations for the future. And I share this, too. But they are not my children, and I have not given them to Mama. And sometimes this hurts me terribly. Sometimes it feels that nothing I ever gave to Mama was ever of any use or value when I could not or would not give her the thing she wanted most... grandchildren. Or maybe *because* she wanted it so much, it was the one thing I could refuse to give to her, the one way that I could assert utterly and authoritatively that I was not her, that I was separate, that I was different, that I was *me*. And I rejected everything she tried to give me because I was so afraid that I could not separate, that I could not survive if I stayed with her, or survive if I left her.

And so it is now, with the handbag. Except that it is not. I visited the States again recently and bought myself a lovely bright red handbag with lots of zips and pockets and little secret places. It is a great bag, a complex bag, a grown-up woman who knows her own mind kind of bag, and I love it.

Mama saw this bag and sniffed at it. "How much did you pay for that?" she said in a voice that suggested she knew they had seen me coming. Mama never pays full price for anything and thinks that anyone who does is a fool.

I smiled at her and put my arm around her thin, frail shoulders. "I got twenty-five percent off," I whispered, and she nodded approvingly. After all, I am my mother's daughter.

But I never told her the price, because she might have fallen off her chair. And she does not need to know what it cost me. Because I know what it has cost me. And it would have been worth it at any price.

Glossary

Abba father, Dad.

aggadah (adj. aggadic) story, or non-legal rabbinic literature.

Akedah binding an animal for sacrifice; specifically, Abraham's binding of Isaac for sacrifice to God.

aliyah; to make aliyah literally, ascent. To be given an *aliyah* is to be called up to the *bimah* in synagogue; to make *aliyah* is to emigrate to Israel.

aron kodesh literally Holy Ark: the cupboard holding the Torah scrolls in a synagogue.

Ashkenazi referring to Jews whose origins are in northern and eastern Europe; compare *Sephardi*.

ba'al koreh a lay person who reads from the Torah scroll during synagogue services.

ba'al tefillah prayer leader.

bar/bat mitzvah son/daughter of the commandments: the ceremony at age thirteen for boys and twelve or thirteen for girls which marks the beginning of adulthood.

bashert predestined.

BCE "before the common era", equivalent to the Christian BC.

Beit Midrash house of study, or synagogue.

Beth Din literally, House of Law; rabbinic court where judgments are made according to Jewish law on issues such as *kashrut*, Jewish status, divorce and conversion.

bimah the raised platform in a synagogue from which the Torah is read.

bris, brit, brit milah circumcision ceremony representing the covenant, or promise, between God and Abraham (*brit* = covenant). Usually carried out on the eighth day after a boy's birth.

Carlebach minyan Orthodox service with a somewhat bohemian aura and lots of music, particularly songs and tunes by Rabbi Shlomo Carlebach (1925-94).

CE "common era" — equivalent to the Christian AD.

chag (pl chagim) festival.

cheder Hebrew school.

Conservative Judaism movement that originated in the United States in the early twentieth century, partly as a response to the modernising influence of Reform Judaism. Conservative Jews are bound more closely by Torah ritual and tradition than Reform Jews, but less than Orthodox Jews: men and women sit together in the synagogue, some prayers are said in the vernacular and women can become rabbis.

erev evening before.

frum observant.

gabbay honorary synagogue official.

get Jewish ritual divorce.

haggadah the text recited at the Passover seder.

halachah Jewish law.

Hanukkah, Chanukah winter festival commemorating the Maccabees' victory over Syrian Greeks and the rededication of the Temple in 165 BCE. Candles are lit every night for eight nights, celebrating the miracle of one day's oil lasting for eight days.

Hasidic belonging to Hasidism, an ultra-Orthodox mystic movement which began in Poland in the second half of the eighteenth century.

havdalah literally, differentiation, between Shabbat and the rest of the week; marking the end of Shabbat by blessing wine, spices and lights.

heim the home — usually used to mean "the old country".

High Holidays Rosh Hashanah (New Year) and Yom Kippur (Day of Atonement), Judaism's most significant festivals, which occur in the autumn.

Ivrit Modern Hebrew, the language spoken in present-day Israel.

Kabbalistic referring to Kaballah, a Jewish mystical tradition.

kaddish prayers recited by mourners when a close relative dies, and on the anniversary of a death.

kashrut Jewish dietary laws; food that complies with these laws is said to be *kosher* (literally, proper, suitable, or correct).

ketubah traditional marriage contract.

kibbutz; kibbutznik communal agricultural settlement in Israel; someone who lives on a kibbutz.

kiddush ritual blessing over wine.

kindertransport children's transport; trains which in 1938-39 brought unaccompanied children out of Nazi-occupied Germany and neighbouring countries to safety.

klezmer traditional Jewish music from eastern Europe, usually including violin, accordion and clarinet.

Knesset Israeli parliament.

Kol Nidre synagogue service on the eve of Yom Kippur.

kuchen cake.

kupple skull cap.

kvell to swell with pride and delight, "until your buttons burst".

kvetch to grumble, carp and criticise.

latkes fried potato pancakes, traditionally cooked at Chanukah.

leyn to chant a passage from the Torah scroll.

Liberal Judaism (or *Progressive Judaism*) modernising movement in which men and women are treated equally and sit together in synagogue, and women can become rabbis.

Magen David literally, shield of David; six-pointed star that is widely recognised as an emblem of Judaism.

mamzer bastard, child of an adulterous relationship.

matzah unleavened bread eaten at Passover.

matzah brei matzah omelette, traditionally cooked at Passover.

mazel tov Good luck! Well done!

mehitzah the screen or curtain which separates the women's section in an Orthodox synagogue.

mezuzah small container attached to doorposts containing a scroll with Biblical passages written on it.

midrash story that elaborates on a biblical text, usually to demonstrate or provide a moral lesson.

mincha afternoon prayer service.

minyan the minimum of ten adult males required for Orthodox prayer services.

Mishnah compilation of legislation on Torah principles,

concluded about 210 CE by Rabbi Judah the Prince.

mitzvah commandment; also used to mean an honour or act of virtue.

mohel ritual circumciser.

moshav a co-operative settlement of small individual farms or industries in Israel.

Orthodox Judaism traditional Judaism, accepting the total body of Jewish law. Men and women sit separately in Orthodox synagogues, and only men may become rabbis.

Pesach Passover, spring festival commemorating the Exodus from Egypt.

Purim Festival of Lots, commemorating Queen Esther rescuing her fellow Jews from destruction by Haman.

rebbetzin wife of a rabbi.

Reform Judaism modernising movement begun in nineteenth-century Germany. Men and women sit together in synagogue, and women can become rabbis.

Rosh Chodesh new moon, start of the new month. Rosh Chodesh is traditionally seen as a special time for women, and many women's Rosh Chodesh groups meet at this time.

Rosh Hashanah Jewish New Year, in the autumn. Rosh Hashanah begins the Ten Days of Penitence, ending with Yom Kippur. During this period, it is traditionally believed that God inscribes the names of those destined to live through the next year in the Book of Life.

sandek godfather, who holds the boy during circumcision.

schlep to drag, carry, with great effort.

schmaltz literally, rendered chicken fat, often used to describe excessive sentimentality.

seder the ritual Passover meal, during which the story of the Exodus from Egypt is retold. The text includes four children (usually "sons"): one who is wise, one who is wicked, one who is simple, and one who does not know how to ask. Each of the four children learns a different lesson about the Passover story.

Sefer Torah the Torah scroll.

Sephardi referring to Jews whose origins are in Spain, Portugal, North Africa, or the Middle East. Compare *Ashkenazi*.

Shabbat (pl. Shabbatot), Shabbas Sabbath.

Shaddai "Master", "Destroyer", a name of God.

shaliach tzibbor leader of the prayers.

Shavuot Feast of Weeks (Pentecost), occurring seven weeks after Passover.

Shechinah the Divine Presence in the world and all living things.

Shehechianu a blessing giving thanks to God "who has kept us alive to this season". Recited when one takes possession of or begins something new. Also recited at holidays and to mark other special events.

Shema one of the most important prayers in the Jewish liturgy, traditionally recited at daily prayers and before death. It begins, "Hear, O Israel: the Eternal One is our God, the Eternal God is One..."

Shemonah Esrai literally eighteen; the eighteen prayers central to Jewish liturgy, recited in silence while worshippers stand, also called the *Amidah*.

Shir Ha-Kavod — Anim Zmirot hymn sung on Shabbat and holidays, often at the end of services.

Shoah the Holocaust.

sitting shiva seven days of mourning for a close relative, when family and friends come to the mourners' home for prayers.

shtetl little town or village in central or eastern Europe inhabited by Jews before the Holocaust.

shul synagogue.

siddur literally order of prayers, or prayer book.

simcha literally joy; used for celebration such as a wedding or bar mitzvah.

simchat bat welcoming celebration for a daughter.

Sukkot, sukkah Feast of Booths, or harvest festival. It is traditional to build a hut or *sukkah* outdoors, through which you can see the stars. Meals are taken in the sukkah through the eight days of Sukkot.

suvganiot doughnuts or sweet fritters popular with Israeli Jews as a traditional Hanukkah treat.

tallis, tallit prayer shawl.

Talmud writings of Jewish tradition, comprising the Mishnah and Gemara, or commentary.

tefilla prayer.

tefillin small leather boxes bound to arms and head by Orthodox Jewish men during daily morning prayers. Each box contains quotations from the Bible.

tikkun olam mending the world.

Torah the Pentateuch or Five Books of Moses, written on the scroll; the source of all Jewish law.

Ushpizin spiritual guests who visit the sukkah.

Workmen's Circle (Arbeiter Ring) North American Jewish and Yiddish cultural, educational and social care and action organisation based in New York.

yachna loud, shrewish woman; busybody.

yeshiva Talmudic school of higher education.

yishuv a Jewish settlement in Israel.

Yom Kippur the Day of Atonement, ten days after Rosh Hashanah.

yomtov a Jewish holiday or festival.

z'l abbreviation for the Hebrew words *zichrono livracha*, "May his/her memory be a blessing."

Authors' Biographies

Lucy Abrahams is a twenty-two-year-old Jewish daughter who works in book publishing and is just starting out as a writer. She grew up in a loving and supportive Jewish environment in north-west London and has recently left Radlett and Bushey Reform Synagogue for Northwood and Pineral Liberal. She is in a relationship with an American non-Jewish man, also a writer. She dedicates this poem to her mother.

Julia Bard is a freelance journalist. She grew up in a traditional Jewish home in suburban north-west London and spent her teenage years in the 1960s in Habonim, a socialist Zionist youth movement. Her first marriage took her to Zambia and Israel, an uncomfortable place for a socialist and feminist who, by that time, was no longer a Zionist. She left her husband, returned to England, trained as a journalist and, in 1985, helped found *Jewish Socialist* magazine. She and her second husband live in north London, where they are both active members of the Jewish Socialists' Group. Their twin sons are at university.

Rebecca Bender was born and raised in Brooklyn, New York, as a secular Jew with a very strong sense of Jewish identity and culture but no religious affiliations. Her grandfather and parents were active members of the Workmen's Circle (*Arbeiter Ring*). Rebecca is a psychotherapist in her late fifties and has lived and worked in England for many years.

Sally Berkovic grew up in Melbourne, Australia, and lived in Jerusalem and New York before settling in London in 1993. She is the author of *Under My Hat* (Joseph's Bookstore, 1998), which explores the impact of the tensions between Orthodox Judaism and feminism on the raising of her daughters. She currently works at the Big Lottery Fund managing health-related grants.

Isobel Braidman grew up in north-west London in a traditional Jewish family, but she became interested in Progressive Judaism while a student. She is married to Rabbi Dr Reuven Silverman, who serves Manchester Reform Synagogue, and they have three sons in their twenties. Isobel is Senior Lecturer in Cell Biology at Manchester University Medical School, and has a major interest in innovations in teaching and learning, both in her work at the university and dissemination of Torah within the congregation.

Sarah Ebner is a journalist who has been shortlisted three times at the British Press Awards. She was a graduate trainee on the *Daily Express*, a feature writer on the *Daily Mail* and then moved into television to be a producer on BBC's *Newsnight*. She now freelances for a variety of newspapers and magazines. Sarah lives in north London with her Glaswegian husband, Brian Statt, and their three-year-old daughter, Jessica. The family are traditionally Orthodox – they belong to a United synagogue.

Angela English works at Birkbeck College as an administrator and lecturer, having graduated in 2000 as a mature student with an MA in film studies, including extensive research into Yiddish film. Until recently, she worked at the London Jewish Cultural Centre in London, and was involved in their Access to Jewish Studies programme, the first of its kind in the UK. She was born and brought up in Edgware, north London, and now lives in south London with her (non-Jewish) partner. She has one son, who is in his thirties.

Shirly Eran has worked for an Israeli human rights group for more than a decade. Born to secular parents in Jerusalem in 1967, she was active as a girl in the youth section of the Israeli Movement for Progressive Judaism. She lives in Jerusalem, and is the mother of an eight-year-old son and a four-year-old daughter.

Berta Freistadt is a Londoner in her sixties. She is a writer and a teacher and enjoys living alone with her cat. She belongs to Beit Klal Yisrael, a radical Jewish congregation, is a feminist and spends much time gardening (when it's not raining) and working on her family archive. Her book of poetry, *Flood Warning*, was recently published by Five Leaves.

Masha Gessen's memoir, *Two Babushkas*, is published by Bloomsbury in the UK and Dial Press in the US as *Ester and Ruzya: How My Grandmothers Survived Hitler's War and Stalin's Peace.* She lives in Moscow.

Glückel of Hameln was born in Hamburg around 1646. She was betrothed at twelve, and went on to bear fourteen children. She began to write the book of her life after she was widowed in her early forties, when she took over her husband's business. She remarried in 1699, and died in 1724, aged seventy-eight.

Sara Goodman lives in the West Midlands with her partner and young son.

Michele Hanson is a freelance writer and journalist. She was brought up in Ruislip, Middlesex, and now lives in north London with her daughter, two boxer dogs and mother, aged ninety-seven, whom she often writes about in her weekly column in the *Guardian*.

Anne Harris is thirty-seven and has lived with her partner for eleven years. They have a three-year-old son. She converted to Judaism in 1997 and became the secretary to a small Progressive Jewish community almost immediately afterwards. She grew up in the north-east of England and now lives in Birmingham, where she is a member of Birmingham Progressive Synagogue. Anne is a director of an educational programme in a local authority.

Kitty Hart was born in Poland in 1926. She survived the war with her mother, and in 1946 arrived in Britain, where eventually she settled in Birmingham. In 1949 she married Ralph Hart and qualified as a radiographer. They have two sons, one a doctor, the other a physics graduate. Kitty has written two books about her experience, *I Am Alive* and *Return to Auschwitz*.

Brenda Heller was born in north-west London. She did not know she was Jewish until, at the age of six, she asked to go to Sunday school with her friends and was sent to cheder instead. She now lives with her family in Leyton, East London, where they are members of a Liberal synagogue. Brenda works as a midday assistant in a secondary school.

Margaret Jacobi is the rabbi of Birmingham Progressive Synagogue. She grew up in London and studied medicine at Birmingham University. After a career in medical research, she entered the rabbinate and shortly afterwards met her husband, David. Having thought it might be too late for children, she feels doubly blessed to be the mother of Yoni, five, and Tali, two.

Batya Jacobs is a social worker, freelance writer and therapist. She grew up in Cricklewood, north-west London, and belonged to the Walm Lane United Synagogue. She spent her student years in Cardiff and was well looked after by the Jewish community there. She spent her "newlyweds" in Birmingham, and now lives in Israel on Moshav Mattityahu with her husband and the six as yet unmarried children of her family of nine boys and one girl.

Ann Joseph has worked in social care all her adult life. She grew up in north-west London and married her Jewish husband in the mid-1960s. They live just north of London and are members of a Liberal synagogue.

Susie Kaufman lives with her husband and daughter in a provincial English community, where she teaches children with special educational needs. Her son is at present working abroad.

Sidura Ludwig, twenty-nine, is a Canadian writer who recently spent three years living in Birmingham, England. Her fiction has appeared in a number of anthologies including *Are You She?* (Tindal Street Press, 2004). She grew up in Winnipeg, and currently lives in Toronto with her husband.

Shana Mauer is a doctoral candidate in English Literature at the Hebrew University in Jerusalem, focusing on contemporary American Jewish fiction. She reviews books for the *Jerusalem Post* and *Jewish Book World*, and has published *The Female Threat in Genesis* with the University of Toronto's On-line Resource for Jewish Feminism.

Rachel Montagu teaches extra-mural Biblical Hebrew at Birkbeck College and is education assistant at the Council of Christians and Jews. She grew up in South London Liberal Synagogue and West Central Synagogue, and later studied at the Leo Baeck College and Machon Pardes Jerusalem. She worked as a rabbi at the Cardiff New Synagogue and the North Western Reform Synagogue. She lives in London with her husband, a homeopath, a member of the Spanish and Portuguese Synagogue, and their two sons, aged eleven and six.

Grace Paley was born in New York in 1922, the child of Jewish parents who arrived from Russia at the turn of the century. She grew up in the poor quarter of the Lower East Side of Manhattan. She has a son and a daughter. She had little formal education – she was too busy writing poetry and reading voraciously to finish school – and began to write fiction in the 1950s. She has taught literature at Columbia University, Syracuse University and Sarah Lawrence College in Bronxville, New York. Actively involved in anti-war and feminist movements, Grace Paley regards herself as a "somewhat combative pacifist and co-operative anarchist". Her books of short stories include *The Little Disturbances of Man* (1959), and *Enormous Changes at the Last Minute* (1974). Other books are *Just As I Thought* (collected essays, 1999), and *Leaning Forward* (1985), a collection of her poetry. Included among her awards are the 1992 REA Award for Short Stories, and the 1993 Vermont Award for Excellence in Art. In 1994, her *Collected Stories* was nominated for the National Book Award.

Marcia Plumb was ordained at Hebrew Union College–Jewish Institute of Religion in New York in 1988 and currently lives in London with her British husband, Michael, and their two children, Anya and Micah, aged five and two. Having served as a full-time congregational rabbi for fifteen years, Marcia became a "freelance rabbi" three years ago in order to better balance her own needs and those of her family with her calling as a rabbi. Among her many rabbinic jobs, she is the director of the Spirituality Programme at Leo Baeck College–Centre for Jewish Education, a seminary for training rabbis and Jewish educators. She is proud to be a Progressive Jew because it allows for creativity within Judaism.

Rosalind Preston describes herself as a "professional volunteer" and has been actively involved in both the Jewish and non-Jewish voluntary sector all her adult life. She was born in the East End of London and grew up with a strong Jewish-Zionist background which has been the major influence in her life. She has two children and four grandchildren, and considers family life to be of the greatest importance.

Ronne Randall, a freelance writer and editor, has worked in publishing since her early twenties and is now studying for an MA in Folklore and Cultural Tradition at Sheffield University. Born in 1947 in Brooklyn, New York, to immigrant, Yiddish-speaking parents, she was raised in a traditional Jewish home. She came to Britain in 1985, and lives with her British Jewish husband and teenage son near Nottingham, where she and her husband belong to Nottingham Progressive Synagogue.

Mandy Ross writes and edits children's books and educational publications. She grew up in Manchester and now lives in Birmingham, where she is a member of Birmingham Progressive Synagogue. She lives with her non-Jewish partner and their six-year-old son.

Sibyl Ruth has a German-Jewish mother and a Welsh father. As a child she was taken to Quaker "meetings for worship", and Quaker beliefs and practices continue to be a strong influence.

Her partner has a similar background – Jewish mother and gentile father. Sibyl is in her mid-forties with two teenage stepchildren. Her daughter, Hannah, was born in 1997.

Lisa Saffron was born in 1952 in the United States and grew up in a middle-class, liberal, non-religious Jewish family. She has lived her adult life in southern England, working as a health researcher, feminist information worker, writer and lesbian mother activist. The family she created is made up of her Irish Catholic woman partner, her nineteen-year-old birth daughter, a twelve-year-old in foster care, two cats and two chickens. The community she identifies with has no name and consists of a wonderfully diverse mix of people sharing similar humanistic values.

Ayala Ronen Samuels was born and raised on Kibbutz Shamir, Israel. The kibbutz offered her a strong Socialist-Zionist education with intensive Israeli secular Jewish culture. Following four years of civilian and army service, Ayala opted to expand her Jewish knowledge and practice, acquiring a BA and teaching certificate in Jewish Thought from Haifa University, and a PhD in Jewish Education from the Jewish Theological Seminary in New York. After moving to Luxembourg for a year, she now lives in Caesarea, Israel. Married and the mother of three boys, she teaches, writes, and is a part of various teams working to develop and enhance non-Orthodox Jewish education and culture in Israel.

Beatrice Sayers lives in Highbury, north London, and works as an editor and sub-editor. She has a three-year-old daughter and is a member of North London Progressive Jewish Community.

Marlena Schmool is now a freelance research consultant, having formerly worked with the Board of Deputies of British Jews since the mid-1980s, serving first as Community Research Director and then Community Issues Director. She had a traditional Jewish upbringing in Leeds, studied sociology at Birmingham University and the London School of Economics, and has published widely in Jewish social demography. A widow with two adult children, she is a regularly attending member of the Spanish and Portuguese Jews' Congregation in Maida Vale.

Anne Sebba is a journalist, biographer and former foreign correspondent for Reuters. She has written eight books and sits on the board of two charities – the PEN Writers in Prison

Committee and YaD, a charity promoting cross-fertilisation among Jewish, Arab and other cultures. She grew up in Surrey in a moderately observant Jewish family and has now returned there with her husband and eleven-year-old daughter. She is also the mother of two "twentysomethings", who no longer live at home.

Ruth Shire came to England as a Jewish refugee from Germany. She trained as a nurse during the war. Recently widowed, she was married to a Jewish GP in Birmingham for fifty-six years. Their Jewish life revolved around the Birmingham Progressive Synagogue and general community as active members. Ruth has a family of three children and four grandchildren.

Elly Stanton is a GP in central Birmingham. She is married to Alan, a paediatrician, and they have three children, aged six, seven and eleven.

Anna Sullivan was born in 1939 in the East End of London. Her mother was Jewish and her father was non-Jewish and a socialist. She has three children and eight grandchildren, of whom four live in Israel. She was a teacher for many years, and has been a painter all her life. Her stories and poetry have appeared in *Poetry Now, Mustn't Grumble* (Women's Press), *One Heart, One World* (a collaboration of poetry and art), and most recently *Mordechai's First Brush with Love* (Loki Books).

Elana Maryles Sztokman is a doctoral candidate in education at Hebrew University, researching the identity development of adolescent religious girls, and currently lives in Melbourne, Australia, with her spouse and four young children. She has worked as an educator in New York, Jerusalem, and now Melbourne; has written for various publications on subjects around education, women, religion, and Israel; and is an advocate for Jewish women. Since 1996, Elana has been an active volunteer for Mavoi Satum, the organisation working to help *agunot* (women denied a religious divorce) in Israel.

Nadia Valman is Research Fellow in English Literature and Jewish Studies at the Parkes Institute for the Study of Jewish/non-Jewish Relations, University of Southampton. Her current research focuses on the figure of the "Jewess" in English literature. She erratically attends a range of synagogues and, in 2005, will become a first-time mother in a queer Jewish family.

Michelene Wandor is a playwright, poet, critic, and short-story writer. Her most recent collection, *False Relations*, is published by Five Leaves. Her parents came to England from Russia and Poland, and she considers herself to be a good Jewish atheist. She has two extremely grown-up sons, and (to date) one delicious granddaughter. She lives in London.

Karen Worth is a lifelong social activist and Progressive Jew. She grew up in North London and now lives in Nottingham, where she leads the Social Action Group at Nottingham Progressive Synagogue. She was a founder member of Nottingham Jewish Peace Campaign and Nottingham Jewish-Muslim Dialogue group. She works as a general practitioner and lives with her partner and baby son.

Rakefet Zohar, a teacher and writer, was born and raised on Kibbutz Bar-am in the north of Israel. She studied history and culture at Tel Aviv University and spent one very educative year in London, on a mission for Hashomer Hatzair Zionist youth movement. Over the last fifteen years she has had several regular columns in the Israeli press, and has published three novels, including *The Shusters Get Pregnant*, a successful novel focusing on three sisters who all get pregnant at the same time. She has also published a book series entitled *Greek Mythology for Children* and is soon to launch a new series, *Bible Stories for Children*. She lives with her husband and four young sons on Kibbutz Ein-Shemer, where she teaches literature and gender studies to high school students.

Sheva Zucker is the author of the textbooks *Yiddish: An Introduction to the Language, Literature & Culture, Vols. I and II* (Workmen's Circle, 1994). She has taught Yiddish and Yiddish literature in the Uriel Weinreich Summer Yiddish Program in New York City and at Duke University in Durham, North Carolina, for many years. She has taught and lectured on Yiddish language, literature and culture on five continents and at major universities, including Columbia, Bar-Ilan, and Russian State Humanities University. She was, for several years, translation editor of the *Pakn Treger*, the magazine of the National Yiddish Book Center and is now editor of the journal *Afn Shvel*. She writes and translates mostly on topics related to women in Yiddish literature. Sheva thinks she can safely say that she has the only Yiddish-speaking children in Durham, North Carolina.

Chicken Soup Recipe
Ronne Randall

There are probably as many different ways to make chicken soup as there are chicken soup makers — and they're probably all equally good. But this is how I make it. You need:

1 large stew pot or Dutch oven

1 chicken, cut up into pieces (in my experience, a kosher boiling fowl makes the tastiest soup)

2 large onions, halved

Several garlic cloves, peeled

6–8 medium carrots, peeled. Chop half of them into big chunks, and the other half into rounds about an inch thick

2 parsnips, peeled and chopped into chunks

3 celery sticks, cut into chunks

1 medium tomato (This idea came from the late Evelyn Rose, the doyenne of Anglo-Jewish cookery)

1 chicken stock cube

Salt and pepper to taste

Paprika for a little extra colour (you can be adventurous with seasoning: I have heard of people putting pinches of spices such as chilli powder or ginger in their chicken soup. Do not be afraid to experiment!)

Egg vermicelli or Manischewitz egg noodles

1. Put the chicken pieces in a large bowl and pour boiling water over them. After about a minute, pour out the boiling water, and repeat the process once or twice more. This is an important step to reduce the amount of scum that surfaces when the soup boils.

331

2. Put all the ingredients except the carrot rounds into your large pot (which my Yiddish-speaking mother would have called a *shissel*), and fill with enough water to cover the chicken.
3. Cover and bring to the boil.
4. Skim any scum off the surface, then reduce heat and simmer for two to three hours, until the soup is golden in colour.
5. Taste and adjust seasoning.
6. Strain the soup into a large bowl. If you wish, you can remove some chicken meat to put back into the soup. But discard the vegetables, because they will have had all the flavour cooked out of them.
7. Rinse your *shissel* and put the soup back in with the carrot rounds. Simmer for about 30 minutes, until the carrots are soft.
8. Meanwhile, in a separate pot, cook the egg noodles or vermicelli according to the packet instructions. (I haven't specified a quantity of noodles because some people like a lot, some less — you'll have to judge for yourself.)
9. When the carrots are soft and the noodles done, add the noodles to the soup.
10. Serve and enjoy.
11. Leftover soup keeps well in the fridge for a few days, and can be frozen for ages. It will taste even better when it's reheated.

*Vegetarian "chicken" stock is widely available, in good kosher shops for example, for those who want to make chicken soup without the chicken.

Five Leaves titles by *For Generations* contributors

False Relations
Michelene Wandor
190 pages, 0 9087123 20 1, £7
Michelene Wandor's new collection of short stories ranges from biblical to modern, from Renaissance Italy to modern day Israel. The story of Esther liberates the voice of Queen Vashti, Henry Vlll and Isabella d'Este enjoy a clandestine encounter while the dilemmas of being Jewish thread their way between the fifteenth century and the present Middle East.

"This is a sensual anthology in which the reader eats with the narrators, listens to music with them, watches the moonlight, lies at night with illicit lovers, or lies thinking about them... whose interesting images will stay in the reader's mind."
JEWISH RENAISSANCE

Gardens of Eden Revisited
Michelene Wandor
172 pages, 0907123 33 3, £7.99
"...a gossipy, irresistible send-up of the Old Testament"
VOGUE
"Strong on dialogue, the conversations between Eve, Lilith and God are compelling, witty and wise..."
POETRY QUARTERLY REVIEW

I Could Become that Woman
Sibyl Ruth
34 pages, 0 907123 54 6, £4
Sibyl Ruth celebrates desire and the way it disrupts our lives, turning friends into lovers, partners into parents.
"Her poems are informal, direct and street-wise. Her best poems have an urgency, wryness and indeed poignancy that will resonate with many readers. Her musings on the discrepancy between the real and imagined in the erotic life address more than her specific experiences."
CRITICAL SURVEY

Flood Warning
Berta Freistadt
36 pages, 0 907123 94 5, £4.50
"...demure men may well be embarrassed by Berta Freistadt's lesbian love poems. However, the erotic and elegant verses can be unashamedly enjoyed as aesthetic delights"
JEWISH CHRONICLE

Five Leaves titles are available from bookshops or, post-free, from Five Leaves, PO Box 81, Nottingham NG5 4ER, UK. Overseas orders add 20% for postage, US$ cheques accepted.